Images of Terror

SOCIAL PROBLEMS AND SOCIAL ISSUES

An Aldine de Gruyter Series of Texts and Monographs

SERIES EDITOR

Joel Best, *University of Delaware*

Joel Best (ed.), **Images of Issues: Typifying Contemporary Social Problems** (Second Edition)
Joel Best (ed.), **Spreading Social Claims: Studies in the Cross-National Diffusion of Social Problems Claims**
Joel Best (ed.), **Troubling Children: Studies of Children and Social Problems**
James J. Chriss (ed.), **Counseling and the Therapeutic State**
Donatella della Porta and Alberto Vanucci, **Corrupt Exchanges: Actors, Resources, and Mechanisms of Crime, Deviance, and Control**
Jeff Ferrell and Neil Websdale (eds.), **Making Trouble: Cultural Constructions of Crime**
Ann E. Figert, **Women and the Ownership of PMS: The Structuring of a Psychiatric Disorder**
Mark Fishman and Gray Cavender (eds.), **Entertaining Crime: Television Reality Programs**
James A. Holstein, **Court-Ordered Insanity: Interpretive Practice and Involuntary Commitment**
James A. Holstein and Gale Miller (eds.), **Reconsidering Social Constructionism: Debates in Social Problems Theory**
Philip Jenkins, **Images of Terror: What We Can and Can't Know about Terrorism**
Philip Jenkins, **Intimate Enemies: Moral Panics in Contemporary Great Britain**
Philip Jenkins, **Using Murder: The Social Construction of Serial Homicide**
Valerie Jenness, **Making It Work: The Prostitutes' Rights Movement in Perspective**
Valerie Jenness and Kendal Broad, **Hate Crimes: New Social Movements and the Politics of Violence**
Stuart A. Kirk and Herb Kutchins, **The Selling of *DSM*: The Rhetoric of Science in Psychiatry**
John Lofland, **Social Movement Organizations: Guide to Research on Insurgent Realities**
Donileen R. Loseke, **Thinking About Social Problems: An Introduction to Constructionist Perspectives** (Second Edition)
Donileen R. Loseke and Joel Best (eds.), **Social Problems: Constructionist Readings**
Leslie Margolin, **Goodness Personified: The Emergence of Gifted Children**
Donna Maurer and Jeffrey Sobal (eds.), **Eating Agendas: Food and Nutrition as Social Problems**
Gale Miller, **Becoming Miracle Workers: Language and Meaning in Brief Therapy**
Bernard Paillard, **Notes on the Plague Years: AIDS in Marseilles**
Dorothy Pawluch, **The New Pediatrics: A Profession in Transition**
Erdwin H. Pfuhl and Stuart Henry, **The Deviance Process** (Third Edition)
Theodore Sasson, **Crime Talk: How Citizens Construct a Social Problem**
Wilbur J. Scott and Sandra Carson Stanley (eds.), **Gays and Lesbians in the Military: Issues, Concerns, and Contrasts**
Jeffrey Sobal and Donna Maurer (eds.), **Weighty Issues: Fatness and Thinness as Social Problems**
Jeffrey Sobal and Donna Maurer (eds.), **Interpreting Weight: The Social Management of Fatness and Thinness**
Robert A. Stallings, **Promoting Health Risk: Constructing the Earthquake Threat**
Frank J. Weed, **Certainty of Justice: Reform in the Crime Victim Movement**
Michael Welch, **Flag Burning: Moral Panic and the Criminalization of Protest**
Carolyn L. Wiener, **The Elusive Quest: Accountability in Hospitals**
Rhys Williams (eds.), **Cultural Wars in American Politics: Critical Reviews of a Popular Myth**
Mark Wolfson, **The Fight Against Big Tobacco: The Movement, the State and the Public's Health**

Images of Terror

What We Can and Can't Know about Terrorism

Philip Jenkins

Aldine de Gruyter
New York

About the Author

Philip Jenkins is Distinguished Professor of History and Religious Studies at Pennsylvania State University. Among his earlier books are *Intimate Enemies* and *Using Murder*.

ALDINE DE GRUYTER
A division of Walter de Gruyter, Inc.
200 Saw Mill River Road
Hawthorne, New York 10532

This publication is printed on acid free paper ♾

Library of Congress Cataloging-in-Publication Data

Jenkins, Philip, 1952–
Images of terror : what we can and can't know about terrorism / Philip Jenkins.
p. cm. -- (Social problems and social issues)
Includes bibliographical references and index.
ISBN 0-202-30678-X (hardback : alk. paper) — ISBN 0-202-30679-8 (pbk. : alk. paper)
1. Terrorism. 2. Terrorists--Psychology. 3. Political violence. 4. Terrorism and mass media. 5. Terrorism--Government policy. 6. Communication--Social aspects. I. Title. II. Series.

HV6431 .J46 2002
303.6′25—dc21

2002013178

Manufactured in the United States of America

10 9 8 7 6 5 4 3 2 1

CONTENTS

ACKNOWLEDGMENTS

As always, I thank my wife Liz Jenkins for all her advice and encouragement. I would also like to thank Kathryn Hume and Patricia Loveless for taking the time to read the manuscript, and offering many valuable suggestions. Finally, my thanks to Richard Koffler, of Aldine de Gruyter, for the help and advice he has given me over the years.

Portions of chapter five originally appeared in my article "Under Two Flags: Provocation and Deception in European Terrorism," in *Terrorism: An Interdisciplinary Journal* 11(1989): 275–287. I am grateful to Frank Cass Publishers for permission to use this material here.

PREFACE

The literature on terrorism was already vast before September 2001, and it has been growing steadily ever since. Thousands of books and articles have explored the issue of terrorism in general, as well as specific terrorist acts and movements, and these topics have attracted the attention of able and distinguished scholars. I have no wish simply to add another drop to that ocean. I wrote this book because of my conviction that sometimes, scholars and journalists accept uncritically the interpretations of terrorism they receive from governments and official agencies. Our perceptions of terrorism are formed by the interaction of bureaucratic agencies, academics and private experts, and the mass media: the images and stereotypes that we are offered do not necessarily reflect objective reality.

Central to my approach is the notion that terrorism, like any other problem, is socially constructed. By that, I certainly do not mean that terrorism is not a *real* problem, an authentic menace, or that society should not respond promptly and effectively to terrorist threats. Rather, I mean that terrorism is not something like a chemical formula that would be understood identically by people in all different societies, and different eras. The concept is shaped by social and political processes, by bureaucratic needs and media structures. This process of construction applies both to the overall concept of terrorism, and to specific movements, groups and their actions. We need to understand how we form our stereotypes of terrorism and how we come to see certain terrorists or militants as demon figures, while giving a virtual free pass to other groups or states that are just as dangerous.

Even the matter of defining what one means in speaking of *terrorism* and a *terrorist act* is anything but simple. As we will see, the definition of terrorism is a highly political phenomenon, a subjective, complex and often self-contradictory process; and common perceptions to the contrary, the stigma is applied in a thoroughly selective and partial way. I shall argue that we can arrive at a definition that would achieve quite a wide consensus: to anticipate, such a consensus definition would emphasize not the fact of violence, but rather its indiscriminate character and its political motivation. But even when such a definition is formally adopted, governments and bureaucratic agencies still exercise enormous latitude in deciding who is or is not a terrorist.

As in the study of any social problem, we must understand the rhetorical processes by which certain interest groups and bureaucratic agencies present their particular views of terrorism, and try to establish these as the ones that come to be accepted as obviously correct. We also need to consider the audiences that receive these statements. Why do the media accept or reject certain views of terrorism? Why does the public accept one kind of rhetorical presentation rather than another? How are popular attitudes shaped and reshaped by the images and stereotypes offered in the mass media, and in popular culture? When we appreciate the processes involved in making news about terrorism, we are better able to sift critically the claims that are made, and to evaluate policies.

For the foreseeable future, terrorism is likely to remain a dominant issue in the political life of the United States, and indeed of much of the world. It is all the more important, then, to understand how we form our notions of the enemy to be confronted—how, in short, we form our images of terror. When we make statements about terrorism—about terrorist groups, or even terrorist states—just how do we know what we think we know?

1

Knowing About Terrorism

> Terrorism is like beauty. It is in the eye of the beholder.
>
> —Zacarias Moussaoui

However familiar the word may be, it is far from obvious what terrorism actually is. To illustrate this, let us take a specific incident that occurred in the Middle East in June 2002. A 22-year-old graduate student named Muhammad al-Ghoul boarded a bus in Jerusalem and he detonated explosives that were packed around his body. The bombing killed nineteen Jewish Israelis, including an eleven-year-old girl and several high school students. The bomb maker had packed the device with ball bearings, in order to kill the largest possible number of people (Beaumont 2002).

This particular incident was in no way unusual, given the time and place. Muhammad al-Ghoul, a Palestinian Arab, was a member of the radical Islamic fundamentalist group Hamas, one of several organizations that over the previous years had undertaken many such suicide attacks against Israel. (Hamas is an acronym for *Harakat al-Muqawama al-Islamiya*, or Islamic Resistance Movement, but the word also means *Zeal* in Arabic.) (Mishal and Sela 2000; Katz 2000) As in the Jerusalem incident, young men—or sometimes, women—strap powerful explosives around their bodies, and enter crowded public places like malls or clubs that are full of Jewish civilians. Such suicide bombings naturally cause immense fear among the Israeli public, while boosting Palestinian morale. Just in the first six months of 2002, the suicide bombing campaign claimed almost two hundred lives, and helped bring the entire region to the verge of outright war. This kind of tactic has proved extremely frightening and effective (Rubin 2002; Bennett 2001, 2002).

Every observer can agree on such a basic description of the phenomenon in reporting where and when attacks occurred, or counting the number of victims, but beyond this, virtually every detail of the story is open to debate. Even in a case that seems to be simply and undeniably terrorism, many diverse views are possible. Israelis obviously characterize these attacks as terrorism, and the description would be echoed by the vast majority of Americans. Yet many millions of people around the world reject such a negative term, preferring to describe the bombers in heroic terms as guerrillas, partisans, or freedom fighters.

Palestinians and other Arabs see each bomber as a religious martyr, or *shahid*, for the cause of Islam, and glorify his deeds in songs, parades, murals, and graffiti (*Shaheed* 1996). By late 2002, an opinion survey showed that over eighty percent of Palestinian Arabs favored the use of violence against Israel: two-thirds of respondents supported the use of suicide bombings (Lahoud 2002). Celebrating recent actions, Palestinian poet Ayman al-Skafi wrote in 2001,

> Because I am a Palestinian
> Because I bear the flag . . .
> I will place the parts of my body as bombs
> In your hatred, in your origin
> In your accursed fruit
> And in spite of you, they will germinate the most beautiful of flowers
> They will germinate the most
> Beautiful Palestine
> Because I am a Palestinian. (al-Skafi 2001)

Support for such actions even comes from leading intellectuals like Egypt's Naguib Mahfouz, a Nobel Prize-winning novelist, who describes the bombers as "people defending a cause by sacrificing with their souls, and this is the highest level of noble resistance" (MacFarquhar 2002).

Hamas is funded and actively supported by Arab and Muslim states, including Syria and Saudi Arabia: the Saudis even use telethons to raise money for the families of "martyrs." Both Iraq and Iran cooperate closely with Palestinian extremist groups, including Hamas and Palestinian Islamic Jihad. The official declaration of the Arab states condemning terrorism specifically excludes from this term the acts of "peoples [who] combat foreign occupation and aggression by whatever means, including armed struggle, in order to liberate their territories and secure their right to self-determination" (Arab Convention 2000). And that is taken to exclude groups like Hamas.

Even many Europeans who condemn the violence respect the cause for which the bombers act, and accept their self-description as resistance fighters. This is a potent term, since it conjures up images of World War II guerrillas rebelling against Nazi oppression. If the Palestinians represent a resistance, then by implication the Israelis must be the modern counterparts of the German occupiers (Carey 2001). When a leading Egyptian *mufti*, or spiritual leader, was asked about the morality of suicide bombing, he used the analogy of wartime resistance: "If Israel is the aggressor and the American government is behind it, and the West stands by observing, it is the Palestinians' right to blow up whatever they want. I ask [the French]: If, say, Germany were to again attack France and occupy your land, would they refrain from resisting?" (http://www.memri.org/bin/latestnews.cgi?ID=SD40202).

Even if we agree that the suicide bombings are terrorism, experts and journalists take very different approaches to questions like the causation of the act, or who might be responsible. Some experts would emphasize individual or social factors, seeing the attacks as the product of frustration and anger of those living under Israeli occupation: Muhammad al-Ghoul was one of many Palestinians living in squalid refugee camps. Other observers stress the role of organized movements that brainwash vulnerable people into committing outrageous acts of violence, often by stirring up religious fanaticism.

But if a group was to blame, which one? Hamas claimed the act, but were they solely responsible? Were the acts organized or permitted by the Palestinian Authority, the mainstream government of the Palestinian Arabs, headed by Yasser Arafat? Or were they done by other groups, without the knowledge or consent of that Authority? Some would see the suicide bombings as organized by outside nations determined to destroy the Israeli state.

How one approaches these issues profoundly affects the appropriate responses to any new bombings. If attacks arise from injustice and oppression, then the proper response would focus on social and political reforms. If the violence were directed by a state or an organized conspiracy, then military counter-action would be necessary and justified. Should the Israeli government try to attack one group rather than another? Should it launch a military action against an outside state? Should it reduce the burdens faced by Palestinians under occupation? Debates over the attribution and causation of terrorism are not merely a matter of academic curiosity since they might well decide, crudely, who gets bombed in retaliation.

Alongside the problems involved in using the terrorist label, debate surrounds virtually every word used to describe the participants in political violence. Are those involved militants or guerrillas, soldiers or terrorists? Do they *commit crimes* or *launch attacks*? Can we even speak of the *victims* of an attack? The question sounds callous, but if one supports the action as a legitimate act of war, then the targets are not viewed as innocent victims. Some American media refuse to use the phrase *suicide bombers* since that term places the emphasis on the self-sacrifice of the attacker: they prefer to speak of *homicide bombers*, stressing instead the criminal nature of the act. Words are everything.

Even the most basic ways of approaching such events are debatable. Depending on which news media you read, you will find a very different interpretation of what is happening. And the suicide bombings should be among the most straightforward kinds of terrorism in understanding motivation. In this case at least, we can be fairly certain that the attacks were the works of Palestinians targeting Israel. But imagine another incident elsewhere in the world, such as the bombing of a United States embassy in a Third World nation, where the only claim of responsibility involves a hitherto unknown "World Revolutionary Front." Media reports may suggest that a particular group or country is responsible, but how do they know this? Should we believe what we are told? If even experts studying terrorism can disagree so greatly on what seems like a straightforward set of events (and they often do), it can be almost impossible for ordinary consumers of news to find out accurately what is happening, and what should be an appropriate response. As terrorism has become a critical issue in public debate with vast implications for foreign policy, law enforcement, and constitutional rights, such confusion is alarming.

THE WAR AGAINST TERRORISM

We can see some of these policy consequences from what has become the central fact of U.S. foreign policy, namely the War against Terrorism, which was launched following the attacks of September 11, 2001. The need for some forceful response was beyond argument, but the way in which U.S. policy was phrased left many critical questions unanswered. Semiseriously, some critics suggested that it was foolish to try and launch a war against a noun. More troubling, the whole war presupposed a certainty of identification and of the assignment of blame, which was not always convincing. And since terrorism is a *tactic* employed in a wide variety of causes, it is questionable to imagine it as a *movement*, with a specific leadership or structure. Individual organizations like Hamas or Hizbullah might have such a structure that in theory can be identified, fought, and destroyed; *terrorism* as such does not. We should not think in terms of a state with its capital, as in the analogy of Berlin or Tokyo in 1941. For the same reasons, terrorism can never be eliminated in the same way that German Nazism or Italian Fascism was utterly uprooted. As long as war and revolutionary violence exist, so will terrorism (Pillar and Armacost 2001).

In addition, it is misleading to speak of terrorism in a way that suggests that the world can be neatly divided into straightforward good and evil, without any shades in between. That the September 11 attacks were an unqualified evil, a grotesque crime against humanity, would be widely accepted, but other violent acts are more open to shades of interpretation.

Equally, not all groups that practice terrorism can be viewed as the incarnation of darkness in the way this would suggest. This is not just a philosophical or theological objection, but rather gets to the core difficulties of mounting a counter-terrorist offensive.

Above all, what should we be fighting? It is far from obvious what groups or organizations should be our enemies, and even more so, whether they have any connections in states and governments. Well-informed people can disagree fiercely on these issues. Imagine that a group carries out some terrorist acts, but the bulk of its actions fall within some other category, such as resistance or guerrilla warfare. Is this still a terrorist group? Suppose terrorism only constitutes five or ten percent of its activities. Can we talk of a group as being partially terrorist, or terrorist for half the time? This may seem like logic-chopping, but in a world in which the U.S. has declared war on terrorism, it is essential to know just how many enemies and friends we have. If a group has ever engaged in terrorism, does that mean that it cannot be an ally in our current war? As we will see, many of the West's allies would certainly fall into this ambiguous category, groups that have made at least some limited use of terrorism. Individuals and groups do not make a simple and irreversible decision to wage war from the dark side of the force: there are many shades of gray.

During the 1980s, the U.S. had a lively subculture fascinated by survivalist and paramilitary matters, and this interest sustained an active trade in weaponry and military equipment. One such catalogue of the era sold an "antiterrorist knife," a complex (and expensive) weapon loosely modeled on the knife made famous in Sylvester Stallone's *Rambo* films. The description of the object was interesting. Admittedly, if one ever was in single combat with a terrorist, the weapon might be invaluable, but it was never entirely clear what particular features of the blade fitted it for antiterrorist warfare. This ludicrous object sometimes comes to mind when we hear discussions of terrorism that assume without question or discussion the exact shape of the problem. Perceptions of terrorism are conditioned by ideology and interest group politics, which form our views not only of what terrorism is, but also which specific terrorists deserve our attention (compare Herman and O'Sullivan 1989).

WHAT WE CAN'T KNOW

In many ways, terrorism poses unusual difficulties for any kind of academic analysis. It differs from other problems in that the official agencies we depend on for information have a powerful vested interest in not revealing the full extent of the information available to them. In saying this, I am not arguing for a conspiratorial view of government behavior, but rather remarking on the nature of the law enforcement response to terrorism. Since so much official action involves clandestine methods or sources, even the most reputable and responsible agencies will on occasion present less than the full truth, or actively give false information in order to protect their methods or sources. Deception is a basic part of the territory, and it is naïve to suppose otherwise. When dealing with regular forms of criminality like drugs or homicide, official agencies might well present misleading statements, generally to gain some political advantage, but in such cases it is possible for critical academics or journalists to reinterpret the evidence to form a more reliable picture. In the case of terrorism, we can be far less confident. To describe the unreliability of media accounts of terrorism is not to suggest any ill will or incompetence on the part of journalists or editors. For excellent reasons, it is simply very difficult for them to analyze these matters in the way they would when approaching "regular" crime.

Before we can legitimately speak of "terrorism," we have to know that the offender acted with a particular motivation or intention. We can illustrate this point by drawing a contrast with conventional crimes such as bank robberies. If someone enters a bank with a weapon and demands money, then that is a robbery, pure and simple. We do not have to know the names of the culprits or their motivations. We can find statistics that a given number of such actions have occurred, though we can disagree at length what these numbers actually mean. By most definitions, though, we can only speak of terrorism when a specific political intent is involved, and that means that we have to know the person or group responsible. Let us imagine that the president of a bank is killed by a bomb placed under his car. Police subsequently find that the act was the work of a radical political group seeking to destroy American capitalism, and the crime is therefore labeled as terrorism. The act would not however be terrorism if it proved to be the work of a jealous husband, or an insane person who felt that the president was beaming telepathic rays at him, or if it was part of a nonpolitical extortion plot. In other words, before we know whether the act falls within the scope of terrorism, we have to know both who did it, and why they did it. These are often very difficult matters to determine. In this type of crime, we depend on law enforcement to confirm that John Doe carried out the act, and what he wished to achieve at the time.

This can be illustrated by a recent example that is all too real. In October 1999, a Boeing 767 owned by the Egyptian national airline EgyptAir, flight 990, crashed in the sea near Nantucket, Massachusetts, killing all 217 people on board. Beyond this agreed fact, we are in the realm of interpretation and speculation. The cockpit voice recorder indicated that, shortly before the crash, the plane had gone into a steep dive as the copilot, Gameel al-Batouti, began repeating an Arabic phrase that roughly translates as "I put my trust in God." One explanation holds that the plane encountered a mechanical problem, and as al-Batouti tried to solve it, he automatically began repeating a phrase commonly used in Egyptian Muslim culture during moments of difficulty. It would be like a worried or frightened American Christian or Jew repeating "Oh, my God!" Others believe that al-Batouti deliberately crashed the aircraft in an act of suicide, perhaps because of depression or derangement. That would make the act criminal rather than accidental (Langewiesche 2001).

Often investigators have a simple choice of two interpretations, but in this case a third view is also possible. Perhaps al-Batouti was motivated by political, Islamic fundamentalist, sentiment of the kind that gained popularity in Egypt during the 1990s (*al-Gama'a al-Islamiyya* n.d.). This Islamist upsurge led to the creation of ruthless guerrilla groups that carried out brutal attacks against Egyptian authorities and Western visitors. (We recall that Mohammed Atta, probable commander of the September 11 hijackers, was also Egyptian.) Bolstering this possible motive, we note that several highly placed Egyptian government officials were among those killed on flight 990. If that interpretation is correct, then the crash was politically motivated violence against civilians, or in other words, a massive act of Islamist terrorism comparable in scale to the attack on the Pentagon. But the categorization of terrorism depends on our understanding of the motivation of one man who is no longer available to be questioned or cross-examined.

To take another and fortunately less bloody example, in 1998, eleven new luxury homes in the Phoenix area were destroyed in a series of arson attacks. Letters to the media claimed the assaults in the name of the Coalition to Save the Preserves, a hitherto unknown example of a militant activist group determined to preserve the environment by violence if necessary. (This is usually known as eco-terrorism.) The group's communiqués announced, "Warning! Thou shalt not desecrate God's creation . . . We won't hurt neighbors or endanger firefighters. But God's work has to be done." Developers were warned that, "If you build, we will burn." For a while the attacks won the sympathy of radical environmentalists, but in 2001 it appeared that the fires had no political motivation whatever. They were in fact the work of a local businessman obsessed with fire-setting, who concocted the eco-terror connection as a means of covering his tracks (Sterngold 2001). In striking contrast to a bank robbery, we only know whether such an act represented terrorism after we have identified the culprit, and discovered his or her likely motives.

For anyone trying to study terrorism in an academic setting, these are fundamental issues. Most social science begins with statistics, which permit a quantitative analysis of a topic or problem, but until we have decided what terrorism is, we can hardly count terrorist incidents, whether in the

United States or globally. For instance, every year the U.S. State Department issues figures for the number of international terrorist attacks over the previous twelve months, together with the number of fatalities. The figures seem remarkably precise: these reports assert that there were 426 such incidents in 2000, and 348 in 2001—although the carnage on September 11 meant that 2001 was the bloodiest year on record. It is tempting to analyze these statistics in the same way that we break down figures for street robberies or drug arrests, and map the changing volume of terrorist activity through charts or graphs. As we have seen, though, terrorist acts simply cannot be counted in this way. Some argue that the State Department counts as terrorism some acts that should really be described as resistance, while failing to count blatant terrorist violence carried out by groups allied to the U.S.

Equally, we need to be very careful about using figures that claim to report the number of attacks associated with a particular group or state. In the annual State Department reports, a major section concerns the activities of "bandit states" like Libya, Iran, and Cuba in supporting international violence and mayhem. Following major terrorist attacks over the past twenty years, the U.S. media have been full of elaborate flow charts depicting the dissemination of money and techniques from particular countries to international groups and individuals. This material permits governments to declare that action X can infallibly be associated with Group Y, which serves as a surrogate for nation Z; which might well become the target of American bombs or cruise missiles. At every point though, we need to ask not only how the agencies involved know this information, but also whether they would be expected to report it in a frank or objective way. The U.S. government is one of many that in recent decades has experienced lengthy debates over the nature, scope, and origins of terrorism, and the picture presented to the public is generally the outcome of a complex process of debate and negotiation. When we are confronted with data, whether official materials or media reports, at every stage we have to ask the fundamental question: how do they know?

METHODS AND APPROACHES

At this point, the reader should certainly be asking a very proper question, which is, how do *I* know? What gives me the right to challenge the standard accounts of terrorism published in leading media outlets by experienced journalists who have excellent and highly placed contacts in intelligence?

In response, I would say, first, I am less concerned with trying to say "what really happened" in any given incident, but rather to note that several competing versions of reality were available, and that bureaucratic agencies chose to accept one rather than another. For my purposes, it does not matter whether the explanation chosen was indeed the correct one. I am mainly concerned with observing the processes of discussion and negotiation that led to a particular outcome. We will for instance trace the way in which U.S. law enforcement agencies decided that the anthrax attacks of 2001 were not linked to the Middle East, and how that interpretation came to be accepted by the mass media. In studying the process by which problems are constructed, I draw on my earlier studies of issues like child abuse and serial murder (Jenkins 1992, 1994, 1996, 1999a, 2000; P. Jenkins 1998). In this work, I explored how bureaucratic agencies respond to social problems, how the news media operate, and how they deal with official sources.

Second, I approach these matters from a historical background. Though intelligence and counter-terrorism officers are reluctant to discuss operations in progress, they are often happy to discuss the activities of bygone years. We now have a vast library informing us of the workings of both terrorism and counter-terrorist policing in the past, including the recent past, and this record suggests certain consistent patterns of operation. The actual weapons may change—nobody before the 1990s had used an airliner as a guided missile against high-profile targets—but the organizational techniques and tactics of both sides have not changed enormously since World War II, or even before that. To understand terrorist warfare in classic campaigns like Algeria in the 1950s, Northern Ireland in the 1970s, or South Africa in the 1980s is likely to shed light on current realities, especially since modern-day terrorists and counter-terrorists were both trained using examples from those older movements. In the American context, we can also find extensive materials about the workings of covert policing from the mountains of documents made public during the intelligence scandals of the 1970s. Among other things, these historical accounts offer rich materials on the uses of tactics of deception and media manipulation.

Third, as a historian, I claim expertise in the selection and handling of sources. We can learn a great deal about terrorism by using a wide range of sources that draw on diverse and mutually independent authorities. The question of diversity has nothing to do with the sheer number of sources we use. If we are following a terrorism story in the U.S. media, we might easily find two or three hundred news outlets all basically presenting the same point of view, although they represent a huge variety of media corporations or news networks. If though, all are drawing their material from the same two or three official sources in U.S. government and law enforcement, then we are inevitably going to be reading a fairly uniform picture. When we read or watch news stories about terrorism, we soon find that the number of experts and agencies quoted is remarkably small and, with a little practice, we can almost predict which of the very limited number of likely faces will appear to comment on a given incident. This does not mean that these familiar sources are necessarily inaccurate, and we might eventually conclude that they are offering the best and most authoritative views; but on occasion, we will find some interesting contradictions in their opinions and (sometimes) biases.

If we want to move beyond simple reliance on U.S. government sources—which in practice means the State Department, Central Intelligence Agency and Federal Bureau of Investigation—then we need to cast our net much wider. Imagine for example that we are trying to understand the motivation of the Palestinian suicide attacks. Instead of relying just on U.S. sources, we should draw on Israeli and Palestinian media, and as many international sources as we can find, especially from Egypt, Lebanon, the Arab Gulf states, and the nations of Western Europe. The process of finding such materials has been made vastly easier by the coming of the Internet. (Apart from newspapers and periodicals, many web sites present the views of terrorist groups themselves, often in English.) We quickly find that accounts of particular events differ enormously from one country or media outlet to another, partly because of different political attitudes. European media for instance are much more sympathetic to Arab political causes than are U.S. sources. More important, the various news media draw on the knowledge and expertise of different authorities, different governments, and intelligence agencies, some of which have excellent connections in the regions where terrorist groups operate.

Some accounts in the foreign media we will find to be largely worthless, including blatant propaganda and easily disprovable misstatements. (The range of bizarre conspiracy theories concerning the September 11 attacks is a case in point: see Brisard and Dasquie 2002). Just because a source offers a radically different perspective does not make it right! Over time, though, we find that some sources are far better than others in the information and interpretation they offer, generally because they are closer to well-informed agencies. We can judge the worth of these sources by observing their track records over a period of years, and noting how their evaluations and analyses compare with the actual course of events.

In other words, we are treating contemporary sources exactly as a historian would evaluate documents or materials of bygone ages. In both cases, we want to ask the same questions: Are the authors of the document in a position to make well-informed comments? What are their biases and limitations? Can we trust them more on some issues than on others? To take a well-known example, Israeli sources have proved to be very well informed on most aspects of terrorism, especially where Middle Eastern groups are involved (Posner 1987). At the same time, any reading of Israeli media or government sources must take account of their natural self-interest, their tendency to place their own country's actions in the best possible light, while making Arab enemies seem uniquely dangerous. As with any historical source, critical reading is essential.

Finally, much can be learned by the application of human memory. If we trace coverage of a particular terrorist group or issue over the years, we can often see sharp and even irreconcilable differences in how matters are discussed. Sometimes, matters change because analysts learn new facts, or reinterpret existing evidence. To take a painful example, through 2000 and the first half of 2001, a number of well-informed writers dismissed the possibility that Osama bin Laden and his al-Qaeda network might pose any serious threat to the West, and specifically to the United States. On September 11, we learned through bitter experience that our fears were in fact fully justified, and later accounts changed accordingly.

On other occasions, though, attitudes change not because of any new information, but rather because of shifting political and bureaucratic influences, through new constructions of a particular problem. Often, those offering a particular interpretation do not acknowledge that it does represent a major change from older views, or even a complete flip-flop. They simply act as if their view has always been the accepted one. By critically observing how presentations of terrorism change over time, we can learn a great deal about the process of construction.

CHANGING HISTORY

As an example of this process, we might take the bombing of Pan Am flight 103, one of the most horrible terrorist attacks in modern history. Shortly before Christmas 1988, the flight blew up over Lockerbie, Scotland, killing 270 people, mainly Americans. Nobody questions the finding that this act was the result of criminal violence, but beyond that fact, much about the crime remains uncertain. Through the 1990s, the consensus interpretation was that the bombing was carried out by the Libyan government, under its dictatorial ruler Muammar Qaddafi, and two Libyan intelligence agents were put on trial. One was convicted in 2001, and Libyan responsibility for the act has become historical fact. In an attempt to remove international sanctions, the Libyan government has been negotiating a settlement under which it would acknowledge guilt, and in that case, nobody is likely to argue with the simple interpretation that "Qaddafi did it" (Walls 2001; Gerson and Adler 2001).

Matters are more complex than this simple resolution would suggest. This is not to say that the Libyan government is not morally capable of such a crime—it undoubtedly is—but we actually have quite strong evidence for involvement by other culprits. Within a few months of the crime, blame had been unequivocally laid at the door of two other nations, Iran and Syria, which have long formed a close military and diplomatic alliance. At that point, all experts accepted an interpretation of the crime that was just as open and shut as the later linkage with Qaddafi. (For the Libyan context, see Bearman 1986; Blundy and Lycet 1987; Jenkins 1988b; Davis 1990; for the Syrian background, see Seale 1988.)

According to this original view, the Iranians were outraged at an incident in mid-1988 when a U.S. warship had mistakenly shot down one of their airliners. Determined to get revenge, the Iranians used their Syrian friends to contact an international terrorist group with long experience in bomb-making and airline attacks. This was the Popular Front for the Liberation of Palestine-General Command (PFLP-GC), headed by Ahmad Jibril (Katz 1993). The group mobilized a cell based in Frankfurt, Germany, which used a legendary bomb maker to construct the device that brought down the Pan Am flight. The man made several bombs, which were to be concealed in radio-cassette players, and they used a barometric trigger that ensured they would go off only when the plane reached a given height. Ideally, this would mean that the airliner would be destroyed over the open sea, making it difficult to retrieve evidence. The triggers of the unexploded devices found in the cell's possession were set to go off at 31,000 feet—which was the actual height at which Pan Am 103 exploded. This information, we were told at the time, was all confirmed by forensic evidence, and from the testimony of informants within the PFLP-GC cell, who were also working for governments friendly to the United States. Moreover, several bombs almost identical to the Pan Am device were discovered in Germany, always in the hands of groups related to that Palestinian network. This PFLP-GC story was the one then believed by U.S. authorities, and by German and British intelligence (Emerson and Duffy 1990).

Throughout 1989 and 1990, this scenario represented uncontested historical fact. We knew—or thought we knew—precisely which Palestinian group had committed the crime, and for what motive. We even had the specific names of the individuals believed responsible, and how they had placed the bomb in a particular type of radio/cassette recorder. Critically, we also knew the state sponsors involved, namely Syria and Iran. Books, documentaries, and television movies all presented the same account, naming specific names. Movies dramatized the scene in which an Iranian minister gave a terrorist leader the multi-million dollar payment for carrying out the deed. The only debate was whether the PFLP-GC group was actually involved, or whether another Palestinian group might have acted as surrogates. Shortly before the legendary Palestinian terrorist Abu Nidal died in 2002, he reputedly admitted that his forces carried out the Lockerbie bombing (Pyke 2002). Alternatively, Iran might not have used Palestinian intermediaries, but operated directly through its own forces, through

Hizbullah or the Revolutionary Guards. Recently, Iranian defectors have explicitly confirmed that their nation sponsored the attack (Baer 2002). The case for some kind of Iranian role in this atrocity is very strong.

Today, though, not only are Syrians and Iranians not blamed for this crime, but it appears that they never were. In late 1990, history changed, and the explanation for this new reality is a little surprising. Reportedly, British investigators searching over the vast debris field left by the destroyed airliner found a remarkable clue, namely a few clothing fragments stained with the residue of the plastic explosive Semtex. Miraculously, one of these tiny items bore the label of a firm based in the Mediterranean island of Malta. Investigators traced the clothing to one Maltese store, where the owner claimed to remember the sale from two years before. The storekeeper later identified the alleged Libyan agent as the purchaser. The new break in the case thus looks like a triumph of forensic science.

Observers can disagree as to whether the new chain of evidence is any more convincing than the old orthodoxy, whether the Libyan connection rests on grounds any stronger than the old Syrian connection. Very few of us have the forensic skills that allow us to assess the technical details in either instance, though we do know enough to be suspicious of convictions based on identification evidence. Conceivably, we are not dealing with a simple choice of either/or, either Libya or Syria: perhaps there are elements of truth in both the old and new interpretations of the attack. Terrorist groups often serve more than one master at a time. Yet the Libyan theory does have real problems. In order to believe it, we are asked to accept that two totally separate and unconnected terrorist groups were both at exactly the same time planning to attack a U.S. transatlantic flight that passed through Frankfurt. Both groups were using the same sophisticated barometric-pressure bombs, set to detonate when the aircraft reached the exact same altitude; both also planned to conceal their bombs in radio-cassette players of identical make. To say the least, the story inspires skepticism.

What can be said without any question is that the reported new interpretation in late 1990 was enormously valuable for the United States government at precisely that time. Some political background is needed to appreciate this. In August that year, a major political crisis had erupted when Iraq's Saddam Hussein invaded the neighboring oil-rich state of Kuwait. The U.S. desperately wanted to evict Iraq, and then-President George Bush cobbled together a large but fragile global coalition, which ultimately fought a successful war against Iraq, Operation Desert Storm. The most delicate negotiations in coalition-building involved the Arab states, because if they were not allied to the U.S., the war would look like a cultural and religious confrontation between the West and Islam. It was crucial to bring the powerful state of Syria into the alliance, but U.S.-Syrian relations were poisoned by charges that that government had helped murder Americans over Lockerbie.

Just as the diplomatic process was becoming hopelessly entangled, rescue came in the form of the reported discovery of new forensic evidence that purported to show that the actual Lockerbie culprits were Libyan, and Libyan alone. Syria was off the hook, and could become a useful diplomatic partner for the West. Perhaps this new interpretation of the crime was fortuitous, a very lucky break for U.S. diplomacy, but the case also suggests the political processes that might be involved in the attribution of terrorist acts. Responding to the change of scenario, terrorism experts Robert and Tamara Kupperman (1991) argued "American authorities have found it politically expedient to indict two Libyan intelligence officers . . . rather than to pursue the real masterminds."

The Pan Am case is by no means unique in illustrating how the interpretation of a terrorist act changes over time, and in which bureaucratic and political factors shape the allocation of blame. As we will see in the course of this book, many other instances could be chosen. They demonstrate how political pressures affect not only the grand picture of terrorism, but also the investigation of specific terrorist acts. Contrary to the rhetoric of impartial science and forensic investigation, such reconstructions of events are a profoundly political process. Results are arrived at through negotiation, and evidence is then highlighted or discarded to achieve and publicize a desired result. The resulting interpretation then enters the realm of the universally acknowledged fact, and in turn shapes future investigations. As the cynical phrase has it, if I hadn't believed it, I wouldn't have seen it with my own eyes.

"REAL" PROBLEMS

In working from the social constructionist perspective over the years, I have occasionally been charged with denying the existence of problems like rape, child abuse, and so on, and I imagine the same objection could be raised to a study of terrorism. Such a critique would however be quite wrong, in this case as in others. We have to draw a distinction between the objective core of a problem and the layers of interpretation with which it is surrounded—and, often, obscured. To take the example of Acquired Immune Deficiency Syndrome (AIDS), no reputable observer denies that such a disease exists, that it causes immense harm, and that finding a cure or an effective treatment is an urgent necessity. At the same time, it is quite possible to speak of the AIDS *problem* as socially constructed. Social, cultural, and political factors determine how we respond to the disease, what aspects of it we regard as most serious, what rhetorical strategies are used to portray the issue to the public.

Serial murder represents another model example of a socially constructed problem. Every society has individuals who murder repeatedly, and it is difficult to imagine a community that could tolerate such behavior. Yet this kind of activity can be understood in different ways, in religious, psychological, or political terms. It is equally open to debate how extensive the issue is, how seriously it should be treated in comparison with other types of deviance. Our present-day concept of serial murder represents only one possible interpretation among many, and when we portray a problem in one particular way, we are by definition shutting off other potential lines of inquiry: to define is to exclude. When we have determined that the offense of serial murder is especially associated with white men, we tend to ignore similar actions by women, or by racial minorities (Jenkins 1994). We have constructed the problem in such a way that we are literally unable to see these other aspects of the issue.

The example of serial murder offers a powerful analogy to terrorism, another form of behavior that, however we label it, involves grossly unacceptable acts of destruction and violence. To say that terrorism is socially constructed does not mean that the problem is not real or that it does not require an effective response. That the behaviors and actions exist is beyond question: people are murdered, airliners are hijacked, bombs explode. Nobody is denying that the attacks of September 11 occurred, or that Israel faces a suicide bombing campaign, or is arguing that such acts should be either ignored or tolerated. Somebody gave the order to destroy Pan Am flight 103, and that group or nation should pay for its crime, whether we believe that such action should be taken on grounds of retribution or deterrence.

Speaking personally, I was a strong supporter of the military campaign launched by the U.S. government after the September 11 attacks, and in fact, do not see how any administration could have acted otherwise. Unless one is a complete pacifist, who denies any right of self-defense, failing to strike at terrorist networks in Afghanistan and elsewhere simply was not an option. While I might argue with aspects of the government's analysis, such as the language of the war against terrorism, I believed that the underlying policy was appropriate and necessary. I would probably be considered a hawk on aspects of Middle Eastern policy, including the need for confrontation with powers like Iraq and Iran. Yet if military force is necessary, we must be absolutely certain about the appropriate targets, and stories like the Pan Am 103 investigation indicate the difficulties involved in achieving this kind of certainty.

To argue that terrorism is socially constructed does not necessarily favor any political perspective. It is not to propose a weak political response, still less to suggest that the underlying issue should be ignored. Ideally, this approach should lead to a more effective policy in pointing out the difficulties that stand in the way of an accurate understanding of the problem. The greatest advantage of this critical strategy is to stress the need for debate, for asking fundamental questions, rather than simply accepting the consensus view of terrorism so often heard in public discourse.

2

Another Man's Freedom Fighter?

> What occurred in Oklahoma City was no different than what Americans rain on the heads of others all the time, and subsequently, my mindset was and is one of clinical detachment. The bombing of the Murrah building was not personal, no more than when Air Force, Army, Navy or Marine personnel bomb or launch cruise missiles against government installations and their personnel.
>
> —Timothy McVeigh

> My ideological commitment is total and the reward of glory for this relentless battle is to be called a terrorist. I accept the name of terrorist if it is used to mean that I terrorize a one-sided system of iniquitous power and a perversity that comes in many forms.
>
> —Kamel Daoudi, Algerian member of al-Qaeda

Since the word terrorism seems so highly subjective in nature, it is important to say here just how I will be using the term. If indeed the word means whatever anyone wants it to mean at any given time, is my definition anything more than my particular opinion, subject to my political and cultural background, my own personal prejudices? I want to argue, though, that we can formulate a definition that would achieve a widespread consensus. At least we can agree in principle what we should be talking about. (For the historical development of terrorism, see Clutterbuck 1980, 1990; Laqueur 1987, 2001; George and Laird 1996; Simon 2001; Schweitzer and Schweitzer 2002; Hewitt 2002; Carr 2002.)

THE PROBLEM OF DEFINITION

The enormous variety of responses to acts like the Palestinian suicide bombings reminds us that the whole language of "terrorism" is politically loaded. As terrorism has been so much in the news in recent years, many writers have reminded us that "one man's terrorist is another's freedom fighter." Recognizing the intense worldwide debates on this issue, the BBC World Service—one of the world's largest news organizations—simply refuses to use the word "terrorist" for any group or individual, no matter how extreme their actions: in this view, even the September 11 attacks should not be labeled "terrorism." To quote one editor, "In BBC World Service reporting, the word 'terrorist' is not used, no matter who plants bombs, kills or murders" ("BBC's Double Standard" 2001). Osama bin Laden "attacked" the United States, and the U.S. in turn "attacked" his bases in Afghanistan; Palestinians "attack" Israelis, and vice versa; Hamas are "militants." From the BBC's perspective, to use other words would imply improper value judgments. (The organization has of course been vigorously criticized for its failure to draw the obvious moral distinctions in such cases.)

Even within the United States, the term "terrorism" means very different things to different people. While most people would agree that certain actions indisputably represent terrorism (the horrors of September 11 being an obvious example), other actions are treated much more diversely. Real controversy also rages about other actions that at first sight seem to fit the customary images of terrorism, such as the violence carried out by Irish Republicans fighting British rule in Northern Ireland. While some observers at least would characterize these acts as terrorism, others would disagree just as strenuously, and would use alternative descriptions.

While some observers refuse to apply the term terrorism to such armed fighters, others try to expand the description to fit groups and actions that would not normally be categorized by such a damning term. Commonly, activists wishing to point out the evils of some problem they wish to denounce stigmatize it by applying the most harmful label possible, and in contemporary usage, that term is often terrorism, which is perceived as a kind of ultimate evil. Such labeling places a given problem on a par with the obvious evils of armed violence. Some months after the September 11 attacks, for example, the United Nations agency UNICEF proclaimed that the commercial sexual exploitation of children was a "form of terrorism," which needed to be combated by a kind of global war ("U.N.: Child sex trade a form of terrorism" 2001). Some feminist militants regard rape as an act of "gender terrorism" or "sexual terrorism". Even mainstream union activists refer to "corporate terrorism," citing the deaths and injuries arising from unsafe working conditions, especially in the Third World.

THE CRIMES OF THE POWERFUL

One common means of expanding the definition is to suggest that states are by far the worst terrorists, and that compared to their crimes, the activities of sub-state groups fall into insignificance. The notion that states can use terrorist methods is scarcely controversial—think of Hitler's Germany or Stalin's Soviet Union—but modern radicals often apply the same critique to Western democratic nations, especially the United States. Over the past quarter century, the use of the "terrorism" card has become quite commonplace in radical denunciations of US foreign policy.

The vision of the liberal democratic state as uniquely violent grows out of the Marxist vision of the state as the servant of the capitalist order, which is founded upon exploitation. From this perspective, state violence and terror are implicit to the structure of capitalism, and will assuredly increase as social conflict grows more intense. At the same time, the Marxist vision sees the media as part of that same capitalist order. Putting these facts together, we would expect media reports to condemn the violence of those seeking to overthrow the capitalist order, rather than those using far more savage terror to uphold it. A Marxist would expect the capitalist state both to use terror, and to lie systematically about the nature of terrorism. From this perspective, the term "terrorism" is no more than a political label, which basically any powerful group applies to others that it dislikes and wishes to condemn, so that any official analysis of the "terrorist threat" would contain a large measure of hypocrisy. In the furious debates over terrorism in the early twentieth century, revolutionary Leon Trotsky (1909) commented, "The only question remaining is whether the bourgeois politicians have the right to pour out their flood of moral indignation about proletarian terrorism when their entire state apparatus with its laws, police and army is nothing but an apparatus for capitalist terror!"

Convinced Marxists are not common today, but in somewhat diluted form, the idea that Western states are the worst terrorists has influenced large sections of the liberal left. The theory has gained influence because of the left's concern with Third World issues, since colonialism and imperialism seem to offer such obvious manifestations of Western state terrorism in action. In recent years, too, liberal academics have drawn heavily on Edward Said's theory of Orientalism, which describes how Western culture imagines other non-Western societies as primitive and violent (Said 1978). In reality, Said suggests, the West is doing no more than projecting its own violence onto other communities, partly to justify Western imperial exploitation of the rest of the globe. From this perspective, it is only logical that the West would imagine the worst terrorism as coming from outside its borders, and would imagine Middle Eastern peoples, for instance, as fierce and violent barbarian attackers. (Said himself is of Palestinian origin.)

Once again, the dominant Western vision of terrorism is portrayed as cynical and hypocritical. This approach is popular because it is so rhetorically powerful. Whenever a terrorist action occurs, and is condemned by Western media, Leftist critics can use the public attention to gain a platform for their own distinctive critique.

Within the U.S., long-running controversies over defining terrorism reached a new intensity following September 11, when the government declared its "war on terrorism." In using this term, U.S. authorities—and mainstream media—generally had a very clear idea of the kind of groups they were targeting. They were usually thinking of sub-state movements like al-Qaeda whose activities were directed against the West, often with the support of radical Middle Eastern governments and intelligence services. Though this categorization seemed obvious, it was bitterly attacked by radicals and extreme liberals, who had spent many years criticizing the U.S. for illegal acts of violence against civilians in Third World nations like Vietnam, Guatemala, Chile and El Salvador. In the leftist view, moreover, such violence was commonly undertaken in the interests of established wealth and corporate interests. How, then, can the US criticize bin Laden? Even in the aftermath of an outrageous attack like September 11, and the deaths of thousands of civilians, a left-wing discourse identified the United States government as quite as much a terrorist organization as al-Qaeda or Hizbullah. The U.S., it seems, is as truly a rogue state as Libya or Iraq. In terms of the harm inflicted (it is claimed) terrorist groups do not approach the scale or savagery of states, including the U.S. and its allies. The US thus had no moral authority to denounce anyone else as a terrorist.

Often, these views stemmed from long-time veterans of anti-war campaigns, dating back to the Vietnam era. At a peace rally in Washington DC in 2002, Catholic pacifist Philip Berrigan asked the crowd, "How can the number one terrorist nation [that is, the U.S.] wage any sort of realistic war against terrorism?" (Quoted by O'Neill 2002; compare Lernoux 1980). Left-wing journalist John Pilger argues that "Al-Qaeda's training camps in Afghanistan were kindergartens compared with the world's leading university of terrorism at Fort Benning in Georgia. Known until recently as the School of the Americas, it trained tyrants and some sixty thousand Latin American Special Forces, paramilitaries and intelligence agents in the black arts of terrorism" (Pilger 2002. Compare Herman 1982; Anderson and Anderson 1986; Herman and O'Sullivan 1989; Zinn 2002). Against this background, terrorist attacks might even seem like justified revenge against Western oppression. Leftist veteran Tariq Ali claims that on September 11, "the "subjects of the Empire had struck back" (Ali 2002). Speaking of the evils of globalization and corporate centralization, leftist film maker Oliver Stone declared that "The revolt on September 11 was a fuck you [to the New World Order]" (Grossberg 2001). If acts like the destruction of the World Trade Center are seen in terms of a "revolt," of a blow against imperialism, the speaker is coming perilously close to justifying the attacks.

Probably the best-known exponent of this kind of moral equivalence is academic Noam Chomsky (Chomsky 1988, 2000, 2001). Chomsky was not arguing that the September 11 attacks were justified—he calls them "horrifying atrocities"—but he urged that they must be set against the U.S. record as a leading terrorist nation. Basic to Chomsky's critique is the claim that the U.S. government itself has been officially adjudged guilty of international terrorism by the International Court of Justice, and that it is indeed the only nation ever so condemned. In fact, Chomsky's statement is false, as we can see if we trace the background to his charge. In 1986, the nation of Nicaragua complained against the U.S. for its military and economic campaign against the leftist Sandinista government, which was friendly with the Soviet bloc. Nicaragua brought a legal case to the International Court, over the objections of the U.S. government, which denied that the Court had jurisdiction. The U.S. accordingly boycotted the proceedings, and was condemned in its absence. The verdict mentioned the "unlawful use of force" by the U.S., never mentioning the concept of terrorism. (Robbing a bank involves "unlawful force," but it fits nobody's definition of terrorism.) Nevertheless, the claim that the Court condemned the U.S. for "international terrorism" is often cited by Chomsky, Pilger and others, and has acquired the character of a political myth, a kind of left-wing urban legend. (The claim is cited frequently in Chomsky 2001; Pilger 2002.) Chomsky blames the US "terror state" for millions of deaths around the globe, in Iraq, Latin America and elsewhere, violence that in some cases (he claims) amounted to genocide.

Views like Chomsky's were highly unpopular, and were denounced by conservatives like William Bennett, who saw the conflict with Middle Eastern terrorism in terms of "moral clarity": the West was right, and the terrorists were wrong (Bennett 2002). But the far-Left critique also angered many liberals, for in effect offering a kind of support to terrorism. Also, the Left was failing to define what terrorism actually was, as opposed to merely using it as a shorthand for extreme violence, without taking account of the nature of the violence or its victims. For several months after September 11, the liberal magazine *New Republic* ran a regular series of the most outrageous quotes from the far Left on these issues, under the evocative title "Idiocy Watch."

While not exonerating U.S. misdeeds over the years, these liberals felt that groups like al-Qaeda did represent an authentic menace to peace and world order, and which needed to be combated and destroyed. From this point of view, leftists like Chomsky allow their visceral hatred of U.S. policies to blind them to the genuine evils perpetrated by terrorist movements.

As Michael Walzer argues, no matter what the alleged evils of past U.S. administrations, "none of this, however, excuses terrorism; none of it even makes terrorism morally understandable . . . The only political response to ideological fanatics and suicidal holy warriors is implacable opposition." "The murder of innocent people is not excusable" (Walzer 2001, 2002). Walzer, like other liberals, was arguing that the label of "terrorism" was more than simply a question of where on happened to be standing on the political spectrum: it described conduct that was wrong and immoral, or—if one chooses to use the word—evil.

In recent years, the debate about the relative evils of states and revolutionaries—of which side is in fact the terrorist—has most often surfaced in the context of the Middle East. Here again, the charge is that "terrorism" is just a convenient label used by the strong against the weak, by established states against their enemies. Commenting on violent Palestinian actions, the Palestinian Authority's chief representative to the United States, Hasan Abdel Rahman, has said "if I were Arafat, I would support the right of the Palestinians to defend themselves against Israel's occupation. The British called George Washington a terrorist. The white South Africans called Nelson Mandela a terrorist. . . . The white South Africans lied about the African resistance. The British lied about American resistance. When you are a colonial power, in order to delegitimize you, suddenly you are accused of being a terrorist" ("A Closer Look" 2002). In this view, George Washington was in exactly the same moral category as Ahmad Jibril or Muhammad al-Ghoul.

Even in the U. S., Ted Turner, head of the CNN network, has declared that the Palestinian fighters were no worse than the Israelis they were targeting, He said, "The Palestinians are fighting with human suicide bombers, that's all they have. The Israelis . . . they've got one of the most powerful military machines in the world. The Palestinians have nothing. So who are the terrorists? I would make a case that both sides are involved in terrorism."

HARD CASES

Also, the division between terrorist/nonterrorist is not as simple as the media might lead us to think. Though we speak of "terrorist groups," some groups use terrorist methods part of the time, but on other occasions engage in regular warfare. We might take as an example the African National Congress (ANC) that led the struggle against the white minority regime of South Africa from the 1960s until its victory in 1994, under the leadership of Nelson Mandela. Most people worldwide would see the ANC as a legitimate resistance movement, fighting for liberation through its military wing, *Umkhonto we Sizwe* ("Spear of the Nation"). The old

South African regime was obviously unjust and oppressive, while Mandela himself was a statesman who exercised enormous moral authority. Generally speaking, even though it was a banned underground organization, the ANC tried to operate according to the Geneva Conventions regulating warfare. When in 1985, the group succeeded in bombing South African air force headquarters in Pretoria, most would agree that the target met customary definitions of a military target—even though nineteen civilians were killed (Davis 1987; Kasrils 1993; Younis 2000).

Nevertheless, ANC fighters did on occasion engage in acts of savage random violence against civilians, and thus engaged in terrorism. In 1986, a guerrilla attacked two Durban bars popular with young white people, using an explosive device designed to cause the maximum number of casualties. (In addition to a hundred pounds of explosives, the bomb included bags of machine gun bullets and metal scraps, to serve as shrapnel.) Three women were killed, and seventy injured (Keller 1992). Do acts like that mean that the whole ANC was a terrorist organization? Some extreme conservatives in the U.S. felt so, though their views never gained much support.

To take a related example, we have already noticed American ambiguities over whether the Irish Republican Army (IRA) can properly be characterized as terrorists. For many Americans, and not just those of Irish origins, the IRA should rather be seen as heroic guerrillas, and it is imperative for the British government to accommodate at least some of their political demands. Throughout the long years of the "Troubles," from 1969 through 1998, the IRA survived chiefly from U.S. support and donations by private groups and individuals. On many occasions, the IRA have undoubtedly fought as guerrillas or partisans, with British soldiers and police officers as their targets of choice. At times their acts have just as certainly merited the label of terrorism. Just to take one example, in 1987, the IRA planted a bomb at a Remembrance Day parade for veterans in the Northern Ireland town of Enniskillen. Eleven were killed, and dozens mutilated or severely wounded (McDaniel 1997). By most definitions, that was terrorism. Even if the IRA had carried out no such other attacks (and there were many, usually with fewer casualties), should that event alone make the group a "terrorist organization"? In placing the terrorist label, it is no defense to argue that the authorities committed crimes as bad as or worse than those of the IRA or the ANC—as British and South African forces assuredly have done on occasion. The fact remains that even these favored guerrilla organizations have on occasion carried out blatant terrorist attacks (Bishop and Mallie 1989; Stalker 1989; Dillon 1990; Geraghty 2000; Bell 2000).

Just as controversial is the question of whether terrorist acts by one organization discredit a whole cause. The worst single event of the Irish struggle to date occurred in 1998, when a bomb in the town of Omagh killed 29, including many women and children. This act was not the work of the IRA, which had officially renounced violence for political methods. The organization condemned the crime, which was undertaken by an extremist sect called the "Real IRA." Yet is it still legitimate to denounce the whole of Irish Republicanism for its ideological linkage to the Omagh attack? Equally, should the suicide bombings carried out by Hamas discredit the whole militant Palestinian movement?

To take an analogy from that same region, the state of Israel itself was created in the 1940s following a guerrilla war by underground Jewish organizations like the *Haganah*, in what modern Israelis call their War of Independence. These movements generally fought a guerrilla war, a military resistance movement, against British occupying forces and rival Arab fighters. In 1945, the militant Jewish *Irgun* killed eight British soldiers in a bomb attack on a Jerusalem police station. (The *Irgun Zvai Leumi* was the "National Military Organization.") Yet some wings of the Jewish resistance were prepared to use overtly terrorist tactics, including the *Irgun* itself and especially the so-called Stern Gang (the "Fighters for the Freedom of Israel"). In 1946, these groups were responsible for blowing up the King David Hotel, which served as British headquarters in the area. Ninety people were killed, including many civilians. On a single day in 1947, Jewish terrorists bombed buses in Haifa and Ramleh, killing twenty Arabs, five Jews and two British soldiers. In 1948, the same groups undertook massacres of Arab villagers, killing hundreds of unarmed civilians. They also engaged in international terrorism, blowing up the British embassy in Rome in 1946 (Clarke 1981; Levine 1991; Zadka 1995; Bell 1996).

If Palestinian Arabs undertook acts like that against Jewish targets in Israel today, they would be described as outrageous terrorism. Such violence would provide the grounds for massive retaliation against not just the specific group that directed it, but against the whole Palestinian movement. In the Israeli case, however, most observers draw a careful distinction between the legitimate activities of the *Haganah* and the fanaticism of the Stern Gang or the *Irgun*. Terrorist acts by one group did not extend the terrorist label to the whole cause for which they were fighting. Two of the most notorious Jewish extremists of that era, Menachem Begin and Yitzhak Shamir, would go on to become Prime Ministers of Israel, and both would be noted for their extremely hard line against Palestinian Arab terrorism. The *Haganah* itself became the core of the Israel Defense Force, that is, the army of the state of Israel.

NAMING AND NOT NAMING

The decision to name a particular group as terrorist is complicated by the policy implications of such an act. In different circumstances, these consequences can lead governments to apply the term where it should not properly be applied or, in some cases, fail to use the term where it would seem to belong. Labeling a group as terrorist is such a potent act because of the absolute condemnation that the word suggests. Unlike other descriptions like "guerrilla," it is rare for any group to describe itself overtly as terrorist, or as using terrorist tactics. Terrorist groups virtually always describe themselves through a more acceptable term, such as "army," with its its "soldiers" or "guerrillas" (this is the terminology preferred by the Irish Republican *Army*). The full name of Hamas includes the word for "Resistance," and the leader of the group's military wing declared that "In general, the Brigades are a small army subject to political decisions, like any [other] army in the world. It has all the kinds of divisions and structures that an army has. We are soldiers" ("Interview with Salah Sh'hadeh" 2002). In practical terms, this implies that fighters deserve the protections of international law, either the full rights of captured combatants, or else some more limited form of consideration. Governments usually resist such a classification, and terrorist wars often involve prolonged struggles over the granting of prisoner of war status (Delgado n.d.; Beresford 1997). Any group categorized as terrorist is denied any legitimacy, and the public tends to feel that no measures are too severe to deal with it. It is almost as if the group has been read out of the human race.

In some cases, even regular armed forces can be delegitimized by these means. In World War II British and U.S. forces launched highly effective commando warfare against Germany, using hit and run tactics, and operating behind enemy lines. The Germans wished to respond to this challenge without openly violating international law. This concern may sound strange given the horrific atrocities that the Nazis committed, but for diplomatic reasons, they were anxious to maintain a pretense of legality when dealing with the Western powers. To solve the problem, the Germans declared that these commandos were in fact terrorists, "terror and sabotage troops," who were for this reason not covered by the laws of war. Hitler complained that because "the members of the so-called Commandos behave in a particularly brutal and underhand manner . . . all men operating against German troops in so-called Commando raids in Europe or in Africa, are to be annihilated to the last man," that is, always executed without mercy. "Under no circumstances may it be allowed that a troop sent to carry out explosions, sabotage or acts of terrorism simply surrenders and is taken into custody, and is then treated according to the rules of the Geneva Convention" ("Hitler's Commando Order" 1942).

In modern times, too, states facing revolutionary challenges have used a similar tactic, declaring all enemies of the state to be terrorists, to be treated as wild animals. This kind of approach lay behind the savage brutality of the "dirty war" in Argentina in the 1970s, when some thirty thousand people were forcibly "disappeared." Some of those killed may indeed have fitted the terrorist description, but many more did not (Marchak 1999; Lewis 2002).

On other occasions, some regimes have been reluctant to classify groups as terrorists because doing so would bring undesirable policy consequences. Once a group is so labeled, that discredits other causes or issues that they support and, in some instances, a government might actually sympathize with that cause, even if they condemn the violent methods. We have already seen that Arab governments refuse to condemn Palestinian acts as terrorism. The U.S. government faced such a dilemma in Central America in the 1980s, when the region was swept by revolutions and civil wars. In Nicaragua, the U.S. supported counter-revolutionary forces, the "Contras," who were trying to overthrow the left-wing government. The Contras carried out many acts of brutal violence, including acts against civilians that fit the definition of terrorism. Anti-Contra groups in the U.S. and overseas had no difficulty in declaring the group terrorists, but the U.S. strenuously resisted such a label, and President Reagan famously declared that the Contras were heroic freedom fighters, "the moral equivalent of our Founding Fathers." If Contra fighters were terrorists, then the cause they were fighting for was discredited, and so, in effect, was a cornerstone of U.S. foreign policy.

TOWARD CONSENSUS

Historically, attempts to find a legal definition of terrorism have often been questionable. Often such laws have erred in the direction of classifying most violent opposition to a state as terrorist activity and thus illegitimate, leaving no justifiable grounds for resistance even to the most savage dictatorship. In 1937, a League of Nations Convention offered a widely influential definition of terrorism as "All criminal acts directed against a State and intended or calculated to create a state of terror in the minds of particular persons or a group of persons or the general public" ("Definitions of Terrorism" n.d.). The date alone should point out some of the problems with that phrasing: the governments in power at that time included the brutal dictatorships of Germany, Japan, Italy, and the Soviet Union, which to modern eyes *should* have been opposed or overthrown, by armed force if necessary. By the League's definition though, any clandestine attempt to resist German or Soviet authorities through violence would have been illegal terrorism.

Not much better is the modern FBI definition. This presents terrorism as "the unlawful use of force or violence against persons or property to intimidate or coerce a government, the civilian population, or any segment thereof, in furtherance of political or social goals." Once again, all governments are set on a moral par, so that an act of resistance against the most savage dictatorship is treated as indistinguishable from that against a liberal democracy. Moreover, "unlawful" could mean an act contrary to any nation's laws, however repressive. It would, as stated, certainly define as terrorism the ANC resistance in the South Africa of the 1980s. The definition makes no allowance for justified resistance to tyranny, and uses terrorism as a blanket term for any act of political violence that the U.S. government happens to dislike.

With all the obvious difficulties involved, it may seem impossible to find even a loose definition of terrorism that would be widely accepted. Yet we need not fall back on total subjectivity, since the concept does have some commonly accepted features, which it has maintained over a lengthy period of time.

We can begin by looking at the origins of the very word *terrorism*. The word was coined in the 1790s to describe the actions of the ruling party during the "Terror" that followed the French Revolution, during the age of the guillotine. By modern standards, this particular repression was not particularly extreme, because it only claimed several thousand lives, rather than the millions of deaths inflicted by recent dictatorships. But it did cause great horror. At that stage, terrorism implied violent acts carried out against certain people in order to frighten and cow many others, or to terrorize a nation. Unlike warfare, killings were carried out against nonsoldiers, and often against people chosen because they represented a particular class or section of opinion. In this sense, the violence involved a good deal of randomness in the selection of victims. In its origins, the term usually meant violence carried out by a government or a ruling order, rather than, as later, the actions of antigovernment rebels. That meaning only became common at the end of the nineteenth century, when left-wing and radical rebels launched violent attacks against European states like France and Russia, using bombs and political assassinations.

Since that era, the word terrorism has commonly come to mean violent acts carried out randomly against nonmilitary, civilian targets, with the aim of inspiring fear in the wider population. Also, the acts are intended to promote some kind of political goals. By that standard, then George Washington was not a terrorist, since he never used violence against civilian or nonmilitary targets. Rather he fought as a soldier in an organized, disciplined army, which happened not to be recognized as legitimate by his British enemies. Nor was Nelson Mandela a terrorist, since his forces usually hit military targets.

THE STATE DEPARTMENT MODEL

One of the best modern definitions of terrorism is that developed by the U.S. State Department, which emphasizes not the fact of violence, but rather its indiscriminate character. In this view terrorism is "premeditated, politically motivated violence perpetrated against noncombatant targets by sub-national groups or clandestine agents, usually intended to influence an audience." (This definition of terrorism is contained in Title 22 of the U.S. Code, Section 2656f(d): see "War on Terrorism" 2001.)

The definition is not perfect, since many writers believe that the worst terrorism is often the work of states rather than "sub-national groups." The violence carried out by the German Nazi regime against its citizens surely fits older definitions of terrorism, as does the repression inflicted by many modern dictatorships. Palestinians would argue that terrorism is the only word to describe Israeli military actions against them. In the Central America of the 1980s, it would be difficult to find a better word to characterize events like the massacre of hundreds of peasants by U.S.-backed Salvadoran troops in the village of El Mozote—one of many such events in the region in these years (Danner 1994). As Michael Walzer argues, such state abuses should certainly count as terrorism if they meet the basic criteria of violence against civilians: "The common element is the targeting of people who are, in both the military and political senses, noncombatants: not soldiers, not public officials, just ordinary people. And they aren't killed incidentally in the course of actions aimed elsewhere; they are killed intentionally" (Walzer 2002).

There are other areas of controversy. What exactly is a *noncombatant*? Technically it means someone not engaged in fighting, but does this term apply to a soldier off-duty, or a soldier engaged in peacekeeping missions? When Shi'ite Muslim guerrillas killed 240 Marines engaged in peacekeeping activities in Beirut in 1983, some sections of the U.S. government decried the act as terrorism, while other officials preferred to see it as warfare against uniformed combatants. A supporter of Osama bin Laden might argue that the September 11 attack on the Pentagon building was not terrorism, since this facility is clearly a major military center, and all of the casualties on the ground were connected with the U.S. armed forces and American war-making capabilities. In some loose sense all were "combatants." (Such a defense would not apply to the passengers on the airliner used to attack the building.)

A similar point is raised when regular military operations cause civilian casualties. During World War II, Allied bombing directed against military and industrial targets caused hundreds of thousands of civilian deaths, though these casualties were not the primary goal of the action. Most observers would not use the term terrorism to describe vastly destructive attacks like Hiroshima or Dresden, though some pacifists would place them in such a category. Nevertheless, such incidents do indicate the dilemmas in drawing a neat line between terrorism and the horrors of modern warfare as conducted by states. Terrorists themselves often cite these events to justify their own actions, and to argue that the West is hypocritical in condemning them. The ANC guerrilla who bombed the Durban clubs asked his critics "What about Nagasaki? . . . What about Dresden and Vietnam?" (Keller 1992). Within al-Qaeda itself, the September 11 attacks were described as the Hiroshima Plan.

Yet the State Department definition gives us a solid working basis for discussion. Critically, too, it does not offer a blanket condemnation for armed struggles against regimes, regardless of whether those regimes are repressive or democratic: it does allow for legitimate resistance, provided that violence is not directed randomly against civilians. It thus provides criteria for distinguishing between terrorism and other types of violent actions, which should variously be categorized as acts of war or resistance, of partisan or guerrilla conflict, of subversion or sabotage. Nor is it suggested that any group that has ever used terrorism is of its nature a terrorist organization. Also, by stressing the political quality of the activity, the definition prevents us expanding the term to cover every form of behavior that we might want to stigmatize, such as child sex trafficking. Since it demands that acts involve violence, the definition prevents the loose rhetorical extension of the terrorism concept to generalized acts of injustice or exploitation.

Finally, the definition usefully demands that the activity should include some degree of organization, should be the work of *groups or clandestine agents*. This prevents us from counting every instance of racially or religiously motivated hate crime as terrorism. Even so, some instances do seem to involve indisputable terrorist acts being carried out by individuals. One noteworthy American example would be Joseph Paul Franklin, a highly motivated ultraright militant who launched a private three-year war in the late 1970s, which involved murdering interracial couples and bombing synagogues. In 2002, again, there was intense debate about whether terrorism was involved when an Egyptian man opened fire at the ticket counter of the Israeli airline El Al at Los Angeles international airport. Though he was not formally affiliated to any known group, he had earlier been linked to the fanatical Islamist organization *al-Gama'a al-Islamiya* (Lichtblau 2002). Moreover, the man's violently anti-Jewish and anti-American ideas fit exactly with those of many established Islamist movements, including many operating in the United States. In considering our definition, we might want to add that individual acts can be counted as terrorism if they occur within the context of an ongoing political campaign, and follow the same goals as established paramilitary movements.

Significantly, the State Department concept is widely accepted even by people who would normally be expected to loathe anything associated with the U.S. government. At least in informal discussions, I have heard radical Muslims and even Hamas supporters strongly agree with the basic idea that an act crosses the line into terrorism when it targets civilians or non-combatants. They believe that this definition reflects the teachings of the *Quran* and the religion of Islam. One of Egypt's leading *muftis*, or spiritual figures, is Dr. Ahmad Al-Tayyeb, who said of the September 11 attacks that "All the Muslims, and the Arab world, rejected and condemned the event, because they wouldn't want it to happen to them, so they don't want it to happen to others. We say this because Islam prohibits such attacks on peaceful civilians" (http://www.memri.org/bin/latestnews.cgi?ID=SD40202). When thousands were killed during the attack on the World Trade Center, the common response among many anti-American Muslims was not to justify the act, but rather to assert that it must have been carried out by some non-Muslim group, namely the Israelis. In other words, they were accepting that the act did constitute illegitimate terrorism, and tried to displace the blame onto others, however unrealistically. For the working purposes of this book, therefore, I will be using the State Department definition.

But even if we can agree broadly what terrorism is, ideological and political considerations still play a huge role in shaping official responses, and that is as true in the United States as in any other society. What seems like a sensible and widely acceptable approach to the concept runs into serious difficulties when it encounters the world of practical politics, and bureaucratic self-interest.

3

The American Politics of Terrorism

> The U.S.—with our open society and huge borders—may seem vulnerable. Not so. It's actually quite difficult for terrorists to enter the country through our well-patrolled airports. . . . Terrorism is horrible, but there's little reason to lose sleep worrying you'll be a victim—especially if you don't leave the good old USA.
>
> —Stan Crock, 2000

To describe terrorism as a political issue requires some justification. In any American election, has one party advocated terrorism, while the other opposed it? Every responsible political figure agrees that terrorism is, of its nature, bad. Yet there is still vast room for debate as to whether particular actions or movements constitute terrorism, and even if they do, which types of terrorism are the most serious. Some terrorist organizations are taken far less seriously than others, depending largely on the political context. Different ideological perspectives try to interpret the activity differently, in ways that offer political advantage to a particular cause. And almost invariably, the word terrorism refers not just to an illegitimate tactic, but to a package of other political beliefs that a particular speaker seeks to condemn.

The particular political direction involved in such labeling very much depends on the ideological coloring of the agencies with the power to impose those categories. An administration of one political shade is likely to respond to terrorist acts differently from another, and that will fundamentally shape the response of federal agencies. The official response will be conditioned by very different attitudes toward law enforcement and policing, and the proper balance between liberty and security, between individual rights and the prevention of terrorist acts.

USING TERRORISM

Terrorism is a very old established part of American life. As we can see from Table 3.1, there are very few periods in American history when terrorist acts have not occurred with some frequency. This table is very selective: a similar picture would also emerge if we traced events occurring before my arbitrary beginning date of 1940. In fact, the volume of activity is a striking rebuttal of the familiar view of terrorism as something either new or foreign to the United States. Admittedly, the most destructive attacks, the ones causing hundreds of fatalities, have generally occurred since the 1980s—the Lockerbie bombing, Oklahoma City, the embassy attacks in East Africa, and of course September 11—but this fact reflects technological change rather than the overall number of incidents. Tragically, several developments have simply made it easier to kill large numbers at a time, including the greater capacity of airliners (and their vast fuel loads), and the use of more powerful explosives and sophisticated demolition techniques (Wilkinson and Jenkins 1999). New military tactics have also played a role, and above all the use of suicide bombers. Yet the increase in casualties in no sense represents an increase in the number of active groups, or of attacks. Arguably, the decade after 1968 was the period in which active groups most proliferated within the U.S., and when attacks (often deadly) most often featured in the headlines. Yet these and other terrorist campaigns of bygone years have largely faded from memory: terrorism is a menace that is discovered anew in each generation, if not in each new decade.

The political uses of terrorism also have a long history. For well over a century, the idea of terrorism has proved to be a potent weapon in partisan debates in the U.S. In no case, of course, has one party actually used terrorism against its rival, but on several occasions both parties and their administrations have used the image of terrorism to attract support for themselves, while discrediting their enemies. In such cases, governments often use a common rhetorical process by which one form of behavior is stigmatized by linking it with another phenomenon that is commonly perceived as far more dangerous. This device is sometimes termed *mapping together*. If a movement associated with a particular cause is commonly agreed to be terrorist, then, fairly or otherwise, that stigma adheres not only to the armed group itself, but also to other peaceful groups that might share its views, whether or not they have any connection with violence. This association gives powerful rhetorical ammunition to the enemies of that cause, who can dismiss their foes as terrorist sympathizers. If a militant Puerto Rican group is seen as a terrorist organization, this has a very damaging effect not just on Americans trying to organize support for that cause, but for anyone campaigning for left-wing or nationalist issues in that region, even if they totally reject violence. If Palestinian movements are classified as terrorist, opponents can then classify any support whatever for the Palestinian cause as giving aid and comfort to international terrorism. The same kind of problem expansion occurs when authorities speak of "eco-terrorism," since this opens the way to condemning peaceful environmental protests. (For the debate over the eco-terror concept, see Bari 1994; Lee 1995; U.S. House of Representatives 2000a; Zakin 2002.)

The terrorist label might also have damaging legal consequences in that supporters of the condemned movement might be subject to criminal penalties for acts like conspiracy, or supporting a terrorist movement. In modern America, the label gives authorities wide discretion in matters of immigration law and deportation. And if a movement is under investigation, it is natural for police to exercise surveillance over likely supporters in related groups. To speak of Puerto Rican terrorism or eco-terrorism authorizes the deployment of a variety of police surveillance techniques against peaceful sympathizers. Conversely, this explains why it is in the interests of political movements and pressure groups of all kinds to resist the application of the terrorist label to other groups that share their general political perspective.

TERRORIST SCARES

Sometimes, concerns about terrorism have been so intense and widespread as if to justify the title of social panic. By using this term, I am obviously not suggesting that governments should not try to suppress actual armed violence against the state, or not defend their citizens. On occasion, though, fears of terrorist violence spill over into exaggerated concerns about the scale of the danger, and into indiscriminate attacks on people wrongly suspected of involvement in violence. Commonly, terrorist scares acquire a powerful social momentum of their own, especially following some sensational crime or exposé. Government and media pay intensified attention to acts that would hitherto have received no more than local notice, which are now contextualized as part of a surging social problem or crime wave. This new recognition in turn arouses greater fear, and greater sensitivity to the existence of moderate or nonviolent groups that share common goals with the perceived terrorists.

Terrorist scares have occurred quite regularly in American history and some have left a lasting impression on the political landscape. In 1919 and 1920, the country experienced what is often known as the Red Scare, following dozens of bombings and bank robberies attributed to anarchist and Communist militants. The terrorist wave culminated in September 1920 when a huge bomb exploded on New York's Wall Street, killing thirty. In response to public fears about revolutionary terrorism, the government began a draconian campaign of mass arrests and deportations that crippled the radical movement and laid the foundation for the conservative politics of the next decade (Feuerlicht 1971). The purges especially targeted foreign radicals and labor activists, many of whom rejected violence. Out of these conflicts came two lasting presences in American life. One was the FBI, hitherto a tiny agency, but which now began its rapid rise under J. Edgar Hoover, who personally organized the raids and deportations. On the other side of the spectrum was the American Civil Liberties Union, which mobilized to resist official repression.

Quite similar events occurred between 1939 and 1941, when the Red Scare was succeeded by a Brown Scare. Just as conservatives feared the red of revolution, so liberals and leftists were alarmed by the brown associated with Fascists and Nazis. (Hitler's street thugs were the Brown Shirts.) And just as conservatives dreaded subversion directed from Moscow, the liberal Roosevelt administration turned the tables by warning of an international terror network controlled by Berlin. At this point, the Democratic administration faced deep internal divisions over intervention in World War II, and many people across the political spectrum favored nonintervention, or isolation. The administration tried to counter them by exaggerating the danger of armed groups on the extreme right, and suggesting that these were about to launch a terrorist war in America. This charge was justified to the extent that armed right-wing militias did exist: there were Nazis like the German Bund, anti-Jewish bands like the Christian Front, and many ethnic fascist groups. And as in the 1990s, this right-wing movement found unity through talk radio, namely the anti-Jewish polemics of broadcaster Father Charles Coughlin. But Roosevelt supporters, assisted by the FBI, made the far rightists look much more competent and threatening than they actually were. This made Americans more concerned about a direct fascist threat to the homeland, while discrediting isolationists and supporters of the antiwar America First movement. Through a kind of guilt by association, people who opposed Roosevelt on reasonable political or constitutional grounds found themselves stigmatized by the rhetorical linkage with Nazi terrorism (Herzstein 1994; Jenkins 1997).

This scare became an immense presence in the mass media, and it was the subject of some of the best-selling books of the era, notably John Roy Carlson's *Under Cover* (1943). In such works, ordinary Americans could read the terrifying statements of extremists warning "Jew hunting is going to be pretty good soon, and we are practicing." According to these hysterical boasts, "the boys" would "dynamite Detroit, Pittsburgh, Chicago—paralyze transportation and isolate whole sections of the country . . . A blood bath is the only way out." Carlson, a gutsy investigative journalist, describes a meeting of the fascist Iron Guard movement, part of the "deeper Nazi underworld" of New York City. Its members used the Hitler salute, and they mapped "every arsenal, subway station, power house, police and gasoline station, public building" in preparation for an armed rising, to be launched with rifles and bombs. The club leader dreamed of the day of action: "I'd like to be able to pick up the paper someday and read 'Grand Central Station Bombed,' 'The White House Blown to Bits,' or '*Queen Mary* Sunk at her Dock'.... Terror! Terror! Terror! That is our watchword from now on" (Carlson 1943). In 1940, the FBI arrested much of the Christian Front leadership for plotting an armed revolution, including acts of bombing and assassination (Jenkins 1997).

Groups like this did exist, and most used outrageous rhetoric: some also acquired weapons. But we have to be very careful about using such accounts, since they stem from sources with a strong interest in making the far right look as dangerous as possible. (Carlson worked closely with the New York City FBI.) And the tactic worked: accounts like *Under Cover* helped to swing political support away from the isolationists and the moderate right, and towards the cause of Roosevelt. Again, the FBI was a beneficiary, and the agency secured even more prestige, and more investigative powers.

The Red and Brown Scares were unusual in the extent of public concern they induced and the strength of the reaction, but events like these have occurred more recently. In the 1960s, for instance, liberals tried to discredit right-wing conservatives by linking them to the Minutemen, an extremist militia that armed and trained to resist a possible Communist takeover in the U.S. (Jones 1968). Again in the 1990s, as we will see below, vastly exaggerated portraits of the right-wing militias greatly advanced the political cause of the liberal Clinton administration. Such scares are the prerogative of no one party or ideological strand. What makes such events possible is the sheer volume of terrorist activities in the United States. Any administration that wishes to choose terrorist movements and list them together as part of a violent wave usually has ample ammunition for its cause.

THE NON-CRISIS OF THE 1970s

Conversely, it is remarkable that the obvious wave of terrorist attacks between about 1973 and 1977 did *not* generate a crisis comparable to those of earlier years. If anyone had wished to argue for a generalized American terrorist crisis, they could easily have done so by citing the violent activities of Cuban, Puerto Rican, Jewish, Croatian, Armenian, Palestinian and African-American extremists, together with far-leftists like the Symbionese Liberation Army, SLA (US House of Representatives 1974; Bryan 1975; Payne and Findley 1976; U.S. Senate 1975b–c; Beal 1976; Frankfort 1984; Castellucci 1986). If circumstances had been different, a terrorist menace might have found a focus in spectacular events like the twin assassination attempts on President Ford (one by an associate of the SLA), and the spectacular political murder of a Chilean exile in Washington DC (Freed and Landis 1980). Of course, terrorist actions drew media attention, especially sensational events like the SLA's kidnapping of heiress Patricia Hearst, and her subsequent conversion to that movement. But militant movements were always treated as discrete phenomena, rather than components of a looming terrorist threat. This is remarkable considering that the number of active movements was far higher in the mid-1970s than in 1920 or 1940, and the tally of deaths was also larger.

The lack of a "terrorist crisis" in 1975–76 requires explanation. Perhaps public attention at this time was so focused on wrongdoing by police and intelligence agencies themselves, acts often undertaken with the nominal goal of defeating subversion. Between 1975 and 1977, the news media were regularly reporting the findings of the Church and Rockefeller Commissions concerning alleged intelligence atrocities at home and abroad. At the same time, the House's Select Committee on Assassinations was exploring whether government agencies might have participated in killing President Kennedy and Martin Luther King (Olmsted 1996). Popular American films about political violence and terror in this period were far more likely to feature as villains "rogue CIA agents" rather than actual terrorists, foreign or domestic. Since agencies like the FBI were in disarray, their opinions commanded nothing like the respect they would have done only a few years previously. Given their record during the civil rights movement, law enforcement claims carried especially little weight in matters concerning African-Americans. This made it difficult to explore possible political motivations in racial murders of the era, like the Zebra killings carried out by the "Death Angels" (Howard 1980). In different circumstances, federal authorities might well have postulated a formidable network of militant black extremists, but in the mid-1970s, this was politically impossible. No claims-makers, no crisis.

Because the terrorist threat remained largely unconstructed, even the largest attacks of this era have faded from national memory. This includes the savage 1975 bombing at LaGuardia airport that killed eleven, more even than the first World Trade Center attack in 1993. (Though technically the case remains unsolved, the LaGuardia attack is generally attributed to Croatian extremists.) It is open to question whether the frequency of violence genuinely is much greater during "terrorism waves" than in other "normal" periods in which government and media have not taken the seemingly arbitrary decision to perceive a wave of terrorism.

LEFT AND RIGHT

Generally in modern America, we can trace an unsurprising partisan division, by which political conservatives are more concerned with dangers from the left, while liberals (predictably) fear attacks from the right. Conservatives stress terrorism as an external threat, while liberals stress internal aspects. Conservatives are more willing than liberals to accept that terrorist movements have international connections. Scares about domestic terrorism tend to occur under liberal administrations; conservatives are more likely to be exercised about externally-based threats. I do not offer these distinctions as a hard and fast rule that is valid at all times and places, but rather as a general conceptual model. And as in most such debates, neither side has absolute truth.

These controversies have their roots in broader debates about the origins of protest and political violence. In any society prone to urban unrest and rioting, responses are likely to take one of two general directions that we can loosely call either liberal or conservative. On the liberal side, observers might feel that the protest reflects authentic social grievances that need to be remedied by reforms, and perhaps political change. While this would not necessarily mean a soft response, the rhetoric would emphasize solving the root problems. Conservatives, on the other hand, use a variety of arguments to challenge the claim of justified grievances. They might emphasize the criminal nature of the looting and violence. If they recognized a political motivation, they would attribute it to the influence of external agitators, perhaps working for some hostile government or other sinister force. From one perspective, there must be something deeply flawed about a society that produces individuals and groups capable of such deadly violence. On the other side, the assumption is that no grievance in a democratic society is sufficiently serious to justify violent protest.

THE TERROR NETWORK

A division of this sort, debating internal and external causation, emerged in responses to international terrorism when that phenomenon revived in the late 1960s (see Table 3.2: Moss 1972; Clutterbuck 1975; Wilkinson, 1975, 1986, 2000; Crenshaw 1983). Though the celebrated terrorist attacks of this era were usually associated with Middle Eastern groups and causes, some conservatives believed they saw the guiding hand of the Soviet Union and the Communist powers, including revolutionary Cuba. Liberals regretted the violence, but rejected the idea of a sinister global conspiracy. Instead, they saw the roots of the violence in social injustice, or perhaps in the psychiatric and pathological disturbances of the guerrillas. (Such explanations were then very much in vogue as a means of explaining crime and deviance.) Within the United States itself, the Nixon administration was convinced that external Communist forces were inspiring the violent protest and terrorism associated with antiwar protesters. Liberals, in contrast, saw it as a regrettable but natural outgrowth of popular anger at the Vietnam war (Bates 1993).

This liberal-conservative division over Communist conspiracies became acute during the late 1970s at a time of intense ideological conflict within the United States. A new conservative right was gaining influence, urging a more intense confrontation with Communism and the Soviet Union. This approach became very influential following the election of President Ronald Reagan in 1980, and the beginning of what has been described as a new Cold War.

In the political debates of these years, terrorism occupied center stage (Livingstone 1982, 1988, 1990; Martin and Walcott 1988). For the conservatives, terrorism represented not just a tactic used by alienated or exploited groups, but rather an organized movement directed ultimately by the Soviets and their satellites, and specifically the KGB (Committee for State Security). This was the model put forward by journalist Claire Sterling in her influential 1980 book *The Terror Network*, and popularized by some best-selling novels (De Borchgrave and Moss 1980). Also active, according to this view, were certain Middle Eastern "bandit states" such as Syria, Iran, and Libya (Sterling 1981). It was widely believed that these countries supplied finance and weaponry, in addition to training facilities and safe havens for fugitives. Terrorism was the chief tool of those seeking to destroy the West, namely NATO plus Israel, in "The Other World War" (Jenkins 1985). The term terrorism now acquired a much more limited sense than hitherto, being confined to acts of leftist and Islamic movements, and not to far right or anti-Communist groups who used almost identical tactics. "Real" terrorism was, by definition, anti-American and foreign, or foreign-inspired (US Senate 1981, 1982; Cline and Alexander 1984–1985; Livingstone and Arnold, eds. 1986; Kempton 1989).

Giving urgency to this issue was the rediscovery of leftist terrorism on U.S. soil, undertaken by groups that had kept up a slow-burning campaign of bombings and bank robberies ever since the collapse of mass radicalism in the early 1970s. In the intervening years, the various factions had formed a broad tactical alliance, including white veterans of the Weather Underground, the Black Liberation Army (B.L.A.), and Puerto Rican movements like the Armed Forces of National Liberation (FALN). This alliance received little attention until one day in October 1981, when a bank robbery in Nyack, New York, went badly wrong. In the ensuing shootout, two police officers and a Brinks guard were killed, and among those taken into custody were several members of the old radical networks, including former celebrities like Kathy Boudin. Suddenly, domestic terrorism was again in the headlines, this time very much in a left-wing context, and with individuals tied at many points to Cuba. One of the best-known leaders of the leftist alliance was B.L.A. member Joanne Chesimard

(Assata Shakur), who killed a New Jersey police officer in 1973. In 1979, she escaped from prison, and was known to have taken refuge in Cuba. The "terror network" thus appeared well rooted in U.S. soil, and the case for Communist state-sponsorship seemed powerful (Jacobs 1971; Stern 1975; U.S. Senate 1975b–c; Tannenbaum and Rosenberg 1979; Frankfort 1984; Castellucci 1986; Shakur 1987; Foner 1995; Jacobs 1997; U.S. House of Representatives 1998; Ayers 2001).

Much of the debate over Soviet manipulation was confused by a lack of definition of what constitutes sponsorship in a terrorist context. Proving that a given terrorist group is in contact with an intelligence agency does not establish that the group is a puppet or creation of that agency. In some cases, that might be a fair analysis, but in others it is not. Intelligence agencies dabble in guerrilla and terrorist conflicts in other countries, in the hope of securing influence with factions that might one day gain power, and also to secure information about possible threats to themselves. During the Algerian struggle of the 1950s, for instance, the American CIA made overtures to the National Liberation Front (FLN), the radical Arab opposition fighting the French colonial overlords (Horne 1977). These contacts do not mean that the U.S. was sponsoring the FLN, but rather that Americans did not want to be excluded from a new postcolonial setup. The same reasons explain why the U.S. tried dealing with Fidel Castro in the 1950s, when he was a revolutionary leader fighting the pro-American Cuban regime (Szulc 1986). During the 1970s, too, the CIA developed an excellent working relationship with sections of the Palestinian guerrilla movement, a link that helped preserve American interests through the Middle East. The key American contact was the head of the much-feared terrorist operation known as Black September. Controversial cases over the years have also suggested a CIA linkage in various instances of IRA gun-running to Northern Ireland (Holland 1988; Loftus and McIntyre 1989). Assuming these stories are true, this would be yet another instance of the CIA trying to work with both sides in a conflict simultaneously. Contact does not mean control.

In fairness to the "terror network" view, Sterling and her allies did have some evidence to support her contention about a Soviet connection with terrorism in the West, and the linkage has become more plausible with passing years. Documents discovered after the collapse of the European Communist regimes confirm the claim that East Bloc intelligence services like the East German *Stasi* (*Staatssicherheit*, State Security) had been lending support to West European terrorist movements (Childs and Popplewell 1996). In retrospect, a senior East German official lamented that the country had become "an El Dorado for terrorists" (Andrew and Mitrokhin 1999). Moreover, Cuban intelligence had certainly cooperated closely with Puerto Rican guerrilla leaders. Still, this does not prove that the Communist states had sponsored or founded these groups, or that their role was anything more than opportunistic. Nor does it mean that the KGB and its allies were any more involved in promoting subversive activities in Europe or elsewhere than were Western intelligence agencies. Even so, the conservative interpretation had enough plausibility to make it convincing.

The terror network view had enormous consequences for other issues debated at the time, and in every case, it favored the conservative side. If in fact the Soviets were trying to overthrow the West through clandestine warfare, then it thoroughly justified the Western response of supporting anti-Communist guerrilla movements throughout the Third World, in countries like Afghanistan and Angola. In this view, the Nicaraguan Contras were a legitimate form of retaliation for the Soviet deployment of terror groups in Italy or Germany. If the West was targeted by terrorists, then these movements should be seen as a component of the general Soviet global campaign. This fact demanded greater arms spending by the West, and an intensification of the cold war, themes that meshed well with Reagan era conservatism. Each new terrorist act, each hijacking or airliner bombing gave new strength to this conservative interpretation (Ra'anan et al. 1986; Netanyahu 1986).

Debates over terrorism became acute following the still mysterious assassination attempt on Pope John Paul II in Rome, in 1981. The actual shots were fired by a Muslim of Turkish origin, but the full scope of the scheme was unclear. For Sterling and her colleagues, the crime was clearly directed by the Soviet KGB, as retaliation for the Pope's efforts against Communist rule in Eastern Europe. As in other recent cases, it appeared, the KGB was operating through a Middle Eastern front-man (Sterling 1984; Henze 1985; Jenkins 1986; West 2000). Liberal and left-wing commentators offered a totally different scenario, suggesting that the Pope was targeted by sinister financiers who had been plundering the Vatican's banking operation to the tune of billions of dollars. These shady figures were tied in with ultraright-wing terrorists, drug dealers, and even Nazi exiles in Latin America. Rarely has a controversy encapsulated so perfectly the ideological assumptions underlying terrorism debates: conservatives look for a Soviet role, liberals point to capitalist machinations. Conservatives sought international connections, liberals looked at conflicts within the society itself. One side saw Moscow puppet-masters; the other saw fascists and bankers.

Conservatives had some merit on their side in the state-sponsorship debate. Problems arose, though, when advocates took their cause to extremes. Sterling even included the IRA as part of the terror network, an idea that was unlikely to shake Irish-American sympathies for the nationalist cause. Somewhat more plausible was the attempt to link the South African ANC to the Soviets, since the Communist Party played a major role in the organization, and particularly in its military wing (U.S. Senate 1982; Morgan 1990; Slovo 1997). By the late 1980s, though, the consensus among U.S. policy-makers was that, as in Ireland, Soviet dabbling was incidental to the major underlying conflict.

Where the terror network idea did cause harm was in the Middle East, where the theory favored the Israeli side in regional conflicts. Israel's deadliest enemies were all aligned with the Soviet Union, the critical enemy of the U.S. in the global cold war confrontation. In the context of the 1980s, the focus on Middle Eastern terrorism made it harder for the U.S. to see shades of grey separating Muslim and Arab nationalist causes, all of which were judged by the standard of where they stood in the clash between terrorism and the West. The resulting policy failures led to disaster in Lebanon (Randal 1983). Arguably, the absolute focus on Moscow's evils also led U.S. administrations to favor the kind of radical anti-Communist Islamism associated with the Afghan resistance, and with leaders like Osama bin Laden (Cooley 2000).

DEBATING CIVIL LIBERTIES

For many other reasons, U.S. liberals disliked the conservative formulation, which contradicted their own political values of antimilitarism and civil libertarianism. Liberals opposed the military buildup of the 1980s, the cold war confrontation, and the aggressive foreign policy that was justified by the terror network idea. Also, a focus on external terrorist threats had significant connotations for domestic policy in matters like immigration policy. If in fact terrorist dangers came from outside the U.S. and were associated with foreign activists, this justified much stricter border and immigration controls.

The implications for domestic law enforcement were far-reaching. During the 1950s and 1960s, agencies like the FBI and CIA had undertaken extensive operations against domestic radicals and dissidents, who were subjected to illegal surveillance, burglaries, and various disruptive dirty tricks (Blackstock 1975; U.S. Senate 1975a; Churchill and Vander Wall 1988, 1990; Mangold 1991; Olmsted 1996; Nutter 2000). Often the FBI was deploying the kinds of powers, legal and otherwise, that it had built up during successive Red and Brown Scares. In the post-Watergate years of the 1970s, Congressional liberals placed severe restrictions on the agencies, curbing their powers to act in this way in future. However, the new construction of terrorism during the Reagan years gave the federal agencies a means to recapture some of their old powers. Congressional restraints applied, *except* where surveillance was required to prevent an imminent act of terrorism. Under Presidential Order 12333, which became the effective charter for federal agencies, no specific evidence of crime was needed to justify domestic surveillance if there was probable cause to indicate a terrorist threat.

The more widely the FBI defined groups as potentially terrorist, the more it was able to intervene in their operations. This especially applied to left-wing groups opposed to U.S. policies in Central America, bodies like CISPES, the Committee in Solidarity with the People of El Salvador. Though the group was apparently peaceful, the FBI claimed to have evidence that CISPES was involved with planned terrorism, including a possible attempt to assassinate President Reagan at the 1984 Republican Convention in Dallas. If CISPES were affiliated with the leftist terror network, that fact would justify intense surveillance and dirty tricks. The federal investigation of CISPES spread to explore the activities of nine other groups and over 160 individuals (King, 1988; U.S. House of Representatives 1989a–b; U.S. Senate 1989a–b). The CISPES issue also had national political implications. For the Republican administration, desperate to arouse public concern about the leftward drift in Central America, it was valuable to link those foreign developments to a potential terrorist threat on U.S. soil. In 1984, the film *Red Dawn* imagined that Central American terrorists armed with backpack nuclear weapons might open the way for a Soviet/Cuban invasion of the U.S. heartland.

Liberals were appalled by what seemed like accusations of guilt by association, which they portrayed as a revival of McCarthyite smear techniques. Particularly sensitive was the issue of investigating religious institutions, which seemed to violate the freedom of religion (Coutin 1993). The FBI's Central American surveillance had indeed covered churches linked to left-wing and pacifist causes, causing liberal critics to bring up memories of the civil rights campaigns of the 1960s. If the police had been able to bug and sabotage churches in that era, the civil rights movement might have been derailed. At the same time, there were and are genuine instances in which religious institutions were used as a cover for political extremism and violence, for instance in the contemporary racist right, and in some of the radical mosques linked to Islamist causes (Downey and Hirsh 2002).

During the years of conservative hegemony from 1981 to 1993, the concept of terrorism was used disproportionately against groups associated with left or radical causes, and not sufficiently against domestic groupings. The best example of this bias involves the anti-abortion violence that flourished in the United States from the late 1970s onwards, and which through the 1980s led to hundreds of arson and bombing attacks against abortion clinics. By the early 1990s, the violence escalated when several abortion providers were assassinated. Most of this activism might appear to fit the bill of terrorism, and it certainly fit the FBI's own definition, as quoted earlier. Surely, this was "the unlawful use of force or violence . . . in furtherance of political or social goals"? (Jenkins 1999b) Yet the FBI steadfastly refused to classify this violence as terrorism until the mid-1990s, which meant that the agency did not become involved in investigating it. Nor did the agency count antiabortion attacks in its terrorist statistics. Anti-abortion "terrorism" only became such when a new political party took power in 1993 (U.S. House of Representatives 1986, 1993; Blanchard and Prewitt 1993; Blanchard 1994; U.S. Senate 1995; McCuen 1997; Solinger et al. 1998; Risen and Thomas 1998; Clarkson 1999; Baird-Windle and Bader 2001; Reiter 2002).

The failure to categorize this wave of violence as terrorism is remarkable. If a group of Middle Eastern or Muslim orientation had carried out assaults against life and property on American soil on a scale far smaller than the actual pro-life extremists, then official agencies would have made their suppression an absolute priority. Congress would have passed whatever draconian legislation might have been perceived necessary for this purpose. How could anyone doubt that this represented a terrorist campaign of the first magnitude? Once the attacks had been constructed as terrorist violence, this problem would not have been permitted to smolder on for decades. Yet the abortion violence inspired no like sense of urgency. The FBI's aversion to focusing on the topic can be understood only as partisan and political. Since targeting antiabortion violence as terrorism would taint or discredit other activists who shared similar goals, any such mapping would alienate the broad right-wing political constituency that supported the goals of the antiabortion movement.

LIBERAL APPROACHES

American concepts of terrorism changed fundamentally during the 1990s, partly due to the eclipse of Soviet Communism, but also because of the election of a liberal Democratic administration in 1993. In other words, a fundamental rethinking of the nature and seriousness of terrorism resulted from a partisan shift, rather than from any significant change in the threat itself.

One aspect of this change was a major reversal of the terror network idea, and a declining concern with international or state-sponsored terrorism. While conservative regimes had chiefly identified terrorism as a problem emanating from the Middle East, and specifically from certain governments, the Clinton administration strenuously sought to avoid pursuing such possible linkages. This approach was especially evident following the first World Trade Center attack of 1993, when the administration actively discouraged any suggestion that the act might have been sponsored by some Arab state. Similar reactions occurred after several international attacks on U.S. interests through the 1990s, in each of which strong evidence pointed to involvement by various Middle Eastern nations. In each case, though, United States military responses were extremely limited, and largely ineffectual; the administration demonstrated little interest in combating major terror networks. When in 1996 the Sudanese government offered to hand over Osama bin Laden and most of his associates, the U.S. declined (Ijaz 2001). Through the decade, too, U.S. policy in former Yugoslavia permitted the massive expansion of radical Islamic networks in Europe—forces that would soon be turned against American interests.

The shift away from Middle Eastern problems is all the more remarkable since the volume and seriousness of anti-American attacks remained steady through the Clinton years, with spectacular events like the embassy bombings in East Africa that killed almost three hundred people (Table 3.3). Also, elements within the government had quite a realistic perception of the scale of the danger. In December 1998, a *Time* story on Osama bin Laden noted that "His operatives might be coming to town soon. Intelligence sources tell *Time* they have evidence that bin Laden may be planning his boldest move yet—a strike on Washington or possibly New York City in an eye-for-an-eye retaliation" (Waller 1998). The following year, a report commissioned by the administration warned that "al-Qaeda could detonate a Chechen-style building-buster bomb at a federal building. Suicide bomber(s) belonging to al-Qaeda's Martyrdom battalion could crash land an aircraft packed with high explosives . . . into the Pentagon, the headquarters of the Central Intelligence Agency, or the White House" ("Early Warnings" 2002). Plenty of academic and political figures continued to press the older Middle Eastern oriented view of terrorism, though they were increasingly embattled (Netanyahu 1997; Mizell and Grady 1998; U.S. Senate 1998; Kushner 1998; Laqueur 1999; Lesser et al. 1999; Lifton 1999; Cordesman 1999; Stern 1999; Advisory Panel 1999–2001; Pillar and Armacost 2001).

Partly, this lack of official response reflected administration fears about U.S. foreign policy, and a reluctance to become engaged in military entanglements. Where at all possible, legal and diplomatic solutions were strongly preferred, emphasizing the work of international alliances and the United Nations in promoting global security. The reluctance to use military methods represented a near-total reversal of the rhetoric of the preceding conservative regimes.

General ideological qualms were reinforced by several specific events of the 1990s, which collectively undermined the bases of the terror network theory, and—at least in the public mind—the emphasis on Middle Eastern dangers. The first was the Oklahoma City bombing of April 1995, which was initially blamed on Middle Eastern groups, but subsequently attributed to domestic militia sympathizers. This apparent error gave strength to Middle Eastern advocates who protested about anti-Arab stereotypes, and the automatic linkage of terrorism to causes based in that region. In fact, there were powerful *prima facie* reasons to suspect an Arab role, since Oklahoma City is a center of Islamist organization, while the methods used in the attack corresponded precisely to techniques pioneered by Hizbullah in attacks in Lebanon, Argentina, and elsewhere (Emerson 2002). Nevertheless, popular mythology assumed that early charges of Arab involvement in the Oklahoma attack arose purely from official prejudice, and made government and media more cautious about repeating this error. This message was driven home by Muslim and Arab-American groups themselves, but also by the strongly entrenched pro-Arab constituency among America's specialists on Middle East affairs, both in think-tanks and universities (Kramer 2001).

The following year, America seemed to be facing a Summer of Terror following several sensational events. In June 1996, a bomb attack in Saudi Arabia killed nineteen U.S. servicemen; a TWA airliner, flight 800, crashed in Long Island Sound on July 17, while on July 27, a bomb exploded in Atlanta during an event in the Olympic Games. The linking of these tragedies seemed ominous, and Congress indicated a willingness to pass get-tough criminal justice legislation conveniently labeled as anti-terrorist measures. The common speculation was that all these attacks might be connected to one of the well-known Middle Eastern causes. Conceivably, flight 800 might have been brought down by a surface-to-air missile, perhaps one of the Stingers that were so easily available to jihad fighters in Afghanistan. Even the *New York Times*, never a friend to conspiracy speculations, headlined that August that "Prime Evidence Found That Device Exploded in Cabin of Flight 800," raising the likelihood of a bomb or missile (Van Natta 1996).

Within a few months, though, these interpretations all seemed highly unlikely. A growing consensus regarded the airliner as the victim of a mechanical failure, while the Olympic bombing was probably the work of a lone domestic ultrarightist. As in the Oklahoma City affair, the terrorist label had been misleadingly applied, and the federal law enforcement bureaucracy had been quite blatant about exploiting public concern to secure legislative advantage. It appeared that the media had cried wolf about the Middle East—a perception that diverted attention from the very real Middle Eastern connection in the Khobar Towers attack. (This was the work of either al-Qaeda, or an Iranian-backed network: Risen and Perlez 2001.)

Two other events influencing public opinion occurred in 1998. One was the release of the film *Wag the Dog* (1998), a cynical satire about how a president threatened by a sex scandal saves himself by generating a bogus international crisis. The film depicts the fabrication of an international conflict through the machinations of the media, and as public interest declines, it is revived by new and entirely fictitious angles, such as the campaign to retrieve a U.S. soldier supposedly missing behind enemy lines. The media were thus shaping political reality, the tail was wagging the dog. The underlying theme of *Wag the Dog* became popular as a means of interpreting official responses to terrorism and other international threats, enhancing suspicion that any kind of military response was an attempt to generate popular support, or even to distract attention from internal crises.

This image gained widespread support very shortly afterwards, when the Clinton administration retaliated for the African bombings. Cruise missiles were fired at targets supposedly linked to Osama bin Laden in Afghanistan and Sudan. Both attacks were ineffective. In the Sudan, the U.S. destroyed a facility at al-Shifa that, according to which source one accepts, was either a legitimate pharmaceutical plant or a biological warfare factory. The evidence was controversial. The U.S. government announced that clandestine agents had taken soil samples near the plant that indicated the presence of a precursor chemical for a deadly nerve agent (Porth 1998). According to critics, the results were misinterpreted. Matters were complicated by the natural U.S. reluctance to compromise active agents or defectors operating within enemy organizations (Halberstam 2001). Whatever the reasons, though, the critical account of the incident gained wide credence, and the media overwhelmingly accepted that the attack was a simple blunder. The popular impression was that the U.S. government had been misled by its obsession with evil Middle Eastern terrorists, and led astray by James Bond methods. The al-Shifa incident survives in left-wing mythology as definitive proof of the reckless foolishness of a purely military response to terrorism, which in practice just wrecked the lives of innocent Third World people (Chomsky 2001).

As to the U.S. motivation, many noted cynically that the president was facing a sex scandal quite as serious as that in *Wag the Dog*, so life was imitating art. A story in *Salon* reported that "It took only a few minutes for one of the reporters in the Pentagon pressroom to ask Secretary of Defense William Cohen the question on many minds: 'Have you seen the movie?' He was referring to *Wag the Dog* and the unsettling coincidence between Thursday's military strikes and a movie in which political fixers concoct a war to distract public attention from a presidential sex scandal." The story was sub-headed, "After Clinton called out the warplanes, Beltway skeptics said they'd already seen the movie" (Corn 1998). The fact that special prosecutor Kenneth Starr was investigating Clinton's misdeeds with a view to possible impeachment proceedings did not escape critics' attention. Responding to the al-Shifa attack, Christopher Hitchens (1998) wrote,

"When Clinton really had to look 'presidential' for a day, he simply launched cruise missiles against a sort of Arab version of Ken Starr." In such commentary, the notion of any legitimate and necessary retaliation against terrorism was eclipsed. What had in the 1980s been the standard analysis of terrorism, would during the 1990s be viewed as the product of racism, xenophobia, militarism, and the cynical manipulation of naïve patriotism.

Just how deep the reluctance to use military methods ran is suggested by the work of Philip Wilcox, who served as U.S. Ambassador at Large for Counter-Terrorism between 1994 and 1997, and who can be seen as a representative of administration thinking. Even following the September 11 attacks, Wilcox rejected any possible military response, calling instead for diplomatic approaches. As the U.S. was preparing its military strike against the Taliban regime in Afghanistan, Wilcox argued that "using military force against terrorists in sovereign foreign states is likely to raise difficult legal issues. Unilateral attacks may violate international laws, including treaties against terrorism that the U.S. has worked hard to strengthen; and they may alienate governments, especially in the Islamic world, whose cooperation we need" (Wilcox 2001). Though different positions are possible on military retaliation for terrorist acts, Wilcox's position at this particular moment represented a remarkably extreme stance. While not denying that Middle Eastern derived violence constituted terrorism, the Democratic administration presented it as far less serious and organized than its conservative predecessors.

A shift to liberal values can also be seen in the methods used to combat the external terrorist threat. As we have seen, liberals had long been suspicious of the tactics used by agencies like FBI and CIA, and their use of infiltrators against suspect organizations (Gelbspan 1991; U.S. House of Representatives 1991). Linked to this nervousness had been hostility to paying informants who were heavily compromised by their involvement in criminality or human rights abuses. While this tactic was logical in terms of gaining influence and intelligence, it also involved serious moral difficulties. Under the Clinton administration, the agency relied more on electronic intelligence and intercepted messages, minimizing the use of human informants. Under new agency guidelines, case officers had to get approval from superiors before recruiting "dirty" informers, people involved in human rights abuses or criminal or terrorist activity. In practice, this meant any informant who might conceivably be of any use in the terrorist world. Again, while not rejecting the seriousness of a terrorism problem, the liberal approach indicated the weight placed on combating it through legal and constitutional means. Moreover, human rights—however defined—represented an absolute value that government and its agencies must respect (Heymann 1998; Dempsey and Cole 1999; compare Pillar and Armacost 2001).

CRYING WOLF

By the end of the 1990s, the recently orthodox focus on Middle Eastern terrorism was all but discredited. The newer and ostensibly more sophisticated view usually stressed that terrorism fears were much exaggerated, especially in the international context. Studies of the statistics issued by the State Department were used to buttress this view, and also to show that the Middle East was not central to the violence that did occur. (These analyses have been much debated, not least because they fail to take account of acts that occurred elsewhere in the world, but were actually linked to Middle Eastern groups, such as the embassy bombings in Africa.) If the dangers were so relatively slight, it made no sense to panic about them, or to worry too much about radical reforms of internal security. And what had once been the liberal view now achieved orthodox status in mainstream and business publications: it was what sensible people believed.

The liberal stance is well illustrated by numerous articles in *Salon* magazine, which through the late 1990s was a major supporter of the Clinton administration. Yet following the U.S. strikes at Afghanistan after the East African bombings, a *Salon* writer dismissed the current charges that major terrorist organizations were plotting against the U.S.: "Bin Laden may be a dangerous anti-American zealot with a mouth as big as his bankroll. But the evidence so far does not support him being a cerebral Islamic Dr. No moving an army of terrorist troops on a vast world chessboard to checkmate the United States" (L. Jenkins 1998). In June 2000, another *Salon* contributor explained "Why a new report on the threat of international terrorist attacks on U.S. soil is a con job. . . . with roughly the veracity of the latest Robert Ludlum novel" (Shapiro 2000). Liberals in these years often cited fiction authors like Ludlum and Ian Fleming, to suggest that accounts of international terrorist plots were the products of immature fantasies. In this view, too, charges about a continuing menace could be traced to retired CIA officers, old hard-liners opposed to the "reformers" now in charge of the agency: they were purely political, right-wing partisan attacks. "By attempting to set off a panic over external enemies, the National Commission on Terrorism is serving those inside-the-Beltway policy goals" (Shapiro 2000).

The lack of concern in some of the articles and op-ed pieces written in this mode make curious reading following the events of September 2001. In the *New York Times,* Larry C. Johnson stated his view that "Although high-profile incidents have fostered the perception that terrorism is becoming more lethal, the numbers say otherwise, and early signs suggest that the decade beginning in 2000 will continue the downward trend. . . . terrorism is not the biggest security challenge confronting the United States, and it should not be portrayed that way." This was written in July 2001.

THE GATHERING STORM

While the Clinton administration heavily played down external threats, it placed far more attention on the danger posed by domestic terrorism, especially from right-wing and anti-government groups. It was in 1993 and 1994 that the government started treating antiabortion violence as terrorism, partly in response to an escalation of violence and the assassination of doctors. The timing contributed to a change of perception, since the first murder of a doctor occurred only two weeks after the first World Trade Center bombing, as a result of which the media had regularly been denouncing terrorism and religious fanaticism on American soil. Late February had also marked the beginning of the Branch Davidian siege in Waco, Texas, an event that culminated in April with the massacre of 75 people. This affair further drew attention to the apocalyptic views and fanatical behavior of the Christian ultraright, no less than its penchant for armed violence. The media now began to depict pro-life zealots in the company of clichéd Middle Eastern terrorists ("Domestic Terrorists at Work." 1993; Jenkins 1999b; Baird-Windle and Bader 2001). In 1998, a man who assassinated an abortion doctor in upstate New York was added to the FBI's Ten Most Wanted List.

This changed perception had immediate policy consequences. In the aftermath of several killings by antiabortion extremists, federal marshals were dispatched to protect clinics across the country. In July 1994, Attorney General Janet Reno created a task force to investigate any organized national campaign or conspiracy in the violence. Though the task force found no such evidence, the mere reporting of its activities served to focus media attention on pro-life violence as a systematic threat, and potentially a form of organized terrorism (Egan 1995a–b). This shift of emphasis can be understood in terms of the different power base of the respective administrations. While the Republican administrations had been aligned with conservative pro-life organizations, the Clinton presidency was heavily supported by feminist groups, for which the right to abortion was a cardinal political belief.

Closely tied to the attack on antiabortion terrorism was a heavy new emphasis on domestic ultraright militancy. In the early 1990s, radical right-wing activism led to an upsurge of militias, paramilitary groups dedicated to resisting what they saw as oppressive actions by the federal government (Gibson 1994; Bennett 1995; Hamm 1997; Barkun 1997; Neiwert 1999; Kaplan and Weinberg 1999; Kramer 2002). Though estimates of numbers are uncertain, militias attracted at least tens of thousands of members and supporters, while related "Patriot" ideologies reached millions of others, particularly through influential media outlets like talk radio. Although no militia was itself implicated in the attack, both government and mass media repeatedly used Oklahoma City as a rhetorical weapon against the militia movement, suggesting that militia supporters were terrorists or terrorist sympathizers (U.S. House of Representatives 1996a–b; U.S. Senate 1997a–b). For some authors, this linkage extended not just to militias, but to the mainstream anti-Clinton Right. In *Salon*, Gary Kamiya (2001) argued that "Timothy McVeigh would most likely have existed even if America's mainstream conservatives did not preach a gospel disturbingly similar to his. . . . But while it would be unfair to blame right-wing ideology for McVeigh, it would be myopic not to see the connection between them. Call it collateral damage." The sequence of events closely recalled the Brown Scare of 1940, and the panic over the Christian Front.

Aggravating such fears were the nerve gas attacks carried out in Japan during 1995 by the Aum Shinrikyo religious cult. The focus on homicidal cults seemed all the more necessary following recent evidence of religious fanaticism within the U.S. itself, notably the Waco siege. The common belief that Oklahoma City had been intended as direct revenge for the Waco raid provided a direct linkage between cults and domestic terrorism, while the Aum Shinrikyo affair raised the likelihood that future attacks might be biological or chemical in nature (Kaplan 1996; Falkenrath et al 1998; Lifton 1999; Juergensmeyer 2000; Reader 2000; Tucker ed. 2000). Might religious groups that believed in Doomsday try and precipitate such an event?

News stories, editorials, and cartoons all presented the view of militias as crypto-Nazis, linked to white racist movements and far right skinheads (Moore 1993; Hamm 1993). An impressive outpouring of books—peaking in 1996—warned of an imminent terrorist disaster from this gathering storm (Berlet 1995; Corcoran 1995; Halpern 1995; Ridgeway 1995; Bjorgo 1995; Abanes 1996; Stern 1996; Ezekiel 1996; Dees and Corcoran 1996; Lamy 1996; Coppola 1997; Dyer 1998; Bushart et al. 1998; Snow 1999; Hilliard and Keith, 1999; Berlet and Lyons 2000; Hamm 2002; Mitchell 2002). Typical titles raised the shadow of *America's Militia Threat*, of *Terrorists Among Us*, of *The Birth of Paramilitary Terrorism in the Heartland*. One book warned of the *Harvest of Rage: Why Oklahoma City is Only the Beginning*. The antimilitia campaign was extremely effective, and most militia supporters withdrew from what they now saw as an extremist movement. By the end of the decade, the militias were largely defunct.

OFFERING A CONTEXT

Just as militias and pro-life groups were obvious casualties of the new mapping of the terrorism problem, so there were obvious beneficiaries, who were also among the leading supporters of the administration. Just as feminists could both use the new stereotypes to link pro-life activism to the armed extremism of the clinic bombers, so too gay rights groups could discredit antigay agitation, and black civil rights organizations could attack their political enemies. In each case, the suggestion was that right-wing activism was part of a spectrum that had at its extremes the naked violence of bombers, militias, or racist skinheads. This broad contextualization helped to justify defensive legal measures, especially in hate crime laws. In the 1980s, when terrorism was seen as made in Moscow, the response to the problem was to be found in foreign policy, intelligence, and military intervention. Now, however, terrorism and political "hate" were to be combated by interventionist political liberalism, reinforced by the courts (Levin, and McDevitt 1993; Jenness and Broad 1997; Jacobs and Potter 1998).

These ideological changes had an impact far beyond the ranks of the federal bureaucracy in shifting what, in the language of constructionist theory, is known as the *ownership* of the terrorism problem. Through the 1980s, conservative pressure groups and think tanks had been regarded as the major authorities on the issue, the experts to whom media and Congressional investigators turned for expert advice. In the Clinton years this role passed to liberal pressure groups like the Feminist Majority Foundation or the Alabama-based Southern Poverty Law Center (SPLC), which monitored racist groups and tried to combat them through proactive litigation.

Though it was not necessarily the most important group of this kind, the SPLC provides a useful illustration of the idea of ownership. If terrorism was a matter of Middle Eastern groups, then the SPLC could have no part of the conversation. Once, though, the administration was devoting attention to domestic rightist violence, the SPLC became a major player, especially through subsidiaries like Klanwatch. While there is no reason to doubt the sincerity of the SPLC's convictions, we can point to many advantages that the group gained from this new emphasis. If militias were a problem, then the SPLC was the obvious source to which the media could turn for information. The SPLC could supply convenient maps and lists of militias, broken down by state and region. They could provide a knowledgeable spokesperson to discuss militia history and ideology (Southern Poverty Law Center 1996). This role also permitted the Center to expand the domain of the terrorism problem to cover other hostile groups on the right that would not otherwise have been discussed in this context. In regular reports, the Center could trace linkages between known violent activists and more obscure groups, suggesting that all constituted a kind of terror network on the racist right. This sort of research constituted superb publicity for the group and its causes, and encouraged public support, moral and material. The more widespread these ideas became, the easier it was to dismiss the older idea that terrorism was ipso facto a Middle Eastern and Arab prerogative. In that case, the response lay not in confrontational military or diplomatic policies, but rather in the enforcement of hate crime laws, and the discrediting of racist ideology at home.

A CARIBBEAN CONTRAST

To demonstrate the thoroughly political nature of labeling in the terrorist context, we can compare official responses to two movements that were at their height in the 1970s and 1980s, the armed militant organizations associated with, respectively, Puerto Rican nationalism and the anti-Castro Cuban cause. Both movements grew out of the politics of the Caribbean region, but developed their armed organizations chiefly on U.S. soil. Both were involved in numerous acts of armed violence within the U.S. and outside, and both were responsible for many deaths, and vast destruction of property. Groups linked to both movements were explicitly identified by federal agencies as dangerous manifestations of domestic terrorism. Yet each strand was associated with quite different political ideologies, the Puerto Ricans on the left and the Cubans on the right, and this distinction goes far toward explaining the markedly different response each received from successive U.S. administrations. Political and electoral considerations account for this differential treatment—and also why neither movement has been constructed as terrorist in the American consciousness in anything like the same way as Middle Eastern organizations.

The Cuban movement traces its origins to 1959, when Fidel Castro took power in that nation and became increasingly aligned to global Communism. Many thousands of Cubans fled, chiefly to Florida, where Miami became a center of exile politics. The exiles formed militias and armed groups, originally with U.S. support, and they began a campaign of violence: in 1960, an attack on a freighter in Havana killed a hundred people. The following year a planned counter-revolution failed disastrously following the landing at Cuba's Bay of Pigs (Corn 1994). Through the 1970s and 1980s, militant anti-Castro groups proliferated, some of the most prominent being Alpha 66, Omega 7, Brigade 2506, and the Cuban National Movement. Some adopted violent tactics, which sometimes shaded into overt terrorism. Targets included facilities and economic interests in Cuba itself as well as Cuban diplomats overseas. Militants also attacked other Cuban exiles who were thought of as soft on Communism, and other states that traded with Cuba, and on occasion, attacks were launched against the U.S. itself. Miami became the heart of a flourishing terrorist and guerrilla subculture, as did the Cuban communities of New Jersey. In 1976, the *Miami Herald* headlined, "Miami a Hotbed for Terrorism" (Crankshaw 1976; Crankshaw and Marina 1976; McGee 1983). By the 1980s, anti-Castro Cuban groups had been involved in hundreds of violent actions in many nations ("Cuban Information Archives" n.d.).

Some of the most spectacular events can be noted briefly. In 1975, Bay of Pigs veteran Rolando Otero launched a one-man bombing campaign in the Miami area, hitting thirteen targets over the course of two days. Targets included federal office buildings and the Miami International Airport. Fortunately, this rampage led to no deaths. The following year, Cuban exiles were involved in a political assassination in Washington D.C., when they helped Chilean authorities murder a prominent leftist exile from that country, Orlando Letelier. The most notorious of the Cuban militants was Dr. Orlando Bosch, who formed CORU, *Coordinación de Organizaciones Revolucionarias Unidas*. Through the 1970s, Bosch and his followers were associated with hundreds of attacks in the U.S., Mexico, Argentina, Venezuela, Chile, and elsewhere. The most notorious attack of this era occurred in 1976, when an airliner belonging to the Cuban national company, Cubana, was bombed over the Caribbean, killing all 73 on board. (Bosch was tried for this crime, but acquitted on three separate occasions, the last in 1987.) In 1980, anti-Castro activists assassinated a Cuban diplomat in Queens, New York (Freed and Landis 1980; Lernoux 1980).

At first sight, the Cuban guerrilla groups look unarguably like a transnational terror network of considerable scale. Within the U.S., though, the terrorist label has been applied only sporadically. Within the Cuban exile community itself, the groups are seen as heroic guerrillas opposing the evil Castro dictatorship, and in 1983, Miami's City Council formally declared "Orlando Bosch Day" to celebrate the extremist then in Venezuelan custody. This sentiment is all the more important because of the wealth and political clout in the Miami community and thus in the politics of Florida, one of the most important states in any presidential election. (We remember the crucial importance of that state in the bitterly fought 2000 contest.) As a result, U.S. politicians have over the years been very nervous about any improvement of relations with Castro's Cuba. A cynical political axiom states that the United States has no Cuban policy, but it does have a south Florida policy every four years—that is, during presidential elections. And the Cubans had other uses. Through the 1980s, the Reagan administration used anti-Castro guerrilla groups to organize armed resistance to Communism in Central America.

Since the U.S.-based Cubans are usually right-wing and anti-Castro, the community tends to support conservative Republicans, who repay this support. In 1989, Rolando Otero was released, strikingly early in view of his career as what local police had called "the mad bomber." Also in 1989, when the U.S. government tried to deport Orlando Bosch, a political firestorm erupted, as leading Republicans pressured the Bush administration to release someone they proclaimed a hero. When some Cuban-Americans began a hunger strike, they received a visit of support from the then-president's son Jeb Bush, later the state's governor. A representative of the Dade County Republican Party declared that "The Republican Party will not abandon Orlando Bosch," who had been conducting "a counter-revolutionary war" (Schmalz 1989). Republican administrations have had to tread very lightly over the terrorism issue in this part of the country—but the close anti-Castro Cuban relationship with government has not changed greatly under Democrats, who also recognize the need to hold Florida.

In short, while federal agencies under both parties have investigated anti-Castro Cuban terrorism and broken up particular organizations, this activity has never enjoyed the high profile of some other movements, and has never featured in the media anything like, say, the Palestinian operations. Agencies are careful not to pursue linkages between the armed anti-Castro groups and the more respectable political organizations. Despite the long track record of anti-Castro violence and extremism, mainstream media have never constructed this kind of terrorism as a major menace. Such an approach is however quite common in leftist and radical literature, which situate the Cubans at the heart of a far right terror network, officially approved by the U.S. government. Arguing against intervention in Iraq and Afghanistan, John Pilger asserts that "There is no terrorist sanctuary to compare with Florida, currently governed by the President's brother, Jeb Bush" (Pilger 2002: compare Herman 1982; Chomsky 1988, 2000). Cuban terrorism has never become the subject of a national scare like some of those described earlier.

At the other political extreme, we find the even lengthier story of Puerto Rican militancy. Puerto Rico was acquired by the U.S. following its victorious war with Spain in 1898, and since that point, island residents have occasionally fought for national independence. Activists believe that the island is an exploited colony reminiscent of European possessions in Africa and Asia, and just as these had become independent in the mid-twentieth century, so Puerto Rico should win the same privileges. In the 1950s, *independencistas* launched armed attacks against both the President and the House of Representatives. By the 1970s, a network of activist groups had emerged, including the FALN and the *Macheteros*. Like the Cubans, these groups carried out hundreds of attacks in both Puerto Rico and on the U.S. mainland. In 1976 alone, the FALN claimed over thirty bomb attacks in New York, Chicago, and Washington D.C. Among the most notorious acts was a 1975 bombing at New York's historic Fraunces Tavern, in which four died. In 1983, extremists robbed a Wells Fargo truck in Connecticut, stealing over seven million dollars to finance guerrilla operations (Sater 1981). Other operations in Puerto Rico itself included a machine-gun attack in 1979 on a bus full of U.S. sailors, killing two, and in

1981 the destruction of nine jets belonging to the Puerto Rico Air National Guard. As late as 1986, extremists tried to detonate ten bombs simultaneously in a coordinated attack on military facilities on the island.

Adding to the potential danger of the Puerto Rican militant movement were its wider connections with armed white and black groups. In 1985, two white veterans of the Weather Underground were implicated in an unsuccessful plot to free a FALN leader from the federal prison at Leavenworth, Kansas. The scheme would have involved using a helicopter landing in the facility's baseball diamond, and a rocket launcher would take out a guard tower. Both the plot leaders were added to the FBI's most wanted list, as was Victor Gerena, leader of the Wells Fargo operation. The FALN also had connections with the Communist regime of Cuba, and one of its leading activists, Filiberto Ojeda Rios, was reputedly a member of the Cuban secret police, the Directorate of Intelligence. In the 1980s both this group and the *Macheteros* would regularly be described as components of the global terror network, directed from Moscow.

The gravity of the terrorist threat was reflected in the desperate means sometimes used by Puerto Rican authorities to combat it. In 1992, respectable U.S. media published an amazing report that read like a fantastic conspiracy theory, claiming that through the mid-1980s, police and federal authorities had collaborated to operate a secret death squad called the Defenders of Democracy. The group was allegedly armed and trained by agents of the FBI and the U.S. Marshals Service. Among other actions, the Defenders might have been involved in the killing of two guerrilla suspects in 1978 at Cerro Maravilla (Weiner 1992). The incident dominated island politics for over a decade and generated a local scandal comparable to Watergate.

Against this background, it is amazing that Puerto Rican activism has not registered more clearly in the public consciousness, or is scarcely mentioned in many accounts of domestic terrorism. The whole phenomenon is virtually absent from popular culture accounts, in which Arab terrorist masterminds are such a tired cliché. As in the Cuban case, domestic politics play some part in shaping perceptions. Since the 1940s, Puerto Rican communities have become influential in areas like New York City, New Jersey, and Chicago, where they constitute a potent voting bloc that overwhelmingly leans to the Democratic Party. They are also strongly represented in the labor movement. While mainstream activists do not support *independencista* violence, many regard the militants as misguided patriots, who should be released after serving reasonable terms of imprisonment. The situation is thus very much like that of the Cubans in Florida. And as with the Cubans, domestic writers and law enforcement officials know that too sweeping a condemnation of the militants will anger powerful elected officials.

This political context underlies the controversy that occurred in 1999 when President Clinton offered clemency to sixteen Puerto Rican militants, on condition that they renounced violence. This resulted in the release of eleven former FALN militants. Clinton's decision was bitterly attacked by conservative politicians as well as by police groups, victims' relatives, and elements of the federal law enforcement bureaucracy. Critics felt that the decision wasted years of effort by police and prosecutors and proclaimed a kind of official approval of left-wing terrorism (Weiss and Orrin 1999; U.S. House of Representatives 1999, 2000b; U.S. Senate 2000).

The president was in part acting for predictable political motives. His wife, Hillary Rodham Clinton, would be running in 2000 for the New York Senate seat, and winning Puerto Rican sympathy was a major step in this process. Granting clemency to the Puerto Rican militants can be seen as a gesture to his core party constituency, since this ethnic community provides so firm a base for the Democratic Party. The decision also won the support of liberals, who supported the anti-imperialist rhetoric of the nationalists, if not their methods. The language employed in media accounts of the clemency decisions significantly omitted the T-word—terrorism—as well as any hints of the Cuban or Soviet links that were so well established for the FALN and the *Macheteros*. Liberal outlets like the *New York Times* spoke consistently of them as "Puerto Rican nationalists" and a "Puerto Rican independence group." The *Los Angeles Times* referred to the FALN as a group "blamed for 130 bombings in the late 1970s and early 1980," implying that charges of violence were baseless or controversial (Lichtblau 1999). As in the Cuban case, even violent activists are viewed much more favorably when one sympathizes with their broader goals.

A similar political pattern can be seen from Clinton's decision in the closing days of his term to commute the sentences of other radical activists from the struggles of the 1970s and 1980s. One beneficiary was Susan Rosenberg who, like the Puerto Ricans, had a powerful record of terrorist activity. She was originally indicted in planning the 1981 Nyack robbery, though charges were later dropped, and in 1984, she was captured in Cherry Hill, New Jersey, in possession of an arms dump of almost eight hundred pounds of explosives, as well as several firearms. (To put this quantity in perspective, the 1993 bomb attack at the World Trade Center used around a thousand pounds of explosives.) Even so, Rosenberg's release also responded to a core constituency, namely those liberals who for years had been campaigning for the release of someone they regarded as a political prisoner.

In 1990, Rosenberg and other leftist women—one was a Puerto Rican leader among those freed by Clinton's clemency order—had been the subject of a highly sympathetic documentary depicting their alleged sufferings in prison. The film, *Through the Wire,* was narrated by the prestigious actress, Susan Sarandon. While not approving the violence of either Rosenberg or her allies, liberals viewed these individuals as falling short of the authentic category of terrorism, very much as some Miami Cubans viewed Orlando Bosch as a hero. (Joanne Chesimard also commands widespread liberal and black nationalist support, ostensibly because of a belief that she was wrongly convicted, and a victim of FBI persecution.) (Freed 1973). A like sympathy would not extend to other activists representing diametrically opposite political causes, so that the liberals who supported Rosenberg would not have favored those far right activists involved in the Oklahoma City attack. Terrorism is something the other side perpetrates.

The analogies between the official treatment of Cubans and Puerto Ricans seem self-evident, but the parallel is rarely drawn in media accounts or political discussions. This is probably because both conservatives and liberals use the respective cases to pursue their particular agendas. Republicans viewed the Clinton administration as soft on terrorism because of the 1999 clemency; liberal Democrats resented the Reagan regime's softness towards anti-Castro activism. Yet when we ignore such partisan approaches, we see some rather consistent patterns in the decision to identify those groups that are to be viewed as the most serious and dangerous terrorists.

SWINGS AND PARADIGMS

We can see a number of swings in the official view of what Americans considered terrorism, and these changes arose from changing ideologies far more than authentic changes in the nature of the menace. In the 1970s, the problem was seen as one of isolated groups; in the 1980s, it was a Middle Eastern phenomenon, part of the terror network. In the 1990s, the main threats were at least as much domestic as foreign. And in each era, the decision to concentrate on left-wing as opposed to right-wing factions was shaped by political considerations. At each stage, believers in the new theory minimized or rejected the old orthodoxy.

In looking at these dramatic changes of opinion, we recall the idea of shifting paradigms, as formulated by Thomas Kuhn to explain the history of scientific revolutions. He attacked the idea that science advanced steadily by the gradual accumulation of information and experiment, and he focused instead on sudden, revolutionary breakthroughs, which fundamentally changed the overarching models (or paradigms) that were used to structure knowledge. Examples would include the Copernican model of the solar system, or the Darwinian theory of evolution. Over time, more evidence emerged contradicting an established paradigm, though mainstream scientists continued to ignore these inconvenient data until eventually, the old model collapsed to be replaced by a new one.

In terms of scale or significance, I am not trying to compare the shifts in understanding terrorism to these epoch-making scientific events, but some parallels do exist. In approaches to terrorism, too, official opinions usually change not because of new evidence, but because of a basic political shift. In this realm too, evidence that contradicts the established paradigm is ignored or underplayed until it becomes so overwhelming as to collapse the older explanatory model. And in each case, in each new paradigm, fundamentally different responses were needed.

In turn, these basic shifts of perception affected the means of knowing about terrorism. We have already noted how panics over terrorism tend to become self-sustaining. When a problem has been defined as particularly serious, agencies tend to investigate it more intensely and find more evidence of that kind of activity. The more we look for something, the more we find it. If we are looking hard at, for example, Islamic extremism in the United States, then we will find more evidence of the behavior, and more evidence of sinister or conspiratorial links. More investigations will produce more court cases, more journalistic investigations and segments on television documentaries, all of which contribute to a public impression that this problem is indeed serious and pressing. That in turn gives added support to the dominant model of the problem. As evidence mounts—and so do arrests and prosecutions—the media misinterpret the growing volume of evidence as signs of intensified activity, and possibly even speak of an epidemic or wave of terrorist organization and activism. This is very much what happened to militias and far right movements in the mid-1990s. Conversely, if we do not identify a problem as terrorism, then it attracts less attention. In the 1980s, no journalist seeking information on antiabortion violence would get any help from the FBI, since that was simply not considered part of the terrorism category. There were no relevant statistics, no ongoing investigations, so obviously, it was not a problem worthy of public attention. Far from being an epidemic, the problem remained unconstructed.

We can also see analogies with the scientific world in the sanctions used to enforce conformity to particular paradigms. In science, a person who does not accept the new model is subject to various stigmas that exclude him from public discourse. The heretic is dismissed for his ignorance—his failure to understand the new methods and insights—or worse, the person is viewed as a crank, someone obsessed with bizarre and irrational beliefs. The implication is that someone who accepts unorthodox views on one key issue must of necessity believe absurd doctrines in other matters, to be a kind of flat-earther. This stigmatizing process has an educative function, in teaching other scientists the painful consequences of failing to operate within the new paradigm.

In the terrorism world, also, we can see a similar process of labeling heretics, those who dissent from the construction that currently enjoys mainstream status. This condemnation can take various forms. Of its nature, studying terrorism means dealing with various kinds of criminal conspiracy, since very few terrorist acts are the work of unconnected loners. If an individual stresses the paramount danger from a terrorist movement that is not of the sort accepted in mainstream theory, then he or she can be dismissed as a conspiracy theorist. Technically the term is accurate, since the person is putting forward theories concerning a conspiracy, but in popular parlance the phrase carries damning implications. It suggests someone who looks for conspiracies as a customary means of explaining events, gives credibility to poorly substantiated evidence, and who accepts wild and unsubstantiated notions concerning historical events like the Kennedy assassination, or the origin of UFOs. It represents someone who takes seriously the kind of bizarre ideas treated as fantastic fiction in a television series like *The X-Files*. The word might even suggest mental instability or paranoia (Fenster 1999; Melley 1999; Goldberg 2001; Knight 2001, 2002).

Also, discussing activities linked to a particular cause or ethnic group can be criticized as arising from hostility to that group. Undoubtedly, much terrorism does arise from a Middle Eastern context, but someone accused of focusing too much on this region can be easily accused of racial or religious bigotry, of anti-Arab prejudice or "Islamophobia." Normally, someone who fails to toe the fashionable line is not likely to be excluded altogether from public discourse, to be barred, for instance, from Congressional appearances or television discussion programs, but that person is less likely to be called on than a mainstream commentator. The heretic is also likely to be introduced in terms that suggest a particular kind of bias.

To observe this process in operation, we can look at a terrorism commentator like Steven Emerson, who has since the 1980s consistently warned of the danger of Islamist terrorism in the United States (Emerson 1988, 2002; Emerson and Duffy 1990; Emerson and del Sesto 1991). In 1994, his television exposé *Jihad in America* warned of the presence of groups like Hamas and Hizbullah on U.S. soil, and in Congressional testimony in 2000, he described how Islamist militants moved freely across U.S. borders, raising the danger of major anti-American attacks. In 1997, he warned specifically, "[The threat of terrorism] is greater now than before the [first] World Trade Center bombing as the numbers of these groups and their members expands. In fact, I would say that the infrastructure now exists to carry off twenty simultaneous World Trade Center-type bombings across the United States." In the aftermath of September 2001,

Emerson's views sound quite prophetic, and *Jihad in America* became required viewing for policy-makers. Yet through the second half of the 1990s, Emerson was subjected to intense abuse as a dissenter from the current orthodoxies. He was vilified as an anti-Islamic bigot by pressure groups like the Council on American-Islamic Relations (CAIR), which sweepingly rejected his claims to be a terrorism expert, as opposed to a crank conspiracy theorist. The leftist group FAIR offered stories under headlines like "Did self-styled anti-terrorism expert Steven Emerson help push the world toward nuclear war?" Even if a media outlet does not believe such charges, it knows that using Emerson will invite controversy, and might well be dissuaded from airing his views, at least without an Arab spokesperson to provide balance. The fewer voices are heard dissenting from a particular perspective, the more that will come to be believed as the only legitimate view.

However impartially we try to define terrorism, the meaning of the word will fluctuate enormously in practice, and over a surprisingly brief time span. Equally subject to change are notions like orthodoxy and heresy, and the relative status of expert or crank. These rapid shifts indicate the intensity of controversies over terrorism, and the critical ideological importance of the concept.

Table 3.1 U.S. Domestic Terrorism Since 1940

1939–1941	Intense media concern over terrorism by extreme right-wing groups like the Christian Front, in alliance with German intelligence and the IRA. Major events include the 1941 wrecking of the Cleveland to Pittsburgh express train in Ambridge, Pennsylvania, killing five
1943	Anti-fascist exile Carlo Tresca assassinated in New York City; John Roy Carlson publishes *Under Cover*, an influential exposé of contemporary American terrorism
1950	Puerto Rican extremists try to assassinate President Truman at Blair House; one Secret Service officer and one attacker are killed
1954	Puerto Rican extremists open fire on U.S. House of Representatives, wounding five
1961	Beginning of wave of airliner hijackings to Cuba, a campaign that would resume at the end of the decade. Most end without casualties
1963–64	White extremists launch several major attacks against black targets associated with the civil rights movement. In 1963 alone, victims include civil rights leader Medgar Evers, and four schoolgirls killed in a church in Birmingham, Alabama
1963–66	Height of extreme-right Minuteman movement; arms raids show the group to be well equipped with automatic weapons
1965	Assassination of Malcolm X
1968	Assassinations of Robert F. Kennedy and Martin Luther King Jr.
1968–1971	Violent protests against Vietnam War lead to hundreds of actual and attempted bomb attacks across the United States: some are claimed by the Weathermen (later the Weather Underground). In 1970, three militants are killed by an explosion of a bomb factory in New York City. A bombing on the campus of the University of Wisconsin in Madison kills one.
1969–1973	Black militant organizations including the Black Liberation Army undertake campaign of assassinations against police officers in New York City, San Francisco, Atlanta, and elsewhere. The B.L.A. also carries out bank robberies. In 1973, Joanne Chesimard kills one police officer and wounds another in a "Turnpike Massacre" in New Jersey
1972–76	Sporadic attacks by Weather Underground and related groups. Targets include the Pentagon, U.S. State Department, police precincts, and corporate offices
1973	Assassination of Israeli colonel in Washington DC, claimed by PFLP
1973	Black Muslims kill eight members of the Hanafi Muslim sect in Washington DC
1973–74	Wave of racially inspired "Zebra murders" by black Death Angels movement in northern California. Other murder series linked to the group would be alleged over the next twenty years
1973–75	Protests by American Indian Movement lead to confrontations with law enforcement and several deaths, including two FBI agents
1974–81	Bank robberies and attacks by Black Liberation Army remnants and white allies, under the name of "The Family"
1974–75	Campaign of assassinations, bank robberies, and kidnappings in California by the leftist Symbionese Liberation Army. Six are killed in a shootout with Los Angeles police
1974–1986	Puerto Rican militant groups carry out over a hundred bombings and other attacks on the U.S. mainland, and on the island itself. Major episodes include the 1975 bombing of the Fraunces Tavern, killing four. The Weather Underground sets off a bomb in a bathroom at the Capitol.

1975	Croatian terrorist campaign: eleven are killed when a bomb detonates in a locker at New York's LaGuardia airport; police officer killed defusing bomb at Grand Central Station. Bombing campaign in Miami area by anti-Castro Cuban, Rolando Otero. Publication of Edward Abbey's novel *The Monkey Wrench Gang*, inspiration for the later ecoterrorist movement.
1975–1983	Anti-Castro Cuban organizations carry out fifty-seven bombings in Dade County, Florida.
1976	Former Chilean ambassador Orlando Letelier and a friend killed in car bombing in Washington D.C., in an act later linked to Chilean intelligence. Croatian militants hijack TWA jet from New York City
1976–80	Joseph Paul Franklin launches single-handed race war, assassinating blacks and Jews
1976–1984	Wave of bombings and bank robberies across the northeastern United States by a left-wing faction, the Sam Melville/Jonathan Jackson group (later known as the United Freedom Front). Victims include a New Jersey State Trooper, killed in 1981
1977–1983	Four Iraqi dissidents killed in Detroit area, presumably by agents of that state
1978	Two Puerto Rican militants shot by police in controversial encounter at Cerro Maravilla, which later becomes a traumatic political scandal. Publication of Andrew MacDonald's novel *The Turner Diaries*
1979	Klan/Nazi attack on leftist demonstrators in Greensboro, NC, leaves four dead. Radical allies help Joanne Chesimard escape from prison
1980	Height of terror campaign by anti-Castro group Omega 7
1981	Bank robbery at Nyack, Rockland County (NY) draws attention to surviving networks of Black Liberation Army, The Family and Weather Underground. Several leaders of these groups are arrested or surrender between 1981 and 1984
1983	Bomb explodes in U.S. Capitol building
1983–85	Neo-Nazi group "The Order" initiates a terrorist campaign involving bank robbery and murders: victims include talk show host David Berg, and police officers. Group plans attacks on nuclear power plants, and major political assassinations
1984–90	Florida cult headed by Yahweh ben Yahweh carries out several racially motivated murders of whites
1984–1994	Prolonged campaign against abortion clinics and providers across the United States, involving over a hundred bombings and arson attacks. Many extreme actions are claimed by the Army of God
1984–87	Series of attacks by militants linked to the Jewish Defense League
1986	El Rukn gang accused of planning terrorist attacks in the U.S. on behalf of Libya
1986–88	Several arrests and prosecutions of leaders of racist right wing and militia groups plotting or perpetrating violence, including the Arizona Patriots. Major sedition trial of leadership of movement. Series of rightist bomb attacks in Idaho
1988	Ju Kikimura of the Japanese Red Army is arrested in an alleged scheme to attack military and political targets in the New York City area. The attacks were to coincide with other bombings carried out by other members of the Japanese network in Naples. These incidents were reportedly ordered by the Libyan government
1988–90	Criminal cases focus attention on ecological activists using violent direct action methods to disrupt logging and other commercial activities in wilderness areas

1989	Publication of Andrew MacDonald's novel, *Hunter*
1990	Assassination of Rabbi Meir Kahane. Bomb destroys car carrying two Earth First! Activists in California
1993	Bombing at World Trade Center in New York City; planned attacks on other New York landmarks. Pakistani national shoots two CIA employees at organization's headquarters in Langley, VA. Group of skinheads and ultrarightists plan to assassinate Rodney King and attack black church in attempt to detonate a race war in California
1993–95	Militia and Patriot groups launch wave of bomb and sabotage attacks against federal targets, mainly in the West and Southwest: agencies attacked include IRS, Bureau of Land Management and Forest Service. Also wave of robberies and attacks by racist groups including Aryan Republican Army, and the Phineas Priesthood
1993–94	Antiabortion attacks escalate to assassination, causing four deaths in Florida and Massachusetts as well as other attempted murders
1995	Bombing of the Murrah Federal Building in Oklahoma City, killing 168; train sabotaged in Arizona by "Sons of Gestapo"
1995–99	Official action against militias leads to numerous raids and prosecutions including Arizona's Viper Militia (1996). In 1995, militia members are accused of plotting to use ricin poison against federal officials. In 1996, an Aryan Nations supporter is arrested while in possession of bubonic plague vials
1996	First violent actions by ecoterrorist organization, the Earth Liberation Front. Arrest of Theodore J. Kaczynski as the "Unabomber," accused of three killings and sixteen bombings since 1978
1996–98	Bombing campaign attributed to Eric Rudolph includes attacks on Olympic Park in Atlanta and Birmingham abortion clinic
1998	Larry Wayne Harris charged with plan to attack New York subway system with anthrax
2001	September 11, airliner attacks leave three thousand dead in New York, Washington D.C., and Pennsylvania

Table 3.2 Major International Terrorist Incidents Since 1968

This is obviously a highly selective list: it also omits acts directed against Americans, which are discussed in Table 3.3

1968	Upsurge of radical political movements across Western Europe, leads to formation of many militant groups committed to violent methods. Popular Front for the Liberation of Palestine (PFLP) pioneer extensive use of airline hijacking
1968–1974	Height of activity by Palestinian guerrilla movements, especially al-Fatah and PFLP, with hundreds of attacks across the globe. Major events include the hijacking and destruction of three airliners in Jordan (1970); Black September raid on Munich Olympics (1972); and massacre on airliner at Italy's Fiumicino airport (1973)
1969	Beginning of crisis and guerrilla conflict in Northern Ireland (through 1998). Violence escalates following the massacre of civilians by British soldiers on Bloody Sunday (1972). In 1972 alone, four hundred and seventy people are killed in "the Troubles"
1969	Start of terrorist warfare in Italy with bombing of a Milan bank that kills sixteen
1969–71	Urban guerrilla movements in Uruguay and Argentina popularize new forms of terrorist warfare
1970	Bombing of Swissair airliner en route to Tel Aviv, first destruction of airliner in the new era of terrorism
1972	Japanese Red Army and PFLP massacre passengers at Israel's Lod airport
1972–73	Israelis use assassination to eliminate leaders of main Palestinian guerrilla groups worldwide
1973	Basque ETA assassinates Prime Minister of Spain
1973–75	IRA begins major bomb attacks on British mainland
1973–78	Height of guerrilla warfare by the Italian Red Brigades
1975	"Carlos" kidnaps leaders of OPEC oil cartel in Vienna
1976	Israeli rescue of hijacked airliner at Entebbe in Uganda heralds new era of counterterrorism
1977	Terrorist crisis in Germany leads to destruction of Red Army Fraction, and suicide of its main leaders; Germans rescue hostages from airliner at Mogadishu, Somalia
1978	Kidnap and murder of former Italian Prime Minister Aldo Moro
1980	Siege at Iranian embassy in London; eighty-five people killed when extreme-rightists bombs rail station in Bologna, Italy
1982–98	Hundreds killed in major IRA bombing campaign against targets in Northern Ireland, the British mainland, and overseas. In 1984, an IRA bomb attack at the Conservative Party convention in Brighton comes close to wiping out most of the British government.
1983	Shi'ite Muslim groups in Lebanon begin to make extensive use of suicide bombing tactic, initially against occupying Israelis, subsequently against Americans and other international forces.
1983–87	Height of activity by leftist *Action Directe* organization in France.
1984–86	Terrorist crisis in Belgium
1985	New upsurge of terrorism across Europe, apparently related to Middle Eastern conflicts. Hizbullah hijack of TWA flight from Athens to Rome; plane taken to Beirut. Palestinian group hijacks the cruise ship *Achille Lauro* in the Mediterranean. In Malta, fifty-seven are killed in botched rescue of an

	EgyptAir flight; Abu Nidal group attacks airports of Rome and Vienna. Sikh terrorists blow up an Air India airliner over the Atlantic killing three hundred and twenty-four, in what was (until September 11) the most destructive terrorist attack in history
1986	Bomb attack on TWA 840 flying from Rome to Athens. Simultaneous attacks against a Pan Am flight in Karachi, Pakistan, and a synagogue in Istanbul, Turkey, both attributed to Abu Nidal; major series of bombings in Paris claimed by CSPPA
1988	Eleven killed in attack on ferry ship *City of Poros* in Greece, allegedly the work of Abu Nidal group
1989	French airliner blown up over Niger, killing one hundred and seventy
1992	Twenty killed in Islamist bombing of Israeli embassy in Argentina
1992–2000	Terrorist war by Islamic militants in Algeria
1994	Jewish extremist murders twenty-nine Muslims in a mosque in Hebron, Palestine; forty killed in Islamist attack on Jewish cultural center in Argentina. Mass hostage-taking by Chechen guerrillas in Russia leads to death of one hundred and fifty
1994–95	Algerian GIA guerrillas bomb targets in France, and attempt to hijack airliners
1994–Present	Islamist guerrillas in Israel begin campaign of suicide bombing against buses and civilian targets
1995	Release of poison gas by Aum Shinrikyo in Tokyo's subway system kills twelve
1996	In Sri Lanka, Tamil Tiger guerillas explode a train bomb killing seventy
1997	Islamist extremists kill over seventy Western tourists in two separate attacks in Egypt
2000	Beginning of "Second *Intifada*" in Israel leads to a massive escalation of suicide bombing by Palestinians
2002	Chechen guerrillas take hundreds of hostages in a Moscow theater. During a rescue attempt by Russian security forces, 120 hostages and fifty guerrillas are killed

Table 3.3 Major International Terrorist Attacks on U.S. Targets Since 1968

1968	U.S. ambassador to Guatemala assassinated
1970	Kidnap and murder of U.S. Ambassador to Uruguay; four U.S. and other Western airliners hijacked, taken to Jordan, and eventually destroyed
1973	U.S. Ambassador to Sudan and other diplomats assassinated by Black September organization
1979	Fifty-two members of the U.S. embassy staff in Tehran, Iran, taken hostage and held until early 1981
1981	U.S. General James Dozier taken hostage by Italian Red Brigades; Red Army Fraction attacks U.S. military targets in Germany
1983	Suicide car bombing against the U.S. embassy in Beirut kills sixty-three, including seventeen Americans; also in Beirut, a second suicide attack kills two hundred and forty Marines
1984	CIA station chief in Beirut kidnapped and later murdered; also in Beirut, sixteen are killed in explosion at U.S. embassy annex
1985	Eighteen killed in bombing of restaurant in Spain popular with American servicemen, in an act attributed to Hizbullah. TWA airliner hijacked over the Mediterranean, leading to death of one U.S. Navy diver. Hijacking of cruise ship *Achille Lauro* in Mediterranean results in death of elderly American Leon Klinghoffer
1985–1990	Kidnapping of twenty U.S. and other Western hostages in Lebanon by groups linked to Hizbullah
1986	Bomb attack against Berlin discotheque provokes U.S. air strikes against Libya
1988	Pan Am flight 103 brought down over Lockerbie, Scotland: two hundred and seventy are killed
1993	Iraqi assassination attempt on President George H. Bush in Kuwait
1995	Seven killed in attack on U.S. personnel in Riyadh, Saudi Arabia
1996	Nineteen U.S. personnel killed in bomb attack at Khobar Towers, Saudi Arabia.
1998	Terrorist bombs destroy the U.S. embassies in Nairobi, Kenya and Dar es Salaam, Tanzania, killing almost three hundred, including twelve Americans
2000	A terrorist bomb damages the destroyer USS *Cole* in the port of Aden, Yemen, killing seventeen

4

Motives

> Mistletoe killing an oak—
> Rats gnawing cables in two—
> Moths making holes in a cloak—
> How they must love what they do!
> Yes—and we Little Folk too,
> We are busy as they—
> Working our works out of view—
> Watch, and you'll see it some day! . . . . .
> We are the Little Folk—we!
> Too little to love or to hate.
> Leave us alone and you'll see
> How we can drag down the State!
>
> —Rudyard Kipling, *Pict Song.*

Rather than offering any kind of manual of terrorist groups or tactics, this book is intended to analyze the ways terrorism is understood in public discourse. Yet having said this, some understanding of the goals and methods of terrorist organizations is essential if we are to explore the process of investigating and reporting their actions. Since one of my central themes in this book is the difficulty of attributing blame for specific incidents, we must appreciate some facts that initially seem counter-intuitive, such as why groups carry out terrorist attacks for which they then try to evade responsibility. When examining why terrorists commit monstrous acts, the media often suggest that terrorists act for publicity, for recognition. If they are not even claiming responsibility, they must fit this characterization of irrational "mad bombers."

Understanding this behavior is all the more important because of a common impression that seems to exist in the mass media, which so regularly suggest that terrorists are insane, crazy, or are acting solely out of a love of murder and destruction, terror for terror's sake. This is very much the notion of destruction for its own sake that we find in the Kipling poem quoted at the start of this chapter. In his novel *The Secret Agent*, Joseph Conrad offered a classic interpretation of the terrorist mastermind as a soulless psychopath: "And the incorruptible Professor walked, too, averting his eyes from the odious multitude of mankind. He had no future. He disdained it. He was a force. His thoughts caressed the images of ruin and destruction. He walked frail, insignificant, shabby, miserable—and terrible in the simplicity of his idea calling madness and despair to the regeneration of the world. Nobody looked at him. He passed on unsuspected and deadly, like a pest in the street full of men" (see also Jenkins 1991b; Scanlan 2001).

During the 1970s and 1980s, a sizable literature developed on this theme of the pathology of terrorism. We could read for instance that "the lengthening list of assassins, hijackers and terrorist groups is packed with the mentally sick" (Watson, and Monahan 1973). In 1986, the science section of the authoritative *New York Times* carried a major story describing recent research into the psychopathology of terrorism, under the headline "The Roots of Terrorism are Found in Brutality of Shattered Childhood" (Goleman 1986, Compare Reich and Laqueur, eds. 1998)

As we will see, though, however repulsive the acts might be, they often do have a rationale, albeit a complex one. Particularly during the 1970s, commentators stressed that terrorists were carrying out attacks for the sake of influencing an audience, and that "audience" was presumed to be the general public. This seemed highly plausible following some of the airliner hijackings of the early 1970s, when Palestinian groups tailored events for the maximum television impact, including the unforgettable scene of three aircraft exploding at an airfield in Jordan (fortunately without any passengers on board). These media spectaculars popularized the idea that most or all terrorism had these public goals. This view placed a heavy responsibility on the mass media in shaping their reporting such incidents. Long ethical debates surrounded questions such as whether television stations should broadcast terrorist communiqués (Miller 1982; Clutterbuck 1983; Alexander and Picard 1991; Paletz and Schmid 1992; Picard 1993; Weimann and Winn 1994; Nacos 1996, 2002). In fact, the audience for such acts might not fit the conventional image of the community watching the six o'clock news, but might rather be a specific government or rival group, or even an individual. If in fact Colonel Qaddafi ordered the destruction of Pan Am 103 as revenge for a U.S. attack on his country, then in a sense, the audience for the act was strictly limited to himself, and perhaps his immediate circle.

However much this contradicts much received wisdom, terrorism is not just a strategy of futility, a last resort for those who can advance their cause in no other way. In appropriate circumstances, it can succeed, to a greater or lesser extent. This is not to deny that some terrorists might indeed be insane, or might act in a way that is disastrously misguided and self-defeating. If we hope to formulate any kind of effective response to this problem, we need to understand that terrorists generally are operating according to their own distinctive rationale and, under the right circumstances, they can achieve their goals. (For the politics and the goals of terrorism, see Laqueur 1979; O'Sullivan 1986; Merkl 1986; Stohl 1988; Rubin 1989; Wardlaw 1989; Vetter and Perlstein. 1991; Wieviorka 1993; Smith 1994; Poland 1997; Reich and Laqueur 1998; Hoffman 1998; White 2002; Dershowitz 2002.)

WHY TERRORISM?

In order to understand the goals of terrorism, let us begin with a specific incident that is relatively straightforward—the 2002 bus attack in Jerusalem by Muhammad al-Ghoul. In this case, we know the identity of the offender, the group, and the cause for which he was prepared to kill and die.

Since the Palestinian cause is so often cited as a factor in contemporary terrorism, some political background is necessary here (Sayigh 1999). During the early twentieth century, the land of Palestine was mainly inhabited by Arabs, who were predominantly Muslim with a sizable Christian minority. However, Jews in Europe and elsewhere wished to establish a national home in that same land, from which they had been expelled centuries earlier, and they began to immigrate in large numbers. Violent conflicts resulted. In 1948, the land was partitioned between a Jewish state of Israel, and the remaining territories under the control of Arab states. During this and subsequent wars, millions of Palestinian Arabs were expelled from their family homes, and many were forced to live in refugee camps on the West Bank of the Jordan, in the Gaza Strip, or in neighboring Arab countries. They saw little chance of escaping from this situation, since repeatedly, Arab states like Egypt and Syria failed to defeat the powerful Israeli armed forces.

As Palestinian despair deepened after the Arab-Israeli war of 1967, there emerged a variety of radical and revolutionary movements pledged to expel the Israelis, and to force the return of Arab lands. Since conventional armed forces could not defeat Israel, Palestinians turned to irregular forces and methods, to guerrilla and terrorist warfare. This decision led to the wave of attacks through the 1970s and 1980s: first the hijackings, later the bombings of airliners and attacks on airports and embassies around the globe. From the late 1980s, the most active and effective guerrilla groups were those preaching Islamic fundamentalism, like Hamas and Palestinian Islamic Jihad (Sivan and Friedman 1990; Miller 1996). In 2000, a new wave of violence broke out, and the fundamentalists began a campaign of suicide bombings (Anti-Defamation League of B'nai B'rith 2002). As of 2002, there were serious concerns that Hamas was seeking to escalate its activities into the realm of "megaterrorism," trying to kill very large numbers of Jews by mass poisoning, or by bringing down skyscrapers (Katzenell 2002).

What did al-Ghoul and the other bombers want to achieve? In trying to explain this, I am not for a moment justifying their acts, but rather seeking to understand what might otherwise seem to be incomprehensible behavior. In essence, Hamas and its followers have the same goals of any nation fighting a war, namely to inflict the maximum possible damage on an enemy, in order to force the other side to surrender or withdraw. To that extent, al-Ghoul's motives were the same as any soldier prepared to kill for his country or his people, who would echo the bomber's remark that he did not want to "kill for the sake of killing but so that others might have life, to kill and be killed for the lives of the coming generation." In his suicide note, he declared, "I am happy that my body will be the response for the attacks conducted by the Israelis, and that my body will turn into an explosive shred mill against the Israelis." In other circumstances, he would perhaps have picked up a rifle to confront the enemy, but given the overwhelming Israeli military superiority, this was not an option. He chose clandestine means, which the Israelis could not prevent. Since he could not fight soldiers, he targeted civilians (Beaumont 2002; Rubin 2002).

Strange as it may appear, al-Ghoul and his kind would have presented their actions in terms of self-defense, or retaliation for previous offenses committed by the Israelis. Of course, he would not have believed that specific individuals on the bus he attacked had done any personal harm to himself or his community, but like other terrorists before or since, he would have justified the violence in terms of acts previously committed by the authorities or the enemy nation. The argument is, "you started it," by occupying our country or by persecuting other activists. Such a moral claim is important for religious activists, who try to justify acts through religious thought and language, but it is also commonplace for secular radicals. Among other things, the idea helps defuse the associations of the word terrorism. Although we are committing a violent act, the rhetoric claims, it is justified as retribution for what has previously been done to us. As Leon Trotsky (1909) wrote, "The most important psychological source of terrorism is always the feeling of revenge in search of an outlet" (Compare Rapoport and Alexander eds 1989; Wright 1991). Oklahoma City bomber Timothy McVeigh explained his action in these words: "Foremost, the bombing was a retaliatory strike; a counterattack, for the cumulative raids (and subsequent violence and damage) that federal agents had participated in over the preceding years (including, but not limited to, Waco)" (Quoted in http://www.backwoodshome.com/columns/duffy010501.html).

Clearly, al-Ghoul did not believe that in setting off his bomb he would end what he saw as the injustices imposed on his people, any more than a soldier in action believes that he single-handedly will destroy an enemy nation. But we can think of several goals of an action like this. Significantly, the terrorists and those who sent them are trying to demonstrate the weakness of the state—in this case, the nation of Israel—and its inability to protect its citizens. They are showing that the state does not have a monopoly of violence. This has the dual effect of encouraging the enemies of the state, realizing that Israel is not as invulnerable as it may appear, while forcing the Israelis to realize that even their military might can be challenged. This was all the more effective at that point in time because the Jerusalem bus bombing occurred just a month after the Israelis had launched a major invasion of the West Bank that was intended to root out terrorism. The intention was to teach Israelis that in order to stop future bombings, they would have to negotiate or make concessions.

Terrorism serves to show that Palestinian issues cannot simply be ignored, in Israel or overseas. When buses and shopping centers are blown up regularly, when death can strike at any moment, it is simply impossible for the state and regular society to continue business as usual. When many people feel that a government can no longer protect the lives of its citizens, that sense obviously has a devastating effect on everyday life. Ideally, the continued violence would provoke a catastrophic social breakdown, out of which the new revolutionary order will emerge. In 2002, Salah Sh'hadeh, leader of Hamas' fighting organization, remarked on the soaring number of candidates willing to undertake suicide missions, with or without official approval, and what that meant for his movement: "If some of the youths do not follow the military apparatus's instructions, and [set out on operations on their own] without being linked officially to this apparatus, this proves that the [entire] nation has become a nation of Jihad on the threshold of liberation, and that it rejects humiliation and submission" ("Interview with Salah Sh'hadeh" 2002). In the years before the great French revolution of the eighteenth century, the queen Marie Antoinette warned, "After us, the deluge." Modern terrorists would rather say, "After the deluge, us." Put another way, the worse the better.

In addition, a movement like Hamas is trying to improve its own political position. The more effective any group is in provoking this kind of disorder, the more it will attract followers and supporters, and probably the financial support of outside governments. And the more a government attacks a group as evil and dangerous, the better the publicity, since it shows that they are having a major effect, and alarming the regime. Once a group is labeled as Public Enemy Number One, it can serve as a focus of dissent and discontent within the larger society. In Palestinian communities, the popular cult of the *shahid*, the martyr-bomber, reflects directly on the movement for which these individuals fight.

WINNING AND LOSING

In all these respects, we can see the suicide bombings as rational, however ruthless and cynical they appear. The point should also be made about another predictable effect of terrorist violence, which is that they incite further repression and violence. Looking at a situation like the Israel-Palestine conflict, Americans are likely to react with puzzlement when they see ever more violent and provocative acts that target innocent civilians. We are tempted to ask: do the terrorists not realize that they will enrage the Israelis, and drive them to new acts of repression? The answer of course is that they know this very well, and this is exactly what they want. From our normal point of view, this seems incomprehensible. If we are doing something wrong, we do not want to invite the police to come in and try and stop us, especially if repression will result in the deaths or imprisonment of many of our followers. In a terrorist war, however, repression is often valuable because it escalates the growing war, and forces people to choose between the government and the terrorists. The terror/repression cycle makes it virtually impossible for anyone to remain a moderate. By increasing polarization within a society, terrorism makes the continuation of the existing order impossible.

Once again, let us take the suicide bombing example. After each new incident, Israeli authorities tightened restrictions on Palestinian communities, arrested new suspects, and undertook retaliatory strikes. As the crisis escalated, they occupied or reoccupied Palestinian cities, destroying Palestinian infrastructure. The result, naturally, was massive Palestinian hostility and anger, which made further attacks more likely in the future. The violence made it more difficult for moderate leaders on both sides to negotiate. In the long term, the continuing confrontation makes it more likely that ever more extreme leaders will be chosen on each side, pledged not to negotiate with the enemy. The process of polarization is all the more probable when terrorists deliberately choose targets that they know will cause outrage and revulsion, such as attacks on cherished national symbols, on civilians, and even children.

We can also think of this in individual terms. Imagine an ordinary Palestinian Arab who has little interest in politics and who disapproves of terrorist violence. However, after a suicide bombing, he finds that he is subject to all kinds of official repression, as the police and army hold him for long periods at security checkpoints, search his home for weapons, and perhaps arrest or interrogate him as a possible suspect. That process has the effect of making him see himself in more nationalistic (or Islamic) terms, stirs his hostility to the Israeli regime, and gives him a new sympathy for the militant or terrorist cause. It might contribute to reshaping and redefining his whole identity, his self-concept. He would be even more outraged and radicalized if the police were arresting, searching, or bullying his family, his wife or children. This is what has been happening among the Palestinians, but it also occurred in many earlier campaigns in South Africa, Northern Ireland, Latin America, and so on.

Far from being a deterrent, arrest and imprisonment are among the most valuable weapons for a terrorist movement. The courtroom can be used as a theater for political statements and media spectaculars, while jailed terrorists can serve as martyrs who are used to inspire new generations of fighters (Hayden 1970). In the Arab nations as well as countless other conflicts, prisoners serve as the focus for potent sympathy campaigns. Many people who would not give money to support overt armed terrorism might well give to a charity that claimed to be helping the families of imprisoned political prisoners—even though in reality, the money would still find its way to buying guns and explosives. During the Troubles in Northern Ireland, the most successful means of fund-raising for the IRA involved requesting donations for "the men behind the wire," the imprisoned guerrillas and their families. Money flowed freely into the organization's coffers when authorities were charged with maltreating the prisoners, and reached a peak in the early 1980s when prisoners died during hunger strike protests (Taylor 1980; Beresford 1997). Even in the United States, a left-wing guerrilla movement that was thoroughly isolated by the mid-1980s won new sympathizers through campaigns on behalf of political prisoners, through films like *Through the Wire.* And imprisonment gives the terrorists other advantages. Terrorists in prison can recruit other inmates to their cause, people who would previously have been non-political criminal offenders. Jailing hundreds or thousands of terrorists will not of itself end an anti-government campaign, but might conceivably keep the flames burning (Page 1998).

The Israeli response to terrorism is also valuable for the terrorists in global publicity terms, since the international media attack Israel for its repression of civilians. Hamas military commander Salah Sh'hadeh, quoted earlier, was killed in an Israeli raid on Gaza in 2002, an act which by any normal standards of warfare would represent a major Israeli victory. In this case though, the killing provoked ferocious criticism of Israel by the U.S. and western Europe, and made Israel's diplomatic situation much more difficult. In short, a terrorist attack itself may or may not attract widespread publicity, but the official response to it very likely will. In saying this, I am not suggesting that governments should not respond to terrorism, or that retaliation is in any sense morally comparable to the original attacks. Many historical examples show that terrorism can be uprooted and defeated, and military action is often an essential part of the official response. But terrorism operates on a logic quite different from that of most conventional politics and law enforcement, and concepts like defeat and victory must be understood quite differently from in a regular war.

A TERRIBLE BEAUTY

Discussions of terrorism generally devote so much attention to Middle Eastern conditions that one is tempted to draw some kind of linkage between the faith of Islam and violence. Yet historically, Muslims were relative latecomers to the ideals of revolutionary terrorism, which in the modern world were evolved in predominantly Christian countries like Russia, France, and Ireland. Today, Ireland is a peaceful and prosperous nation, but its national political mythology focuses on an act of revolutionary warfare, the urban guerrilla rising launched by Irish Nationalists in Dublin in 1916. The rising itself was utterly defeated, and most of its leaders executed. Even so, the ensuing war forced the British rulers to give up power in 1922, ending over seven hundred years of occupation. The fact that the rising itself occurred over the Easter weekend gave immense rhetorical and religious force to the event. Just as Christians believe that Jesus died and was reborn to redeem humanity, so Irish nationalism viewed the dead rebel leaders as martyrs whose deaths had regenerated Ireland. The Easter lily, a token of rebirth, became a symbol of Republican nationalism. (This view would be strongly influential in Irish circles in the United States, as well as in Ireland itself. Compare McCann 1974.) Even those who opposed the rising were stirred by the deaths: W. B. Yeats wrote, famously, that after the executions, the martyred leaders,

> Now and in time to be,
> Wherever green is worn,
> Are changed, changed utterly:
> A terrible beauty is born.

Association with this epic event gave political charisma, and lasting legitimacy. One of the few surviving leaders of the 1916 rising was Eamonn De Valera, who dominated Irish politics into the 1960s. Also, like the former Jewish guerrilla leaders in Palestine, De Valera would be a forceful enemy of ultranationalist terrorism.

Perhaps the greatest of the 1916 martyrs was Pádraic Pearse, whose mystical views on the redemptive nature of violence, bloodshed, and martyrdom sound not too far removed from the theories of modern Palestinians. In 1915, he delivered a speech at the grave of nineteenth century revolutionary hero O'Donovan Rossa, a leader of the nationalist Fenian movement, one of the first modern groups to kill large numbers of urban civilians by terrorist bombing. Pearse's words on that occasion have become among the most famous in Irish history. He concluded "Life springs from death; and from the graves of patriot men and women spring living nations. The Defenders of this Realm have worked well in secret and in the open. They think that they have pacified Ireland. They think that they have pacified half of us and intimidated the other half. They think that they have foreseen everything, think that they have provided against everything; but the fools, the fools, the fools!—they have left us our Fenian dead—And while Ireland holds these graves, Ireland unfree shall never be at peace." As so often in terrorism, it is not so much the violent act that carries lasting historical weight, but rather the official response, and the construction of memory.

THE WORLD OF EARL TURNER

The theories underlying terrorism also influence many non-Muslim Americans. We might for instance look at a book that since its first publication in 1978 has become the bible for the American racist right, *The Turner Diaries*, by Andrew MacDonald—the pen name for neo-Nazi theorist William Pierce. Equally influential, though less familiar to law enforcement, is Pierce's later book *Hunter.* To date, two hundred thousand copies of *Turner Diaries* are in print, and *Hunter* is freely available from the same sources (MacDonald 1980, 1998; Griffin 2001).

The *Turner Diaries* is an imaginary account of a guerrilla war undertaken in the United States during the 1990s by a Nazi movement called The Order. *Turner Diaries* is distinctive in the painstaking detail of its nuts-and-bolts descriptions: how exactly to combine fuel oil and fertilizer to make a powerful bomb; how to sabotage the port of Houston; the best means of sabotaging a nuclear power plant (mortars firing nuclear contaminants). The book tells readers exactly the armaments you need to take out Dallas's telephone exchange ("three 500-foot spools of PETN-filled detonating cord and a little over twenty pounds of dynamite"). At this very moment, in America's extreme right compounds, someone may well be reading the paean to mortars ("marvelous little weapons, especially for guerrilla warfare") and speculating on the best methods for construction and use. In his fantasy, "the great Houston bombings" destroy the metropolitan power system, then bring to a halt both the airport and the freeways: "after Houston, there was Wilmington, then Providence, then Racine." The book reads like a manual for terrorist warfare and has been so regarded by some of its readers who have attempted to realize its lethally dark vision. During 1984 and 1985, a Nazi group called The Order tried to put the theory into practice, initiating a terrorist war across sections of the West and Midwest.

The book attracted notoriety in 1995 when its meticulously described scenario for bombing a federal building was put into practice by the men who destroyed the Murrah building in Oklahoma City. Pierce himself professed himself "shocked" by this "desperate and foolish" attack, though the perpetrators almost certainly borrowed his methodology (Pierce 1995). The book ends on an equally prophetic note with the hero, Earl Turner, flying a nuclear-armed aircraft on a suicide mission against the Pentagon. A 1978 book came close to envisaging the realities of 2001.

However abhorrent their politics and their violent racism, Pierce's books deserve careful reading because of what they suggest about the goals and methods of terrorism. Throughout, Pierce's fictional commandos launch attacks not for the sake of destruction, but for all the goals that we have listed here, in the context of Middle Eastern or Muslim movements. The fictional Order brings chaos to Houston precisely to bring the people to desperation, to force them to choose between the authorities and the revolutionaries, to radicalize the "sheep" that ordinary Americans have become. The violence of revolution is a means of exposing the weakness of the state and its inability to protect ordinary citizens. Violence serves as a purifying furnace in which the people of the postwar society are being forged. These were exactly the ideas held by the creators of modern Islamist terrorism, like the radical Egyptian thinker Sayyed Qutb (who was executed in 1966).

Significantly, Pierce even envisages the American far right moving to a strategy very much like the Palestinian suicide bombings, using lone attackers rather like the techniques of Hamas. In 1989, Pierce published *Hunter*, which portrays a lone wolf terrorist named Oscar Yeager (German, *Jäger*, or "hunter") who assassinates mixed-race couples. The book is dedicated to Joseph Paul Franklin, "the Lone Hunter, who saw his duty as a white man, and did what a responsible son of his race must do." (We recall that Franklin was the racist assassin of the 1970s.) The fictional Yeager also undertakes armed attacks against the liberal media and against groups attempting to foster good relations among different races and creeds. Central to the book is the notion of revolutionary contagion—that the hero cannot by himself bring down the government or the society that he detests, but his "commando raids" can serve as a detonator, to inspire other individuals or small groups by his example. "Very few men were capable of operating a pirate broadcasting station or carrying out an aerial bombing raid on the Capitol, but many could shoot down a miscegenating couple on the street." As racial tensions rise, blacks are provoked into open rebellion, a Day of the Long Knives, in which whites are slaughtered in the streets, and open racial war develops in American cities. Once again: the worse the better.

Following the Oklahoma City attack, Pierce declared that his vision was no mere novelist's fiction: In a radio address he predicted that, "A growing number will turn to terrorism as their only weapon against a terrorist government. And I suspect that we'll see some real terrorism—planned, organized terrorism—before too long. I suspect that a growing number of exasperated, fed-up Americans will begin engaging in terrorism on a scale the world has never seen before . . . There are many Americans who have come to consider the U.S. government their worst enemy." The influence of *Hunter* may perhaps be seen in a number of racially motivated killings through the late 1990s, acts committed by "loners" targeting black or Jewish institutions or individuals. Clearly, the core ideas of terrorism are not foreign to the United States.

THE BATTLE OF ALGIERS

In trying to understand the aims and methods of terrorism, we can do no better than to look at the "classic" terrorist war that occurred in Algeria during the 1950s. At first sight, this might seem like ancient history, and the story of the Algerian war is not well known in the United States. In fact, these events are highly relevant today, particularly since they were commemorated in the remarkable film *The Battle of Algiers*, which is still used as training material for both terrorists and counter-terrorists alike. In a sense, all modern terrorism has its origin in the Algeria of that time.

The basic story can be told quite simply. The North African nation of Algeria was colonized by the French in 1830, and by the 1950s it had a population of roughly ten million Arab Muslims and one million white Europeans. In 1954, the Arabs launched a revolutionary war to win national independence under the leadership of the National Liberation Front, the FLN. Though the war began as a rural struggle, in 1957 the revolutionaries moved their war into the great capital city. Here, they waged a terrifyingly innovative kind of urban guerrilla warfare, characterized by brutal bombing and machine-gun attacks against soldiers, police, and European civilians. This was a straightforward race war, in which people were killed because of their ethnic and religious background (Horne 1977; Crenshaw Hutchinson, 1978).

In response, the French sent in their finest troops, the Paratroopers or Paras, who fought the prototype of modern dirty wars, using torture, assassination, and provocation to destroy the FLN's devastatingly effective network of terrorist cells. By the end of 1957, the Paras had won a decisive victory, and all FLN units in the city were either destroyed, or so thoroughly infiltrated that they were under French control. Algiers seemed secure, and the French thought they had won a decisive victory: the rest of the war should only be a simple matter of cleaning up the remaining guerrilla units in the countryside. But things worked out very differently. In 1960, the revolt broke out again in Algiers itself, and this time as a mass popular movement, not just as the work of a few armed extremists. Algerian resistance combined with the French failure of political will to permit the creation of a new nation. In 1962, Algeria became an independent Arab Muslim nation, and virtually all white Europeans were forced to flee the country. The FLN had achieved its goals.

In 1966, the radical director Gilles Pontecorvo made the film *Battle of Algiers*, which is like no other film ever made about political violence. It tells the story from the point of view of the terrorists, some of whom are actually played by the real-life senior leaders from the 1957 battle, men and women who had much civilian blood on their hands. In one scene, we see women planting bombs in offices and restaurants with the goal of killing and maiming many civilians. Some of the terrorists are played by the real people who had carried out the actual attacks years before. The film makes no pretense that the revolutionaries were innocent, and offers no argument that civilians were only killed in tragic accidents. At the same time, the film does not demonize the French, even the Paras, who are depicted as resourceful soldiers who happen to be fighting on the losing side of history. The film describes countless details about organizing and mounting a terrorist war, including details like the organization of independent cells. This is why the film has so often been used for instructional purposes, in Latin America, Ulster, South Africa, and by some U.S.-based groups.

Amazingly, this proterrorist film celebrates a battle in which the terrorists seem to lose everything. The FLN guerrillas in the film know they are going to die, and their cause will fail in the short term—indeed, the film begins and ends showing the Paras rooting out the last effective terrorist units in the Algiers Arab section, the Casbah. Yet the guerrillas have faith in the future, because they know that their heroic deaths will inspire the people as a whole. In addition, the masses will be radicalized by the French repression. In the right circumstances, losing a battle against hopeless odds may well produce a long-term victory. And the film suggests that they are correct. The closing scenes show the masses of Algiers demonstrating heroically against the French, marching forward into the fire of tanks and machine guns, and sending the message that the deaths of even thousands of people will not prevent the people's victory. Significantly too, the marchers are led by women, for whom the revolutionary struggle has marked a process of social liberation. The closing words tell how in 1962, "the Algerian nation was born." Though the FLN was not a religious party, and did not have the idea of martyrdom that we find among many modern Muslim extremists, their theories did include a notion of "revolutionary suicide," of achieving victory through sacrificial death (compare Newton 1995). Pádraic Pearse would have understood completely.

TERRORISM AND POLITICS

The Algerian story raises other important points about the overall goals of terrorist movements. It shows, for instance, that we are often wrong to speak of "terrorist movements", as if groups fight solely and exclusively by such means. We do better to think of terrorism as one tactic that groups use among many others. Often, this method is used at an early stage in a struggle, when the movement has few supporters, and terrorist attacks are all that are open to it. Sometimes, groups use terrorist tactics against civilians at the same time as they are using non-terrorist methods of regular warfare against enemy soldiers. As time goes by and support grows, the movement develops to become more of a political party or even a regular army, and it might abandon terrorism altogether. In a telling scene in *Battle of Algiers*, journalists ask a captured FLN leader why he fights using women who carry bombs in their shopping bags. He replies that the French use bomber aircraft against his people's villages, and that he wishes he could fight by such means. Give us your bombers, he says, and we will give you our shopping bags.

The Algerian war also showed how resistance or guerrilla groups integrate violent actions with politics, indeed, how they have to do this if they hope to win. One critical concept here is *insulation*, which British counterterrorism expert Frank Kitson (1971) defines as "a functional system of associations, clubs and other groupings designed to carry out specific tasks." It is, in short, a means by which terrorists can hide among the larger population. In an ideal world, terrorists would wear T-shirts with the word TERRORIST printed in large letters, so they can be picked out easily by the security forces. Unfortunately, they do not do so, and strenuously resist attempts to isolate them from the people.

In a situation like Algeria, active terrorists coexist in a wider political world alongside other activists with varying degrees of commitment, and these less committed members provide a cover for the activities of the armed groups. There may be a political party supporting the movement's general goals, as well as dozens of sympathetic organizations appealing to separate constituencies and performing specific tasks. This model grew out of the highly successful pattern developed by Communist parties during the 1920s and 1930s, with their proliferation of front groups, molded further by the experience of clandestine operations during the wartime resistance movements in Europe and Asia. In Algeria, the overall movement, the FLN, worked with groups active in organized labor, education, tenants' rights, women's causes, farm-workers' organizations, student movements, religious bodies, and so on. It also formed and dominated ad hoc groups designed to respond to specific situations, campaigns on behalf of political prisoners, or committees to fight police brutality. Some actual terrorists might pose as members of one of these other groups, as party officials, student leaders, or labor organizers. As time goes by, ordinary people find that many of the most militant and determined activists in these various grass roots causes also support armed resistance, and that helps win support for the rising revolution. The related groups can be used as testing grounds, to observe the efficiency and dedication of young militants who might eventually be drafted into the terrorist organization.

In order to find the terrorists, the armed forces are going to have to arrest and interrogate many people who belong to these aboveground organizations, and in doing so, they will alienate these various communities. This is certainly more likely when the security forces are using torture. The use of insulation will not only protect the terrorists, but will help to radicalize moderates, and win recruits for fighting organizations. Forcing the authorities to raid what appear to be charitable or religious organizations pays rich dividends in public relations, since the international media will paint police and soldiers as bullies and oppressors.

The FLN used these political methods in a very sophisticated way, and the same strategy has been imitated in many other later conflicts, during the prolonged wars in Palestine, South Africa, Ireland, and Basque country. One of the best modern examples of insulation is Hamas, which apart from its notorious suicide bombing activities also runs a wide and effective range of schools, kindergartens, youth clubs, charitable institutions, health clinics, grass-roots development projects, and so on, often connected to mosques. According to one American observer in the 1990s, "Hamas runs the best social service network in the Gaza Strip. . . . Structured and well organized, Hamas is trusted by the poor (Gaza's overwhelming majority) to deliver on its promises, and is perceived to be far less corrupt and subject to patronage than its secular nationalist counterparts" (http://www.leyada.jlm.k12.il/proj/hamas/support.htm; compare Zuckerbrot-Finkelstein 1996). This reputation helps draw well-intentioned people into the organization, some of whom go on to become military fighters.

Even in the U.S. and Britain, some radical mosques and Islamic charities have provided this kind of concealment, such as the Jersey City mosque that was the base of operations for the first plot against the World Trade Center in 1993 (Downey and Hirsh 2002). Sometimes the insulation tactic has been very successful. In other cases though—as in Italy, Uruguay, or Argentina during the 1970s—state repression is too efficient, or too brutal, and the insulated network is destroyed along with the fighting organization.

This political emphasis reminds us that the long-term goal of terrorism is not simply destruction or chaos. These may be the short-term consequences, but ultimately, the terrorists hope to become a serious political force, and often to form a government, as happened to the FLN. Groups are often influenced by the Leninist ideal that the new revolutionary society emerges within the shell of the old, until it finally breaks through and replaces it. In this sense, the network of party organizations and related movements represents a blueprint for the new society.

Several other movements have made the transition from loathed terrorists to respected politicians. At some stages of its history, the African National Congress used terrorist actions, but in 1994, the ANC became the governing party of South Africa, the most powerful state in black Africa. In Northern Ireland, the Irish Republican Army has often employed savage violence against civilians and noncombatants, of a sort that can only be described as terrorism. By the late 1990s, leading IRA supporter Gerry Adams was a prominent figure in Northern Irish politics and a member of the British Parliament. In Israel too, the condemned Jewish terrorists of the 1940s had by the 1980s risen to the status of respected political leaders.

Terrorism can succeed, and the only reason we think otherwise is that observers tend to forget about such terrorist pasts. It is rather like the case of political treason: if a treasonous movement succeeds, it becomes the government, and has the power to declare that what it was doing was correct all along. As the old poem says,

> Treason never prospers.
> What's the reason?
> Why, if it prosper,
> None dare call it treason.

Terrorists can succeed—though if they do, we call them "Mr. Minister" or "Your Excellency," rather than terrorists.

The story of the Battle of Algiers has even greater contemporary relevance for Americans than might at first appear. Apart from the Pontecorvo film, the Algiers experience would reverberate through other works of fact and fiction. One of the most important French commanders in Algiers was Roger Trinquier, whose book *Modern Warfare* (1964) would for many years be perhaps the most important single text on urban guerrilla warfare in military academies around the world. The lessons of Algiers also inspired a new generation of revolutionary activists in the Middle East and Latin America. One was Brazilian radical Carlos Marighela, who encapsulated these themes in his legendary book *The Mini-Manual of the Urban Guerrilla.* This was as important a textbook for would-be guerrillas as Trinquier's was for the soldiers fighting them. Through the 1960s, Algiers itself was a refuge for many of the world's guerrilla and terrorist groups, including the Palestinian *Fatah*, Basque ETA (*Euskadi Ta Askatasuna*, Basque Homeland and Freedom), and the U.S. Black Panthers.

Later generations of radicals would also take close note of subsequent events in the nation of Algeria. The FLN regime established in 1962 survived into the 1990s, when free elections were arranged. An Islamic fundamentalist movement seemed about to win, but rather than face this prospect, the armed forces refused to let it take power. This check provoked an Islamic revolt that led to several years of warfare, in which perhaps a hundred thousand people died—some killed by terrorists, some by the military, and some by actions that cannot certainly be linked to either side (Willis 1996; Stone 1997; Quandt 1998).

The Muslim resistance was led by the fearsome GIA, the *Groupe Islamique Armée.* The GIA fought the government exactly as the FLN had combated the French decades earlier, using the same tactics, and believing in the same goals, of long-term victory through a kind of revolutionary suicide. In 1994, GIA militants hijacked an Air France flight in Algiers, and planned to fly it to Paris with the goal of launching a suicide attack against the Eiffel Tower. Many believe this was the first manifestation of the scheme that would reach fruition with the attacks against the U.S. on September 11 (Wald 2001). By the end of the decade, the GIA was largely put out of operation in Algeria itself, but many of its members joined together with Muslim extremists from Egypt and Saudi Arabia to create a new terrorist network called al-Qaeda, headed by Osama bin Laden. Some GIA fighters in France moved their operations to Quebec and other regions of Canada, giving Islamists a new base within striking range of the United States. Algerian militants have been implicated in many al-Qaeda operations, including a foiled plot to bomb Los Angeles International Airport on New Year's Eve, 1999. The ghosts of the Battle of Algiers are still with us today.

UNDERSTANDING SEPTEMBER 11

These points about the goals of terrorism can be illustrated by what, to date, is undoubtedly the most spectacular terrorist event in history, namely the attacks of September 11, 2001. For the sake of argument, let us assume that these attacks were entirely the work of the al-Qaeda organization, headed by Osama bin Laden, and fighting to promote extreme Islamic fundamentalism. (As we will see later, the truth may be somewhat more complex. My account of bin Laden and al-Qaeda is drawn from Bodansky 1993, 2001; Bergen 2001; Alexander and Swetnam 2001; Reeve

2001; Corbin 2002; Gunaratna 2002; Williams 2002; Jacquard 2002; Landau 2002; Esposito 2002.)

As is all too well known, the attacks destroyed the World Trade Center and a major portion of the Pentagon. If matters had developed only a little differently, the terrorists would have achieved an equally spectacular goal, which was to crash a fourth airliner into the White House or perhaps the Capitol. This scheme was defeated by the heroism of the passengers and crew of Flight 93, who ensured that the aircraft was forced to crash in a deserted Pennsylvania field (Longman 2002). And although September 11 marked for many Americans one of the worst days in the nation's history, it is sobering to realize that matters might have been even worse than they were. Some believe that the original hijack plan involved at least one additional airliner, flying from New York's JFK airport, and possibly two or three more, leaving from Newark, Boston, or Atlanta (Koring and Levitz 2001; Phillips and Eggen 2001; Johnston and Risen 2001). (Though al-Qaeda supporters have stated publicly that only four flights were to be used, this may have been disinformation designed to distract attention from other active units still operating in the West.)

The impact of these events on Americans can hardly be exaggerated. Particularly as new terrorist scares arose over the following months, many people were filled with anger and depression, and had lost much of their sense of the nation's security or invulnerability. For New York residents or visitors, the absence of a massive landmark like the WTC is a daily reminder of the breaching of American defenses, not to mention the ghastly human loss and suffering that occurred (compare Linenthal 2001). At the same time, the events gave great satisfaction to America's enemies, in the Middle East and elsewhere, who rejoiced at this massive American disaster, the proof that the nation was not as strong as it appeared. As happens on a much smaller scale with something like the suicide bombings in Israel, hostile forces gain courage from knowing that even a Goliath Western superpower can be challenged on its home territory. Despite all its nuclear weapons, the U.S. was successfully attacked by men wielding box-cutter blades. For people who know next to nothing about America, the institutions destroyed symbolize the heart of the power and wealth in the Western world: the center of world trade; the stronghold of U.S. military might; and (very nearly) the nation's political headquarters.

At every point, we can see that the goals of this massive attack were largely identical to those of "everyday" terrorist acts. Throughout al-Qaeda's statements and communiques, we can see the same kind of themes and justifications that have already been noted in the context of Palestine. The al-Qaeda spokesman, Suleiman Abu Gheith, declared in 2002 that the attacks were a kind of retribution for U.S. crimes around the globe in Palestine and elsewhere. "The [number] killed in the World Trade

Center and the Pentagon were no more than fair exchange for the ones killed in the al-'Amiriya shelter in Iraq, and are but a tiny part of the exchange for those killed in Palestine, Somalia, Sudan, the Philippines, Bosnia, Kashmir, Chechnya, and Afghanistan. We have not reached parity with them. We have the right to kill four million Americans—two million of them children—and to exile twice as many and wound and cripple hundreds of thousands. Furthermore, it is our right to fight them with chemical and biological weapons, so as to afflict them with the fatal maladies that have afflicted the Muslims because of the [Americans'] chemical and biological weapons" (Abu Gheith 2002).

Americans can understand that the attack expressed the hatred felt for the West in some circles, and perhaps the sense of revenge. But in many ways, the attacks remain mysterious. Beyond their warped pleasure or satisfaction, what on earth could the terrorists hope to achieve by this act? Don't they know they can never defeat the United States? This sense that the terrorists had badly misjudged their enemy only grew over the following months, as U.S. forces removed the Islamic fundamentalist regime in Afghanistan, and rounded up many supporters of the al-Qaeda movement worldwide. President Bush was one of many Americans who mocked the notion of al-Qaeda leader Osama bin Laden skulking nervously in an Afghan cave somewhere. By any customary standard, the September 11 attacks led to a stunning defeat for its perpetrators (Balz and Woodward 2002).

At this point, however, we need to recall the different standards of victory that exist in terrorist conflicts. A case can be made that events as they proceeded in the year following the attacks developed very much as the terrorists wanted. The United States was led to intervene militarily in Afghanistan, an outcome that could not have occurred in any other circumstances, and U.S. troops established a long-term presence in that country. Though U.S. forces in the early stages of the war won overwhelming victories, the terrorists could hope over the coming months and years to entrap the Americans in a long drawn out guerrilla warfare, which in theory could result in a nightmare like the Vietnam war. As in Vietnam or Algeria, democratic nations find it difficult to fight long campaigns against guerrillas or terrorists, since public opinion usually demands peace and negotiations. In a guerrilla war, governments lose by not winning; guerrillas win by not losing. In the 1960s, Cuban revolutionary Che Guevara urged radicals around the world to draw the U.S. into more and more struggles of this kind, which however unequal in the military forces used, would ultimately cause a political defeat for the United States. His slogan was "Create two, three—many Vietnams." This lesson has been enthusiastically adopted by modern Islamic revolutionaries.

Meanwhile, al-Qaeda can report the war in Afghanistan as if it is an unprovoked Western attack on a small Islamic nation, a grievance that can lead a whole new generation of young Muslims to mobilize against the United States. They would be encouraged in this new movement by the proof they have seen that the West is not invincible, proof of the kind the world saw on television sets on September 11. And although al-Qaeda does not operate the kind of structure of insulated party organizations that we saw in Algeria, in many countries movement sympathizers have infiltrated mosques and religious organizations, which can be used to recruit new followers, and to raise money. Police agencies face the danger that in trying to root out these militant networks, they will alienate sincere religious believers, and seem to be persecuting Islam. Increasingly, believers would see their own local fights as part of the global struggle of radical Islamism.

However odd it may sound to Western ears, the United States invasion of Afghanistan was precisely what the al-Qaeda movement wanted to provoke. Whether they will meet any of their broader goals is something that will emerge over the coming years.

CLAIMING RESPONSIBILITY

In the list of goals that terrorists often seek to achieve, we notice that the specific identity of the attackers or the groups responsible is not always relevant to the cause. Sometimes, as in Palestine or Algeria, there is little doubt about the general cause for which the guerrillas are or were fighting. Everyone knew that the FLN was responsible for most of the guerrilla insurgency in Algeria, simply because they were for several years the only fighting force carrying out attacks against police, army, and European civilians. Equally, we can say with certainty that one or more of the various Palestinian radical factions is to blame for all the suicide bombings to date.

In international terrorism, however, claims of responsibility are much less certain. Often, many separate groups make claims in order to gain publicity for their cause, while the actual culprit may or may not speak up at the time. For instance, al-Qaeda never made a direct and overt claim for the September 11 attacks, although subsequent statements and comments leave no doubt of the group's participation. The reasons for this modesty are apparent if we think of the goals of the action, namely to intimidate and demoralize the West, to galvanize the forces of radical Islam, and to generate an armed conflict between Islam and the West, in Afghanistan and elsewhere. From this perspective, it did not matter whether one Islamic faction or another carried out the attacks.

When a terrorist action occurs, the media place great weight on the claims of responsibility which are made, on the assumption that the culprits will wish to be associated with the attack in question. Yet publicity is by no means the only desired effect of terrorist acts. Some goals can only be achieved by publicizing the identity of the group involved; in other settings, that is unnecessary, and even counter-productive. In studying terrorist groups, therefore, we often find evidence of masquerade and subterfuge, basically, of individuals and groups pretending to be someone other than they actually are. This kind of behavior immensely complicates any attempt to attribute responsibility for particular acts, and thus to observe a track record for any given group or nation. It also means that any understanding of terrorism must depend on the interpretive work of official agencies or expert observers, to a degree that is not the case when dealing with most routine crime. Defining terrorism is in large measure a subjective process, conditioned by political and bureaucratic interests.

5

False Flags

> Every thing secret degenerates, even the administration of justice; nothing is safe that does not show it can bear discussion and publicity.
>
> —John, Lord Acton

Though the element of deception is rarely considered in news reports of terrorist incidents, historical observation suggests that it is in fact quite common, and anything but new. Contrary to many accounts, it can be very difficult to determine which group undertook a particular attack, and much harder still to deduce the full meaning of that event. Governments and intelligence agencies frequently use deceptive tactics to conceal their involvement in acts of violence, especially against other nations. The fact that the mass media rarely acknowledge these subtleties seriously impairs the reliability of their comments (Jenkins 1988a).

PROVOCATEURS

The terrorism literature often uses the word *provocation* to describe acts of deception or impersonation. Technically, the term provocateur originates in the practice of police or intelligence agents, though we sometimes use it to describe one terrorist group impersonating another.

At least since the emergence of modern policing two centuries ago, police have used infiltrators and provocateurs, agents who pretend to be something they are not in order to detect criminals or subversives. In modern America, forces like the FBI have regularly used infiltrators or "moles" to uncover the operations of criminal organizations. The term *provocateur* refers to something rather more sinister. In such cases, the police agent creates crime by encouraging a gang to carry out some kind of crime so that they will be arrested. In the U.S. at least, such provocateur activity is illegal, but worldwide, it is nevertheless widely used.

Provocation is a very old tactic of law enforcement and intelligence agencies when faced with violent or subversive opposition. It was especially common during the first great age of international terrorism between about 1880 and 1914, when virtually every modern tactic of terrorism and counter-terrorism was pioneered. Terrorism was as much in the news at the start of the twentieth century as it would at the beginning of the twenty-first. Then as now, groups targeted transportation facilities, bombed public buildings and meeting places, and assassinated political leaders (Heehs 1993). Then as now, terrorism could only be combated by extensive covert policing, through the use of infiltrators, moles, and turncoats, with all the dilemmas posed by these methods. Every modern issue about the goals and morality of terrorism was extensively debated in popular media as much as in expert scholarship, as were issues about the defense of civil liberties. A sophisticated public learned to be skeptical about the claims of responsibility for given terrorist acts, knowing that many violent incidents in Russia, France, the U.S. and elsewhere proved to have been undertaken by police spies in order to discredit radicals.

One of the founding fathers of counterterrorism was Pyotr Rachkovsky, who served as head of overseas operations from 1884 to 1903 for the *Okhrana*, the secret police of Tsarist Russia. Though his career is now known only to specialists in European history, the tactics he devised remain very much in use—and governments still have to grapple with the difficulties they can cause. Rachkovsky's agents extensively penetrated anarchist and revolutionary organizations, in order to identify and prevent terrorist threats against the government. Even revolutionaries like Trotsky were forced to admit that terrorist groups would inevitably be subjected to police control, so long as they concentrated on violence as opposed to broader-based political campaigns. As he wrote in 1909, "The Combat Organization, which the official party hierarchy places under the Central Committee, inevitably turns out to be above it, above the party and all its work—until cruel fate places it under the police department" (Trotsky 1909; Cohn 1996).

Rachkovsky's successes depended on his agents using terrorism themselves. Through the 1890s, he organized at least some of the bombings and assassinations in Western Europe that were commonly blamed on "anarchists" or "nihilists." In other words, a government agent was carrying out attacks in order to cast blame and suspicion on government opponents. Another motive was to promote police cooperation between Western liberal states and the Tsarist government, and to prevent foreign states from tolerating Russian exiles. Within Russia too, the line between police and terrorists was very thin. Of the double agent Azev (exposed in 1908), it has been written: "While he was active, much of the time and energy of the *Okhrana* had to be invested in combating acts of terror they had themselves instigated" (Cohn 1996). Such double agents sometimes ran out of control, to the point of assassinating leading officials in the Tsarist state (Schleifman 1988; Geifman, 1993, 2000). The *Okhrana* collapsed when the Bolsheviks took power in Russia in the revolution of 1917, but many of its ideas and methods were taken over by the new Communist secret police, which became notorious as the KGB (Andrew and Gordievsky 1990; Andrew and Mitrokhin 1999).

Such provocateur activity was not confined to Europe. In the United States at the turn of the century, terrorist activities were quite common, often in the context of labor disputes, and provocation was much used as a tactic (Adamic 1963; Lukas 1997). One of the legendary moments in American labor history occurred in Chicago in 1886 when a bomb exploded near police ranks confronting a massed rally of workers. Several were killed in the ensuing battle, which led to a notorious show trial: a number of union leaders were convicted and executed. Around the world, radicals believed, rightly or wrongly, that the original bomb was the work of a provocateur trying to discredit the labor cause, and the executed leaders became martyrs. (The monument erected on the site to commemorate the dead police officers would itself become a recurrent target for bombers, most recently in the wave of leftist violence in 1969 and 1970.)

The mood of this era is suggested by Jack London's apocalyptic fantasy novel *The Iron Heel* (1907), which imagines the future of America as a bloody series of wars between revolutionary terrorists and a repressive police state. The great attorney Clarence Darrow frequently defended labor or socialist militants on invented charges of involvement in revolutionary violence. In his autobiography, he records how astonished he was to find that in one case, his radical clients really had been guilty of the action for which they were charged, namely a bomb attack on the *Los Angeles Times* building (Darrow 1957). Obviously, as a defense attorney, Darrow had a vested interest in casting doubt on police accounts, but he had ample grounds for suspicion. For Darrow and his liberal contemporaries, the normal assumption was that terrorist actions or movements were invented by police or employers. Though debate still rages over the attribution of particular crimes, we can say confidently that many terrorist attacks really did involve provocateur activity.

This idea was discussed in some classic literary works. In 1907, Joseph Conrad's novel *The Secret Agent* describes a terrorist bombing that seems to be the work of anti-government anarchists, but which is really undertaken by governments themselves in order to discredit the revolutionaries, and to encourage support for greater official repression. In one scene, a government agent promotes terrorist actions to help counter "the general leniency of the judicial procedure here, and the utter absence of all repressive measures . . . What is wished for just now is the accentuation of the unrest—of the fermentation which undoubtedly exists." In 1908, English author G.K. Chesterton published *The Man Who Was Thursday*, a fictional account of an anarchist cell so thoroughly penetrated by the police that every activist is in fact a government agent: all the anarchists are really police officers, and vice versa. The book is still said to be very popular in intelligence circles, as one of the best accounts of the murky subtleties of the espionage world.

CELLS AND COMPARTMENTS

In some circumstances, the use of infiltration and double agents may lead to a situation in which—as in *The Man Who Was Thursday*—whole cells or even larger terrorist units find themselves controlled by the government. This can make it very difficult to assign blame for a given act of violence, while causing the authorities to tell the public considerably less than the whole truth.

A classic example of successful infiltration occurred during the 1957 Battle of Algiers when, as we have seen, the rebel FLN was at war with the French government and military. The French inserted more and more people into FLN ranks, while persuading other rebels to change sides and fight on behalf of the government. Gradually, more and more FLN fighting units fell under the control of French military intelligence. By the end of the battle, the French intelligence chief "found himself, in effect, virtually controlling the FLN apparatus" in Algiers (Horne 1977; Kitson 1971). To maintain an appearance of authenticity, the chief organized bombings himself, one of which destroyed his own headquarters.

Such manipulation is made possible because terrorist militants often do not themselves have a very good idea of who or what they are fighting for. While this concept may initially seem strange, we can usefully draw analogies with legitimate warfare. In Vietnam, an ordinary U.S. soldier would have known that his commander was General Westmoreland and his President was Lyndon Johnson but, beyond this, he would have had no reliable sense of the political or diplomatic context of any particular mission or campaign. Terrorists, similarly, know what side they are on, and they know their immediate comrades and superiors, but beyond that, they know little of the wider context. Information is kept on a strictly need-to-know basis, so that if an individual is captured, then he or she can give little information, even under torture. When a videotape showed Osama bin Laden gloating over the September 11 attacks, he was visibly amused that at least some of the hijackers on that day did not even know they were on a suicide mission. Probably eleven out of the total nineteen thought they were engaged in a regular hijack operation, which they were likely to survive (Rose 2001). This need-to-know standard has major implications for investigating the broader context of terrorist acts. If a captured member of al-Qaeda declared under interrogation that he was acting on behalf of Osama, that statement would be no more than a matter of personal opinion. The al-Qaeda member would have no clear idea of whether any state or intelligence service was directing his actions, because he would have no need for this information.

We also need to be careful in speaking of terrorist perpetrators as "members" of a given group. Some are members but, at least since the 1970s, investigations in Europe and elsewhere have shown that groups have assigned particular tasks to individuals not closely connected with the organization, to individual activists or even professional criminals. This is very much the same process that in the corporate world is known as outsourcing. These subcontractors are paid to carry out a specific act, to carry weapons or to place a bomb in a supermarket, and might never be contacted again. They literally know nothing of the motives or context of an act, and can identify no-one except their immediate contacts. If they receive orders through written or emailed commands, they would not even know those immediate superiors.

Ideally, the actual killers or bombers are chosen from a group with no obvious ties to the patrons who pay for the deeds. Many examples of such "cut-outs" can be cited. For instance, we know with fair certainty that in 1968, James Earl Ray was the assassin of Martin Luther King junior, but the wider ramifications of the plot are obscure. A Congressional investigation in the 1970s assembled convincing evidence that Southern racists and white supremacists might have conspired to kill King, using the low-level criminal Ray as a subcontractor. Ray himself probably had no idea of the politics of the killing, and seems neither to have known nor cared who was paying him to act. In his first interviews with the police after his arrest, he suggested that Black Muslims might have ordered the assassination. He might have been lying to his interrogators, but he may really have believed this story (Wilson 2001). In the mid-1980s, Libya conspired with members of the African-American gang El Rukn to carry out attacks against federal targets in the Chicago area, the actions to be paid for on a contract basis ("Five Draw Long Sentences" 1987).

Recognizing the vital necessity to keep information in watertight compartments, successful terrorist movements normally organize their active members into *cells*. This term has been much misused in recent media accounts, in which it means roughly the same as "units" or "forces," regardless of number. Actually, "cell" has a precise technical meaning. In a classic cell structure, terrorists are organized into groups of four or five individuals, each of whom knows every other member of the unit, but has no idea of the members of other cells. Each cell should ideally be like a hermetically

Table 5.1 Diagram of a Typical Cell System

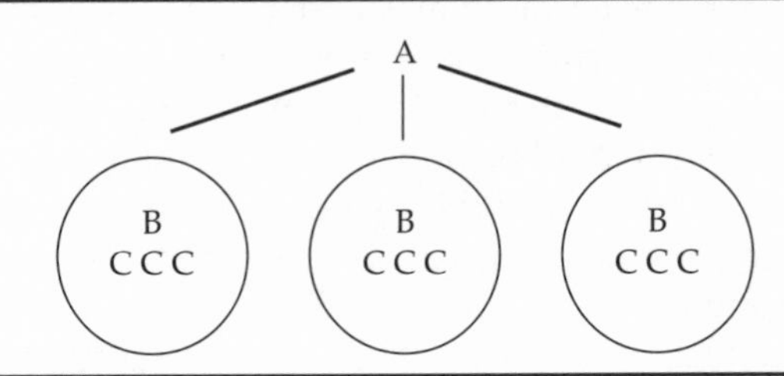

sealed compartment, permitting no contact with its neighbor. A member of one cell can sit next to another on a bus and neither will have the slightest idea that they are fighting for the same cause.

In each cell, only one superior officer has any contact with the higher ranks of the organization, and all orders are channeled through that person. In Table 5.1, the cell consists of three ordinary members (C's) and one superior (B). The superior communicates to a representative of the wider organization, A, who may in turn be in touch with higher levels—though that is not within the scope of what the ordinary cell needs to know. An ordinary C-soldier receives and acts on orders, but has no more idea of their overall purpose than would an American soldier in a rifle company in Vietnam.

The cell idea is over a century old and was used by most of the European groups that proliferated during the early twentieth century. Typical among these was the Serbian movement known as the Black Hand, which enjoys unparalleled notoriety among terrorist groups since its violent campaigns directly precipitated World War I. In 1914, its several hundred members were organized in a strictly compartmentalized model: "The Black Hand was organized at the grassroots level in 3 to 5-member cells. Above them were district committees. Above them, was the Central Committee in Belgrade. At the top was the ten-member Executive Committee" (Shackelford n.d.). This kind of structure was used by the European Resistance movements that fought the German occupiers in World War II, and was subsequently adopted by most Middle Eastern guerrilla groups. Today, Hamas derives much of its strength from its effective use of a cell structure. Hamas' fighting force—which among its other activities, directs the suicide bombers—is the 'Izz Al-Din El-Qassam Brigades. This force is "comprised of a few dozen activists loosely organized into small, shadowy terror cells, at times operating independently of each other" (Zuckerbrot-Finkelstein 1996).

Yet even watertight compartments can leak and cells can be penetrated. Imagine that one of the superior officers, a B, is somehow turned, persuaded to go over to the side of the authorities. Thenceforward, the members of that particular cell would continue operating, though unknown to them, all their operations would be directed by the authorities. This would allow the cell to be used for whatever purpose the agency in question wished. If, though, ordinary cell members were arrested, they would say, with perfect truth, that they believed they were still acting in the revolutionary cause.

Such "turning" is all the more valuable because of the small numbers involved in most terrorist organizations. Commonly, the terrorist groups that have attracted so much attention in Western countries over the last thirty years or so have had remarkably few members. Even significant community-based groups like the Provisional IRA never have more than 500 or so fighters at any given time, actively aided by perhaps ten times that many supporters handling tasks like hiding weapons and helping fugitives. Most groups are far smaller, and the German Red Army Fraction of the 1970s and 1980s usually had around thirty or so fighters. In Greece, the November 17 organization maintained a violent urban guerrilla campaign from 1975 through 2002, though the group seems never to have had more than a dozen members. If we imagine a terrorist group with, say, a hundred fighters—and that would be a formidable organization—then if the authorities secured control over just three or four cells, they would effectively be in charge of a major share of the group's operations, perhaps twenty percent of its frontline troops. (These comments are based on numerous case studies of individual movements, including Pluchinsky 1982; Aust 1987; Farrell 1990; Meade, 1990; Catanzaro 1991; Dartnell 1995; Alexander et al. 2001; Rapoport 2001. See also the essays in Crenshaw 1995.)

Recently, terrorist groups have tried to achieve a still great degree of separation between active units to the extent that the cell itself has literally no contact with any other component of the underground movement. This was in large measure a response to the collapse of many of the best known terror movements in the early 1980s, shattered by new official techniques of surveillance and counter-insurgency. The shifting balance of forces was recognized by the American far right, whose theorists evolved a shrewd if desperate strategy of "leaderless resistance." The core idea is the "phantom cell or individual action." If even the tightest of cell systems could be penetrated by federal agents, why have a hierarchical structure at all? Why not simply move to a *non*structure in which individual groups circulate propaganda, manuals, and broad suggestions for activities, which can be taken up or adapted according to need by particular groups or even individuals? To quote far right leader Louis Beam, "Utilizing the leaderless resistance concept, all individuals and groups operate independently of each other, and never report to a central headquarters or single leader for direction or instruction . . . No one need issue an order to anyone" (Beam n.d.). The idea meshes well with the kind of individual terrorist warfare outlined in William Pierce's book *Hunter.* The necessary diffusion of information is possible because of the rise of the Internet, which since the mid-1980s has been the preferred communication tool for the U.S. far right. In theory the strategy means that attacks can neither be predicted nor prevented, and that there are no ringleaders who can be prosecuted.

The leaderless resistance tactic has obvious advantages for the terrorists and guerrillas. At the same time though, it makes it even easier for security forces, or for rivals, to undertake their own operations and claim them in the name of some hitherto unknown phantom cell. The possibilities for deception and provocation become even larger.

PSEUDO-GANGS

The tactic of "turning" guerrilla groups is well known in the counterterrorism literature. A classic work in this tradition is the 1971 *Low Intensity Operations* by the British Army officer Frank Kitson, based on his experiences in many antiguerrilla campaigns. Kitson (1971) advocated the use of whole units of turned or bogus terrorists, of what he called pseudo-gangs. Depending on circumstances, the proportion of the unit who knew the real nature and purpose of the operation might vary from the whole group to only a handful of leaders. Kitson suggested that American authorities had successfully used such pseudo-gangs in disrupting and ultimately defeating black revolutionary activity in the U.S. in the 1960s, in destroying groups like the Black Panthers. (The Panther organization fell apart during 1970 and 1971, following bloody internal dissension and armed clashes with other revolutionary groups: Horowitz 1999. For the scale of police infiltration into the Panther organization, see Kempton 1974; Zimroth 1974). Such infiltration activity becomes quite easy in the latter stages of a terrorist campaign, when groups often recruit their members in prisons. They are thus drawing on a population that is already under the surveillance of police authorities and the likelihood of infiltration is extreme.

In some cases, terrorist units that have in effect been annexed by police or intelligence agencies can subsequently be used for complex covert operations on behalf of those agencies and their political masters. In the 1970s and 1980s, one of the world's most feared terrorist organizations was the Red Brigades, which undertook hundreds of armed attacks and assassinations in Italy. At the time, the group was seen as an extreme left-wing movement sympathetic to Communism and revolutionary socialism. Even its name was "red," and it certainly had links with the Czech intelligence service, the StB (*Státní Bezpeènost*, or State Security). Many writers then and since have suggested that the story is more complex. In this view, the Red Brigades began their career as an authentic movement of the far-left but as time went on, most of their columns (urban cells) were penetrated and controlled by government agencies. Ultimately, most or all of the movement became a kind of pseudo-gang under the control of sinister forces in the Italian police and intelligence community. As we can imagine, conspiracy theories run wild in such a setting (Jamieson 1989; Collin and Freedman 1990; Meade, 1990; Catanzaro, 1991; Drake 1995).

In such a case, the ideological motivation of particular actions becomes all but impossible to fathom, while police agencies sometimes find themselves investigating crimes connected to other sections of the law enforcement bureaucracy (recall the thorough confusion caused by provocateur policing in Tsarist Russia). Obviously, government forces will not readily admit that their people have been involved in such acts, and will not be able to investigate them freely.

For over a century, every major terrorist crisis has involved some such duplicity, some use of false flags, and these tactics would again be evident during the second great age of international terrorism that began in the mid-1960s. Often, scholars of terrorism speak generally of such false claims as provocateur activity, but as it stands this term is too vague. A better classification would emphasize the wide variety of motives that lead one group to claim an act in the name of another. I have suggested three major factors that often play a role:

1. *Deniability:* To achieve a goal that cannot be publicly acknowledged and in which one's participation is deniable.
2. *Stigmatization:* To discredit one's opponents by blaming them for acts that attract widespread repugnance.
3. *Destabilization:* To provoke a general social or political crisis out of which a group or agency seeks some future benefit.

In each case, the group might be private or public, and its attitudes either pro- or anti-government.

A particular act may have as its immediate or ultimate goal more than one of these aims, and different groups or agencies will differ in the clarity with which they have defined their objectives. However, this classification does serve to distinguish the very different reasons for which false colors may be used.

1. Deniability

Terrorist wars often involve false fronts that can serve the interests of the authorities as much as the terrorists themselves. In Northern Ireland, for instance, the IRA waged its guerrilla war against the British government, on occasion carrying out large-scale terrorist attacks. Politically, it was unacceptable for the government to admit that it was carrying on negotiations with the IRA, though in practice it often needed to talk in order to bring about a political solution. The dilemma was solved by the existence of *Sinn Fein*, an aboveground political party that was the counterpart of the illegal armed movement, the IRA. The British could then negotiate with *Sinn Fein* without seeming to talk to the IRA—though all parties knew that *Sinn Fein* was firmly part of the same movement as the IRA, and that there was massive overlap of membership between the two. A similar method has been used by many groups that notionally separate their political and military wings: ETA (*Euskadi Ta Askatasuna*, Basque Homeland and Liberty) does this, as does Hamas. Technically, Hamas attacks are carried out not by the mainstream organization, but by the 'Izz Al-Din El-Qassam Brigades. Thus "the connections and levels of coordination between the military and political branches are concealed" (Zuckerbrot-Finkelstein 1996).

These cases illustrate the political value of a name, a front, in providing a kind of fig leaf to conceal or justify activities. In the U.S. likewise, the Black Panther Party of the 1960s tried to separate its legal aboveground activities from the terrorism and guerrilla warfare of its military wing, the Black Liberation Army. The Panthers had been deeply influenced by the FLN experience in Algeria, and hoped to achieve a similar kind of insulation. In this case, though, the overlap between the two wings was so thorough and obvious as to deceive nobody, making it easy for police to investigate and disrupt B.L.A. activities.

False fronts also emerge when groups commit acts for which they hope to avoid responsibility—that are deniable, to use a familiar intelligence term. We have already noted the 1981 attack to assassinate the Pope by an unstable Turkish militant named Mehmet Ali Agca. We still do not know who employed Agca, though different observers suggest involvement by the Soviet KGB or else organized and corporate criminals in Italy itself. In either case, the effort to achieve deniability worked perfectly.

In rare instances, we can see the internal deliberations of agencies planning such deceptions. In the 1970s, for instance, Congressional investigators in the U.S. obtained and released materials that showed how the CIA had planned to carry out assassinations some years previously, under a scheme code named ZR/RIFLE. Likely targets would include left-wing rulers like Fidel Castro. When a senior CIA official discussed this scheme, his notes included the following points: "Never mention word 'assassination' . . . no projects on paper . . . . strictly person-to-person, singleton ops. . . . planning should include provisions for blaming Sovs or Czechs in case of blow. . . . no chain of connections permitting blackmail . . . Should have phony 201 in RG [Central Registry] to backstop this, all documents therein forged and backdated.... Should look like a CE [counterespionage/counterintelligence] file" ("James Jesus Angleton and the Kennedy Assassination" n.d.). In other words, the act should be carried out in such a way that even if the assassin were identified ("a blow"), he could never be connected to the United States. No paper record could ever be discovered. In fact the only documents that might be found would be bogus materials such as personnel files (201s) linking the assassin to enemy Communist powers, the Soviets or Czechs. The killing—or other violent act—would be fully deniable.

A terrorist group may wish to distance itself from an act because it is especially likely to cause outrage among the public from which support is hoped, whether that is a local population or the broader public of international opinion. To take an obvious example, if a nation like Iran or Iraq launched a violent attack against a U.S. target, say by blowing up a U.S. embassy, that country would be very unlikely to admit its involvement, since to do so would invite a damaging military and diplomatic response, and perhaps to provoke open war. It would make much more sense for that country to adopt some kind of false front, to claim that in fact the attack was the work of a spurious "World Islamic Front," or else was connected to some other known terrorist group.

The quest for deniability often involves the creation of a bogus front group on which unpopular acts can be blamed. The process can be traced in the Palestinian guerrilla movement in the 1970s, when Yasser Arafat's mainstream organization al-Fatah wished to draw global attention to its cause, yet at the same time hoped to overcome the terrorist label that prevented it from being recognized in political negotiations. The solution was the creation of the front name Black September for Palestinian attacks undertaken outside Israel, especially in Europe. Black September carried out some of the most notorious and bloody attacks of this era, including the taking of Israeli hostages at the 1972 Munich Olympic Games. Black September posed successfully as an extreme militant sect within the Palestinian Liberation Organization (PLO), at the same time that the al-Fatah mainstream courted European opinion, with considerable success. By 1974, al-Fatah leader Arafat was able to address the United Nations as the head of the Palestinian people, a diplomatic triumph that never could have happened if al-Fatah had taken direct responsibility for the violent acts of Black September. When the Palestinians had achieved their major goals, Black September simply ceased to function, because the charade was no longer necessary (Dobson 1974).

Other examples of this kind have occurred in the Middle East. Between 1975 and 1990, the state of Lebanon experienced a bloody civil war, and for several years a number of Americans and other Westerners were held hostage by shadowy Islamic groups with names like Islamic Jihad. This group also claimed responsibility for a series of bloody and controversial operations in Lebanon, Kuwait, and Europe. In Lebanon itself, the Islamic groups blew up the U.S. Marine barracks in Beirut, killing 240 American servicemen, and on several separate occasions bombed the U.S. embassy. On one occasion, the terrorists kidnapped the CIA station chief in Beirut, and tortured him so severely that he died. The hostage crisis became an event of global significance as the U.S. Reagan administration tried all sorts of unorthodox tactics to buy the prisoners' release. This ultimately led to the so-called Iran-Contra crisis in U.S. politics during 1986–87, an affair that came close to causing the president's impeachment.

But, who was responsible for the hostage taking? Several groups claimed responsibility, but it is very unlikely that these existed except as a cover name. When the prisoners were eventually released, it was found that people who had notionally been kidnapped by several totally different organizations had in fact been held together in the same house, even the same room. Even Islamic Jihad, long one of the most feared names in international terrorism, may never have existed as an actual organization. In reality, the kidnappings were the work of well-known Lebanese militias belonging to the Shi'ite Muslim sect, groups like Hizbullah (the Party of God) and Islamic Amal, both of whom worked closely with the Iranian secret service.

But we can easily understand why these groups would want to conceal their identity. If Hizbullah openly admitted that they had kidnapped Americans, the U.S. government would face overwhelming pressure to attack Hizbullah offices, leaders, or training camps, most of which were in well-known locations. Also, since Hizbullah was funded and armed by the Iranians, that linkage could have led to a U.S-Iran war that could have destabilized the whole region. Finally, it would be impossible for the U.S. to negotiate with Hizbullah or Iran on any other issues until the hostage crisis was resolved. For multiple reasons, then, it was essential for groups to operate under names like Islamic Jihad, while Western nations had to pretend to believe that such groups had an authentic existence. (For Iranian-backed terrorism, see Jaber 1997; O'Ballance 1997; Wright 2000, 2001; Baer 2002.)

New information has recently shed light on another Islamic Jihad attack that again confirms the Iranian context. In 1994, eighty-five perished in the bombing of a Jewish center in Buenos Aires, Argentina. At the time the incident was definitely linked to Middle Eastern affairs, but no government complicity was established. In 2002, however, an Iranian defector provided a detailed and convincing account of how his country's secret service carried out the attack. In this instance, the danger of detection was rare since the Iranians had massively bribed the local Argentine police and also paid off the nation's president to the tune of ten million U.S. dollars. Obviously, local authorities would at every stage block any attempt to unravel the truth of the case (Rohter 2002).

The use of false fronts is particularly obvious in the Middle Eastern context, but it has often occurred, in Ireland and elsewhere, and some of these fronts have become notorious in their own right. One important example in Europe involved the Basque peoples of northern Spain and southern France, who for decades have been campaigning for national independence. In the 1960s, Basque extremists organized the famous guerrilla movement, ETA, which up to the present day has maintained a violent campaign against the Spanish government. They have especially targeted police and army units and have caused hundreds of deaths (Alexander et al. 2001). ETA is a quite genuine movement, but much more dubious is another organization that appeared in this region in the early 1980s, GAL, *Grupos Antiterroristas de Liberación*, or Anti-Terrorist Liberation Groups. For several years, radical Basques and ETA supporters were kidnapped and murdered, often on French territory, where ETA had believed they were safe from attack. On each occasion, responsibility was claimed by a clandestine organization called GAL, which seemed to be a far-right terrorist death squad. Ultimately, GAL claimed almost thirty victims (Woodworth 2001).

During the 1990s it emerged that GAL was a bogus front group, a name that had been invented to conceal attacks carried out by the Spanish police and intelligence service. The police could not openly kidnap and kill suspects without trial, especially when these acts took place on the soil of a friendly neighboring country. By inventing GAL, the Spanish thus achieved deniability, or at least, kept up the pretense for several years. The case ultimately led to a devastating scandal for the Spanish government. (It is controversial whether British authorities might also have employed similar tactics in Northern Ireland. See Stalker 1989; Dillon 1989, 1990; Bruce 1992; Geraghty 2000.)

THE PARIS BOMBINGS

Some false front organizations are more convincing than others. In the case of Islamic Jihad, it was a fairly open secret that this was little more than a cover name for Hizbullah. In other cases though, deception can be much more convincing. To illustrate the difficulties involved in such matters, we can look at a traumatic series of bombings that occurred in Paris in the autumn of 1986, which attacked vulnerable civilian targets like supermarkets. The affair generated a sense of political crisis in France because the police seemed utterly unable to stop the attackers. The incidents gained worldwide attention and were covered extensively in the U.S. media.

So, who was responsible? What was known was that the attacks were claimed by a group called the CSPPA, the Committee for Solidarity with Arab and Middle Eastern Prisoners, which was demanding the release of three prisoners held in France. One prisoner was a Palestinian with Iranian connections; the second, a member of the Armenian guerrilla group ASALA (Armenian Secret Army for the Liberation of Armenia), and the third, a leftist Lebanese Christian named George Abdallah. At the time, French law enforcement was convinced that George Abdallah was the key figure in a campaign that was being organized by his supporters and relatives, and the media reported that some of his brothers had been identified at the scene of bombings. French police were issued photographs of the Abdallah clan. Because the Abdallahs were closely tied to Syrian intelligence, it was likely that this nation was participating in the attacks. The French government tried to negotiate with Syria, threatening political sanctions if the attacks continued. This interpretation of the attacks remained unchallenged for several months and was reported unquestioningly in the U.S. media.

It soon appeared, though, that this account was simply wrong. Months later, the French completely changed their views, and placed all the blame instead on Iran rather than Syria. They now charged that the Abdallahs had nothing to do with the crimes, which were instead the work of Islamic fundamentalists working for the Iranian secret service, and allied to Hizbullah (Ibrahim 1990). By the summer of 1987, the French government was blaming the bombings on an alleged Iranian agent and several arrests were made. A diplomatic crisis with Iran followed.

Even stranger than the total shift of interpretation was the account that now emerged of law enforcement politics during the crisis. France has two intelligence agencies, the DGSE (*Direction Générale de la Sécurité Exterieure*), which roughly corresponds to the American CIA, and the domestic agency DST (*Direction De La Surveillance Du Territoire*), which resembles the FBI (Faligot and Krop 1989). It was the DGSE that had believed the Abdallah story, and which had spread this account to the media. Meanwhile, the DST had its own separate contacts and had apparently known all along that the bombings were linked to Iran. They regarded Abdallah throughout as small fry, partly because they had kept him under constant surveillance, and knew that he had no role in the bombings: among other things, they were using his lawyer as an informant. DST thus knew that all the official statements coming from the French government were simply false. Looking at this amazing internal conflict, we should be reminded that French intelligence has a very high reputation: presumably other services are capable of still worse blunders.

The official view of the Paris attacks thus changed utterly within the space of a year. Either interpretation might be correct, either the view held so absolutely in 1986 (blaming Syria) or in 1987 (Iran), but in either case, the creation of CSPPA was a masterpiece of concealment and disguise. At least for several months, some group, or perhaps some nation, appears to have been remarkably successful in using the CSPPA guise in order to conceal its real identity, and thus to maintain deniability.

The later interpretation of the bombings also had larger implications for understanding a number of other terrorist acts during these same years. At the trial of the Paris bombers in 1990, it was argued that the acts had little to do with the prisoner issue, and the campaign was rather intended to prevent France from selling weapons to Iraq for use in its long drawn out war with Iran. If true, this same model would also seem to be more widely applicable. Between 1985 and 1989, Europe was the setting for several assassinations of political and corporate leaders, attacks that at the time were attributed to small left-wing factions, pursuing the logic of their anti-capitalist rhetoric (Dartnell 1995). Those targeted included senior officials and corporate leaders in France, Germany, and Italy, and also the Prime Minister of Sweden, Olof Palme (Table 5.2).

However, what all these figures had in common was that their business concerns were deeply involved in the business of arms trading to one or both of the partners in the Iran-Iraq war, in deals that were highly profitable, but usually illegal. Olof Palme, for instance, had recently reneged on the sale of Swedish surface-to-air missiles to Iran, missiles that the Iranians had already paid for. Participants in an illegal contract have no recourse to law, but (as in organized crime ventures) they must commonly resort to physical intimidation. In this scenario, the still unexplained murder of Palme would have served both as an act of revenge, and a form of intimidation to ensure future compliance with agreements (Jenkins 1989). We recall that at this exact time (1985–1986), Iranian-backed militias in Lebanon were holding Western hostages as a means of persuading the West to deliver sophisticated weaponry to Tehran, the deal that would lead to the Iran-Contra affair. When the Gulf War ended in 1988, so did the need for armaments — and coincidentally or not, so did the recent flurry of international terrorism, which subsided as rapidly as it had begun.

Quite possibly, then, a number of the terrorist attacks and assassinations in Europe in this era were the byproduct of the Iran-Iraq conflict, and should be attributed to Iran or its surrogates. Again, this would be a model example of the use of deniability.

2. Stigmatization

Stigmatization is committing a particularly heinous crime with the goal of placing the blame on somebody else, ideally some leading enemy. In such a case, a left-wing group might carry out an attack in such a way that the political right will attract the stigma, and will suffer for that. To take a modern illustration, defector reports suggest that in 2000 Iraq was plotting to destroy a U.S. warship in the Arab Gulf, using a small boat laden with

Table 5.2 Political Assassinations in Europe During the 1980s

	1985
January	Assassination of General René Audran, head of France's international arms sales organization
February	Killing of Ernst Zimmermann of German arms corporation MTU (*Motoren und Turbinen Union*)
June	Assasination attempt on Henri Blandin, comptroller general of the French armed forces
	1986
February	Swedish Prime Minister Olof Palme murdered
July	Killing of Karl-Heinz Beckurts of German firm, Siemens. About the same time, a bomb attack targeted the Dornier Corporation, which was active in "Star Wars" research.
November	Killing of Georges Besse of French corporation Renault
	1987
March	Killing of Italian general Licio Giorgeri, active in "Star Wars" research.
	1988
April	Killing of Senator Roberto Ruffilli, aide to Italian Prime Minister De Mita
September	Attack on Hans Tietmeyer, senior civil servant in German finance ministry
	1989
December	Murder of Alfred Herrhausen, head of Deutsche Bank (Herrhausen was currently overseeing the merger of German armaments corporations into a huge conglomerate.)

explosives. Iraqi authorities planned to use an Iranian national to carry out the attack, operating from a boat flying the Iranian flag (Peterson 2002). In addition to averting the blame from Iraq, that government would secure the added bonus of provoking a confrontation between two of its worst enemies, the U.S. and Iran.

A number of historical precedents exist for this kind of behavior, including the Reichstag Fire in Germany in 1933. Shortly after Hitler and the Nazi Party came to power, persons unknown burned down the German parliament building, the Reichstag. Though historians are still not sure who was responsible, it is commonly believed that the Nazis set the fire themselves, in order to blame it on their Communist enemies. The act caused enormous outrage, and scared the German people into believing that a Communist revolution was just around the corner. Millions of people who would not have supported Hitler before that point were now encouraged to support the Nazi regime in all its acts of violence against Communists and Jews.

Though the interpretation of the affair is crucial, some observers believe that a similar kind of "Reichstag" provocation may have occurred in Russia in recent history. Following the breakup of the Soviet Union, the Russian Republic emerged as a major state. However, it faced separatist pressures from various ethnic groups, including the Chechens, a Muslim people who live on the southern border. In the mid-1990s, Chechen jihad fighters launched an armed rebellion that Russian forces failed to quell, and the government signed a peace agreement. The whole affair embarrassed and infuriated military and intelligence officials, who feared that Muslim agitation could spread to other parts of the country (Seely 2001; Oliker 2001; Bennett 2001). Matters were fundamentally changed, though, when in the autumn of 1999, Russia suffered a series of dreadful terrorist bombings that seemed designed to cause the largest possible number of casualties. The blasts destroyed two apartment blocks in southern Moscow, a third block in the southwest city of Volgodonsk, and a military barracks. Over three hundred people perished, the great majority of them innocent civilians who were literally killed as they slept. The attacks provoked intense fear because of their randomness as much as their sadistic brutality, and they naturally angered the Russian public. Reversing previous policies, Russian forces now launched a new invasion of Chechnya and the wave of national patriotism helped secure the election of the new Russian leader, Vladmir Putin in 2000.

Initially, Russian authorities expressed certainty that the attacks were the work of Chechen extremists, and this interpretation sounded plausible. The Chechens had used terrorist tactics in the past and many Chechens had joined Osama bin Laden's forces in Afghanistan. But even at the time, some Russians expressed doubt about this attribution, and doubts have grown since. An alternative view holds that the attacks were carried out by Russian intelligence agents themselves, working for the Federal Security Service (FSS), the successor to the KGB. In this view, forces within the Soviet government committed those heinous crimes because they were the only way of galvanizing the Russian public for a new war against the Chechens. If in fact Chechens were responsible for a terrorist campaign, it is odd that they launched it in Moscow (though this would not be the first attack there). And it is doubly strange that they undertook violence that could only have disastrous effects for their cause. Meanwhile, the KGB had a long and bloody record of staging bogus terrorist incidents in order to manipulate public sympathies, and these tactics presumably were inherited by the new FSS (Andrew and Gordievsky 1990; Andrew and Mitrokhin 1999). If we look at the crimes and ask the classic legal question, *Cui bono*?—who benefits?—then the answer looks straightforward. The Russian state benefited, as did the armed forces, and the FSS, which had until recently been headed by Vladimir Putin.

Now, the fact that the apartment bombings benefited one side and harmed another tells us nothing about the actual culprits. People often do things that are ill-judged and that harm their own interests. In the case of the Russian bombings, though, evidence of deception and stigmatization has steadily mounted, until by 2002, responsibility for the attacks had become a significant issue in Russian politics. While Putin and the FSS steadfastly deny involvement, powerful politician and media figure Boris Berezovsky has argued that the attacks were an internal provocation, linked to Russian security officers (Wines 2002; Kishkovsky 2002). This conspiratorial interpretation was popularized through television documentaries and best-selling novels, and today the view is widely held. As in many terrorist incidents, the truth may never be known.

Stigmatization is a common explanation or excuse made by groups that wish to avoid the consequences for some action that has gone badly wrong, and has attracted public disgust. The explanation is that some evil enemy must have done this: as we will see, many Muslims firmly believe that the September 11 attacks were launched not by Arabs, but by Israelis, in an attempt to discredit the Muslim world. Often, such explanations are simply silly, but some must be treated seriously because of their credible sources. In one 1986 incident, a Jordanian man induced his Irish girlfriend to carry explosives onto an El Al airliner at Heathrow Airport, with a view to destroying the plane in flight. The plot was detected, the aircraft saved, and an early consensus placed the blame for the attempt firmly on a Syrian clandestine agency. As a result, Britain severed diplomatic ties with Syria. Within months, however, an alternative theory had emerged that saw the incident not as a terrorist act, but as a charade sponsored by Israeli agents to stigmatize their Syrian opponents as criminal masterminds. This view would sound outrageous, the work of some eccentric conspiracy theorist, but it was actually outlined by the Prime Minister of France, Jacques Chirac, speaking in what he thought was an off-the-record conversation with the German Chancellor (Bernstein 1986). Neither man was given to conspiracy theory, while the French had an intelligence apparatus in the Middle East far better informed than anything the Americans could dream of at that point. However odd the story, it deserves consideration.

3. Destabilization

Closely related to the idea of stigmatization is that of destabilization. In the former, agencies or groups try to pin the blame on some enemy faction in order to discredit them. In the latter, groups undertake terrorist violence that may or may not be attributed to any particular faction. The goal is to create a sense of chaos leading to an overwhelming sense of public fear and outrage, and perhaps to disrupt a hostile state. When the archives of the KGB became available during the 1990s, abundant evidence emerged of Soviet efforts to destabilize the U.S. and other Western powers by such means. Sometimes the activity took the form of circulating bogus literature, as in 1984 when the Soviets circulated violent racist leaflets as a way of stirring up racial strife at the time of the Los Angeles Olympic Games (Leaflets warned "The Olympics—For the Whites only!" and denounced "African monkeys"). Occasionally, though, violence was used. In 1971, at a time of great racial tension, the Soviets set off bombs in "the Negro section of New York," and falsely claimed the acts as the work of the Jewish Defense League, in an obvious attempt to incite "mass disorders" and race war (Andrew and Mitrokhin 1999, 238–39).

Sometimes, especially in some European countries, such tactics are undertaken by internal domestic groups in order to force a radical change in government policies, usually in the direction of severely increased repression and internal violence. In such cases, the culprits are sometimes official agencies themselves, in a kind of *coup d'etat* against an established government. Government agents impersonate terrorists and commit acts of violence in order to demonstrate to the public that law and order have broken down, that the state is incapable of preventing such acts, and that stronger rule is essential. Once again, numerous terrorist actions are undertaken without specific or plausible claims of responsibility.

Italy provides some of the best examples, though one could equally choose examples from other European or Latin American countries. In fact, the idea of destabilization is sometimes described by the phrase *strategy of tension*, which stems from the Italian crisis of the 1960s and 1970s. This began in 1969 with a bombing in a Milan bank in which sixteen people were killed. Two anarchists were arrested for the act that eventually was attributed to fascists closely allied to police and to members of SID (*Servizio Informazione Difesa*, military intelligence). In other words, though the act seemed to be the work of the political left, it was really the work of the far right (Ginzburg 1999; Willan 2001).

This pattern of domestic terrorism sponsored by state agencies recurred several times in the next fifteen years, as terrorist murders claimed hundreds of lives. It is often hard to tell whether any given act was the work of the left or the right. Time and again, we find terrorist acts claimed by extreme factions like the Red Brigades, but more probably connected to elements of the police and intelligence services. Though Italy preserved its democracy by means of a very effective antiterrorist policing, the nation's democracy came close to being snuffed out on several occasions. (For the Italian terrorist crisis, see Silj 1979; De Lutiis 1984; Weinberg and Eubank 1987; Moss 1989; Rimanelli 1989.)

In 1990, new information emerged that confirmed the involvement of official agencies in acts of terrorism during these "years of lead." This was the uncovering of the so-called *Gladio* scheme that had begun in the 1940s, when the West feared a Soviet invasion of Europe. In each country, Western forces established covert networks and arms dumps that could be used after an invasion to resist Soviet forces, just as resistance movements had fought the Nazis in World War II. In Italy, the scheme was known as Operation *Gladio*, or Sword. However, during the 1970s, guns and explosives from the highly secret *Gladio* weapons dumps were being used by Italy's domestic right-wing terrorists, with the connivance of sympathizers in the armed forces, the police, and the intelligence agencies. *Gladio* explosives and members of the *Gladio* network were implicated in terrorist attacks, including the catastrophic bombing that killed eighty-five people in Bologna in 1980.

Another example of a strategy of tension occurred in the early 1990s in the nation of South Africa. At this point, the nation was in the final stages of a revolution against its white minority government, as the opposition African National Congress was making significant political and military progress. (The ANC campaign eventually triumphed in 1994 when the party's leader, Nelson Mandela, was elected president in free elections.) As a last ditch attempt to preserve power, however, the white minority government developed what might be called a strategy of tension. In a terrifying development, mysterious armed thugs boarded commuter trains, killing dozens of travelers with guns and machetes. In 1990, one single incident left 26 dead on a commuter train, and hundreds more mutilated (Wren 1990). The response was, obviously, general fear and panic, which the government hoped would translate into new support for the police and government authority. The violence was never claimed by any group, though the ANC spoke of the crimes as the work of a "hidden hand." Subsequent investigations leave no doubt that the hand belonged to agents of the police and government in a cynical attempt to destabilize the country.

THE BELGIAN EXPERIENCE

Another example occurred in the European nation of Belgium in the mid-1980s. Though the nation had previously escaped most of the serious terrorist violence that affected nations like Italy and Germany, suddenly in 1985, the nation experienced a substantial terrorist crisis. Though the number of victims was not large by the standard of September 11—only some thirty people died in all in the Belgian events—the campaign was deeply shocking and caused a major political crisis (Jenkins 1991a).

The violence apparently had two quite distinct faces. The more terrifying was a series of attacks by masked gunmen on supermarkets, where they would kill several people during what appeared to be robbery attempts. However, the disproportionate violence in itself suggested that motives other than those of "normal" professional crime were involved. Public fear and concern became intense; Belgium differs greatly from the

United States in the frequency of violent crimes especially where guns are involved. Multiple deaths during armed robberies had hitherto been extremely rare, which gave a chilling novelty to the crimes of the so-called Killers of Brabant. The random nature of the crimes gave people a sense that they or their families could be at risk.

At just the same time, many bomb attacks were undertaken by what appeared to be a left-wing terrorist group, the CCC or Fighting Communist Cells (*Cellules Communistes Combattantes*). In 1984 and 1985, CCC attacked the sort of targets that we might expect from such a left-wing group, such as banks, targets associated with corporate capitalism, or with the U.S. military. The campaign effectively ended around Christmas of 1985 with the arrest of CCC leader Pierre Carette and several of his associates. Other leftist groups involved around this time included the shadowy movement FRAP, the Revolutionary Front for Proletarian Action, whose French acronym resembles the word for strike or blow.

At first sight, the overt terrorist violence seemed unconnected with the supermarket attacks, and it was just coincidental that both series of events had happened at exactly the same time. By the end of the 1980s, however, the situation was seen in a very different context. Later analyses suggested that the "Killers of Brabant" were not just gangsters, but were rather far-right terrorists trying to destabilize the democratic Belgian state by creating panic. One clue to this was the dates of their attacks, which proved to have followed the Nazi ritual calendar. The worst of their attacks occurred on November 9, one of the holiest days in the Nazi year. This suggested that the Killers were affiliated with one of Belgium's active neo-Nazi sects.

Even more surprising, though, was the investigation of movements like FRAP and the CCC, which at least pretended to be left-wing in orientation (they were "Communist" cells, after all.) At every point, though, these groups seemed rather to be connected to the far right, to the sorts of group who had undertaken the supermarket killings. Like the Killers, FRAP liked to launch its attacks on dates special to the Nazi calendar, like April 20, which is Hitler's birthday. Pierre Carette himself came from a distinctive background. He was the son of an agent of Belgian state security, while his brother was an army commando and a member of Westland New Post (WNP), a fascist sect linked to the supermarket massacres (Herman and O'Sullivan 1989: 226–227). Of course, the fact that his relatives were on the far right does not necessarily mean that he was too. People often rebel against their backgrounds by turning to the opposite political extreme, and Carette's family links may be purely coincidental. But the close overlap in time between the CCC affair and the Brabant massacres must raise questions.

In hindsight, it seems likely that both CCC and the Killers were working for a common right-wing cause, probably in alliance with elements of the Belgian state security apparatus. In 1990, a parliamentary inquiry confirmed the role of ultrarightist elements in the supermarket attacks. The investigation suggested widespread collaboration between agents of law enforcement and right-wing paramilitaries, and the resulting administrative changes were as far-reaching as any experienced in a Western country in recent years. The national intelligence agency, *Sûreté d'État*, was disbanded and the head of the police anti-terrorism unit was suspended ("Coup Plot" 1990). It was also charged that leading figures in Belgian business were involved in what now appeared to be a far-reaching plot. The CCC should probably join GAL, CSPPA, and Islamic Jihad in the catalogue of terrorist groups who were very different from what they initially appeared to be.

At least some terrorist crimes involve elements of masquerade, crimes that are not in fact the work of the groups who might initially seem responsible. Reading such accounts might initially fill us with a sense of despair: how do we ever know who carried out a particular attack? Fortunately, deception plays a role in only a minority of terrorist cases, so that we need not be unreasonably skeptical about claims of responsibility. We are not dealing with a world in which "things are often not what they seem." As the classic rejoinder to this saying declares, "Of course they are—otherwise, they wouldn't seem that way." We can be quite confident about attributing incidents that occur in the context of ongoing communal struggles that involve large and well-known movements like the IRA or ETA, which carry out hundreds of attacks for every one linked to a shady front group like the CCC or CSPPA. These deeply rooted groups pursue a consistent strategy and operate within a specific community. If a given individual carries out an attack in such a communal struggle, his motives and affiliations will be known to a wide circle of his family and neighbors, and there is little danger of any kind of deception operation.

We can readily accept claims of responsibility if, for example, a military base is attacked in Northern Ireland or the Basque country, followed by an admission from the guerrilla movement concerned. The IRA never has been shy about claiming actions, and the group's behavior is so reliable than if they deny something, even the organization's bitterest enemies acknowledge that they must not have been involved. In Palestine and Israel too, we need not doubt that attacks and suicide bombings really are the work of the groups claiming them. Where there is room for uncertainty is in the wider context claimed for the acts. Hamas, for instance, might indeed have carried out a particular act: but were they working alone, or for some other country or intelligence agency? And how do we know this?

Our skepticism about finding the culprits for terrorist incidents need not apply in every case, or in even a majority of cases, but many recent stories of incorrect and misleading attributions should raise some doubts about the workings of media and law enforcement. Cases like the Paris bombings raise significant questions about the reliability of government statements on terrorist incidents. Though we customarily ask what the government knows about something, this story suggests that different components of government know—or think they know—very different things. Any reading of media accounts, in France or elsewhere, has to take account of the different agendas and interests of rival official agencies.

6

Investigation and Intelligence

Secrecy, being an instrument of conspiracy, ought never to be the system of a regular government.

—Jeremy Bentham

Investigating terrorist attacks is a much more complex and politicized process than regular police work, and far less confidence can be placed in public statements allocating the blame. This needs to be said because popular culture so strongly encourages a public belief in the rationality of the investigative process. For well over a century, police and detective stories have been mainstays of popular culture, and both genres work according to certain well-understood principles. When a crime has been committed, we as readers or viewers can see the processes by which the investigators identify the culprits and try to prove their guilt. Commonly, such stories leave little doubt about the identity of the perpetrators because the audience is often allowed to see the commission of the crime, or if not, then at least any mystery is resolved by a final confession. We know who the murderer is.

Of course, we are not naïve enough to believe that such rationality applies in every real-life criminal case, since we know of countless false convictions and other miscarriages of justice. Yet even though innocent people get imprisoned (or even executed) the common assumption is that such evils result from human fallibility or prejudice. Such exceptions apart, it is believed, the investigative system itself is founded upon an impartial quest for truth. Linked to this belief is a tendency to accept official statements about the culpability for a particular crime.

These assumptions cannot be held with any confidence where terrorist acts are involved. Primarily, the complexity of terrorist organizations means that motivation is often difficult to determine with any confidence, and tracing the full ramifications of an act can be extremely difficult. Also, the explicit political nature of the actions means that investigation will involve a much wider range of competing agencies and interests than would apply in a regular criminal case, even a relatively complex affair like an instance of organized or corporate criminality. These factors make it much more difficult for investigators to know with confidence the real nature of an event. And even if they are confident, political factors make it unlikely that such knowledge will be made public with the same kind of frankness that would apply to say, a case of serial murder or bank robbery.

INFILTRATION

In order to investigate terrorism, law enforcement agencies must use various clandestine methods, including infiltration and double-agent tactics. While these means are essential, they often lead to difficulties in assigning the blame for acts, and raise questions about the reliability of official statements and statistics. Just as terrorist groups practice systematic deception and false flag methods, so do law enforcement agencies. Agencies wishing to suppress terrorism must, of necessity, operate in a complex and dirty clandestine world (Marx 1988). In order to succeed, they must often do things that they cannot publicize frankly.

The best and perhaps only means to defeat subversive or terrorist groups is to penetrate or infiltrate their ranks. This needs to be stated because of the common official emphasis on enhancing security to protect airports and public buildings against antiterrorist attacks. Since September 11, Americans are all too familiar with the vastly increased random searches before flying on commercial airlines. Some of these precautions are useful and necessary—especially the added defenses on cockpit doors—but most have no impact whatever on the likelihood of a terrorist attack. If you fortify aircraft, terrorists attack airports; if you fortify airports, they can bring down aircraft with missiles fired from remote locations; if you defend aircraft, they attack ships; and so on. Overwhelmingly, such security precautions are designed to raise public consciousness, a feel-good strategy without any real effects or benefits. No government can defend itself against terrorism solely by means of protection and security (Carroll 2002).

This is all the more true when we consider the international dimension. Even if we assume the impossible, and the U.S. became wholly invulnerable from terrorist attack, this would still leave an almost infinite number of targets worldwide. Think for example of Europe, an area somewhat smaller than the continental U.S., though divided into over thirty separate nations, with competing police jurisdictions. This alone makes it easy for activists to escape detection, to operate freely across several countries, and to drive across three or more countries in a few hours. Commonly, such illegal transients assume the identity of "student," which gives them good grounds for traveling widely from one European academic center to another. This status also qualifies them for the identity cards that are so essential in European societies. Some of the September 11 hijackers had used such student cover in Germany. Europe also has large Middle Eastern populations, heavily concentrated in some cities, many of which serve as bases for deep-rooted extremist Muslim networks like *Takfir wal Hijra* ("Anathema and Exile") and the Algerian movement known as the Salafists.

Each European country, moreover, has a network of foreign embassies, which can transport weapons or contraband through their diplomatic bags that are immune to search by the host country. Meanwhile, Europe is host to hundreds of major U.S. targets, including embassies, military bases, business offices, airline offices, and tourist resorts (Alexander and Myers 1982; Alexander and Pluchinsky 1992; Chalk 1996; Alexander ed., 2002). And that is just Europe: American targets are just as exposed in the Middle East, in the Asia-Pacific region, or in Latin America. There is simply no way that the U.S. can mobilize forces to defend every single potential target in the world against a global organization like al-Qaeda or Hizbullah, or to place U.S. troops at every port and airport, every embassy and tourist destination. In a terrorist war, any effort that is solely defensive is bound to fail: just to protect is to lose.

The only way to defeat attacks is to prevent them being launched, and that demands the use of infiltrators, what is known as human intelligence. Relying on infiltrators requires many moral compromises, namely that a government has to deal with very dubious or criminal individuals. but realistically, there are few alternatives. In the 1990s, when U.S. intelligence agencies tried to evade this problem by relying more heavily on electronic surveillance, the results were very mixed. We now know that on September 10, the U.S. intercepted messages in which terrorist supporters warned that "tomorrow is the big day" and "the match is on." The messages were not translated until two days afterwards, that is, after the towers of the World Trade Center had fallen. But even if they had been understood earlier, what could authorities have done? Even if every airline pilot in the U.S. had known that an attack was likely somewhere in the world, there is no way that such intelligence would have made the slightest difference to what actually occurred. Would the U.S. have shut down all air travel indefinitely until the alarm was lifted? The only thing that would have helped would have been agents or infiltrators in place.

The more difficult a group is to infiltrate, therefore, the more effective will be its operations, and the longer it will last. This explains why groups like al-Qaeda often use family networks, in which individuals have known each other for many years, and have powerful motives for remaining loyal. Fortunately, not many groups are anything like this close knit, so that it is possible to insert agents or moles, or to persuade members of the group to become double agents. In either case, law enforcement agencies will then have people in place within the group, and will know of its operations in advance.

This in itself suggests a fundamental difference with the world of regular law enforcement. Police normally are happy to announce the arrest of offenders, to report the disruption of a major criminal network. In the terrorist world, however, arrests can in some cases be seen as a kind of failure, especially if they are publicized. In many cases, when a terrorist suspect is detected, the best response is to keep him under surveillance to identify other associates. For the authorities, the ideal solution is if he can be contacted and turned, that is, persuaded to work for them, without his new loyalties being known. In this setting, arrest or trial would be the worst outcome. This helps explain some of the official behavior that became so controversial during the post-September 11 investigations. Many people were appalled to find that the CIA had maintained surveillance on some of the men who had subsequently participated in those attacks, though without detaining them. In fact, this policy was quite in keeping with standard practice. (What was unforgivable was that when the men entered the U.S., the CIA reportedly gave up surveillance on them rather than passing the task to the FBI.)

INFORMANTS AND THEIR DANGERS

Successful terrorist investigations demand infiltration, either by government agents, or by turncoats or defectors within that organization (Grathwohl 1976; Payne 1979; Hill and Bell 1988; O'Callaghan 1998; Johnson 2000; Collins 2002). But this inevitable fact has undesirable consequences because, in order to maintain their credibility, agents may be forced into situations that are difficult legally or ethically. If agents are required to remain in place for months or years, then they can only maintain their credentials by carrying out crimes or terrorist acts. As a situation develops over time, police or government agents will themselves be involved in an ever-growing number of violent acts. This problem is similar to what has often been noted in the world of antidrug policing, in which informants are themselves engaged in illegality, though the crimes involved in the terrorist world are far more serious (Reuter 1982; LaBrecque 1987; Bloom 2002).

Sometimes police effectively allow criminals to operate so long as they are aiding the authorities. This might be tolerable while only minor illegalities are involved, but occasionally official sanction is offered to a major organized crime operation. In Boston, recent scandals have suggested how the FBI worked closely with organized crime groups, over decades, to the point of knowingly permitting an innocent man to be imprisoned for murder. This relationship culminated in 1995 when one of the city's leading gangsters was about to be indicted for racketeering, but was able to escape capture because of a tipoff from high-placed friends in the FBI (Lehr and O'Neill 2001). In such circumstances, the danger is that the police form close personal relationships with criminals, actively defend them from investigation by other agencies, and in some cases, become involved themselves in profiting from crime. After a while, the problem is almost deciding who is informing to whom. Very much the same blurring between police and wrongdoers can occur in the context of political crime or terrorist violence (Greer 1995).

In extreme cases, police or intelligence agencies can find themselves in the position of "going native," to the point of working for and with terrorists or terrorist regimes. One of the worst intelligence scandals in U.S. history involved an agent called Edwin Wilson who in the mid-1970s offered his services to the Libyan regime, helping it to obtain vast quantities of weaponry, and training its soldiers and clandestine forces. Wilson drew other American agents into this network, often on the pretence that he was working under deep cover for the U.S. government. As a result, U.S. personnel and weapons were involved in serious acts of Libyan-backed terrorism and criminality (Goulden 1984; Maas 1986).

INFORMANTS AND THEIR DANGERS

Agencies have many reasons for caution in admitting the use of informants and moles. Regularly over the past twenty or thirty years, scandals have erupted when the media have reported that U.S. authorities have been employing as paid informants some particularly villainous individuals, who have been involved in heinous crimes like murder or drug-dealing. Such figures are aptly known as "dirty" informants. One notorious example of this problem occurred in 1979, when several left-wing demonstrators were murdered in Greensboro, North Carolina, by a group of Ku Klux Klansmen and neo-Nazis. Subsequent investigation showed that police and federal agencies had at least two infiltrators within the attacking force, one of whom was serving the Bureau of Alcohol, Tobacco, and Firearms, while the other was working for the FBI and the local police department (Wheaton 1987). This is not to say that the government supported the attack, but the informer relationship gave credence to suspicions of official misbehavior, and forced people to ask why the crime had not been prevented.

Such scandals recurred in the context of the U.S. covert war in Central America during the 1980s. In 1995, a Congressional inquiry found massive evidence of paid informants being involved in massacres and torture. As the *New York Times* reported, there were "scores of paid informers in the upper ranks of the Guatemalan military, which has killed, tortured and kidnapped tens of thousands of its own citizens in a war against a small leftist guerrilla force." (Weiner 1995: This is somewhat tendentious, in that the leftist opposition to the Guatemalan regime was far more substantial than this sentence would suggest.) Once again, agencies like the CIA faced political demands not to use such people, and CIA officials in the area were demoted or disciplined. It would have been very tempting for the agency to mislead Congress and media about these linkages, if this could have been done without overt perjury.

An equally embarrassing connection came to light during the investigation of the Pan Am flight 103 bombing. At the time the main interest focused on the Syrian-backed faction, the PFLP-GC. Two months before the 1988 Lockerbie attack, West German police had arrested a group of activists related to this organization, and had found sophisticated explosive devices very much like those eventually used against Pan Am 103. However, most of the group were soon released, because at least some of its members were informants for German authorities, and one man—the group's ace bomb-maker—was giving information to the intelligence services of Jordan and perhaps Germany. In this instance, at least one intelligence agency was in contact with a bomb-maker, in a group that planned to destroy aircraft. (Presumably, the bomb was never designed to be used in reality.) If such a connection came to light, it would be enormously compromising, though the uses of the relationship are obvious. Far better to have influence over senior members of a terrorist organization than over low-level associates since that kind of connection is likely to prevent major crimes. Yet we can certainly understand why no police force would under any circumstances admit to having such connections.

In the intelligence world, a well-known maxim states that "Everyone is an informant for someone," and it is commonly assumed that many people will be double agents. Often, though, the issue of who a given person is really working for is so intractable that we may doubt whether the agents themselves have any clear ideas on the subject. One embarrassing saga in recent years involved Ali Mohammed, an Egyptian army officer who moved to the United States and joined the U.S. Army. In the 1980s, he became a member of Egyptian Islamic Jihad, one of the groups that co-founded al-Qaeda, and with his senior military experience, he rose to high rank in the new organization. He trained the personal bodyguards of Osama bin Laden, gave training in terrorist tactics and clandestine warfare, and personally organized the cells in East Africa that carried out the embassy bombing attacks in 1998. In the camps, he was known as Abu

Mohamed al-Amriki—"Father Mohamed the American." However, during the early 1990s, his loyalties seemed more complex. In 1993, when Ali Mohammed entered Canada, he was detained and questioned by the Royal Canadian Mounted Police. However, he rang his handler at the FBI, who assured the Canadians that he was working for the Americans as a double agent. If true, this would have been a wonderful coup, since the Americans would have had a direct conduit to the heart of al-Qaeda operations (Oziewicz and Ha 2001). Later events proved that this was overoptimistic. Ali Mohammed was in fact a triple agent—someone who seems to betray a terrorist group and go over to the authorities, while really working for the terrorists. Looking back, the failure to arrest him in Canada appears a major tragedy. He is now in a U.S. prison.

Sometimes an agency may simply be wrong in assuming the loyalty of someone it believes to be an informant. More often, even if they are not actually treacherous, informants pursue their own agendas, which can be easily understood from normal human psychology. Informants try to make themselves seem more important than they actually are; they tell their handlers things they believe the agency wants to hear; they try to make themselves indispensable; they give information in a way that will harm their personal enemies. All agencies recognize these dangers, and make allowances for them, but sometimes they simply make errors. While trying to deceive their enemies, agencies end up deceiving themselves. One notorious example of this occurred in 1981, when the U.S. believed that it was facing a major terrorist danger from the nation of Libya. That December, the news media were full of what seemed to be a well-authenticated story that a Libyan assassination team was actually on U.S. soil, preparing to kill President Reagan and other senior U.S. officials. The story remained in the headlines for some weeks before fading into oblivion, to the great embarrassment of federal law enforcement. Not until years afterwards was it discovered that the "hit team" story had originated in the fertile mind of a CIA informant, who for personal and ideological reasons wished to make trouble for Libya. Once the story surfaced, other informants tried to get in on the game by feeding supporting pieces of information, so the story became self-feeding (Woodward 1987).

THE NO-WIN SITUATION

Counter-terrorism efforts face what may be an insoluble problem. Infiltration is the only reliable way to prevent terrorist attacks and to disrupt terrorist networks, yet of their nature, effective informants are going to be tainted by criminality. Any highly placed member of a terrorist organization is bound to have been involved in violent or homicidal acts, and it is difficult to imagine that they will be able to renounce this kind of misbehavior when they are placed on a U.S. payroll. Using informants means that law enforcement agencies are dealing with and, effectively, tolerating crime and violence.

This may be a fact of life in the intelligence world, but it is not one that can easily be explained to the public or politicians, especially when both operate on the basis of mixed and contradictory values. People want to be protected from terrorism, and they want to avoid police forces running out of control and violating human rights. Whether both goals can be reconciled is open to question. It is instructive, and depressing, to compare the Congressional hearings into intelligence practices in 1995 and 2002. In 1995, Congressional leaders were appalled to find that the CIA had been so closely aligned with dirty informants in Latin America, and they sent a strong message that such behavior would no longer be tolerated. The agency complied to the extent that the CIA acquired "a risk-averse culture that made the agency hesitant to aggressively recruit informers inside the terrorist network." In 2002, Congressional leaders were equally shocked to find that the CIA had been so timid in hiring dirty informants that would have allowed the organization to keep effective track of al-Qaeda, and thus prevent the September 11 attacks. Once again, CIA authorities were bitterly criticized, this time for doing the exact opposite of what they had been excoriated for in 1995. CIA officials could have been pardoned for asking, "So what do you really *want*?" (U.S. House of Representatives 2002; Risen 2002c).

Equally, agencies face an impossible contradiction when trying to keep watch on terrorist networks. Both public and political leaders demand that such networks be kept under surveillance and ideally, destroyed. Yet experienced domestic groups conceal themselves behind a web of affiliated groups and organizations, through the process we know as insulation. An effective investigation of terrorism must of necessity involve not just fighting organizations but also the whole broader network, which in practice means surveillance and infiltration of numerous innocent-sounding groups pursuing worthy causes like labor organization and women's rights. Yet such an operation carries inevitable dangers, since so many of the people involved in such groups will have no terrorist connections, and agencies leave themselves open to charges of repression, antilabor and antiwomen attitudes, even religious persecution. Rounding up foreign students on American soil sounds like a gross act of intolerance, until we realize how often international terrorists use student status as a cover. If in fact the potential violence of the group has been vastly exaggerated—as seems to have been the case with Central American solidarity groups like CISPES—the odds of scandal become overwhelming. Critics of government have a ready-made arsenal of rhetorical charges in such a situation, evoking the shades of J. Edgar Hoover and the FBI's COINTELPRO (Counter Intelligence Program) scheme to observe and disrupt potential subversives (Blackstock 1975; Churchill and Vander Wall 1988, 1990).

The whole idea of *potential* subversives or terrorists is controversial—some would say, repellent and Orwellian. Counter-terrorism of its nature means trying to prevent actions, rather than investigating them after they have occurred. That by definition means investigating many people who have not yet engaged in violence, on the supposition that they might do so in the near future. This notion contradicts basic democratic beliefs about the role of police, and the investigation of crime. It even evokes the science fiction fantasy of detecting crimes before they happen, as outlined in the film *Minority Report*, with its concept of "precrime"—though in our case, we are speaking of real police forces, real suspects, and the violation of real rights.

In summary, antiterrorism policing of its nature involves agencies in conduct that if made public, would subject them to severe political criticism. This irreconcilable difficulty makes it doubly unlikely that agencies will speak freely or honestly about their actual operations.

DECEPTION

The peculiar realities of undercover policing mean that the public needs to be highly sensitive to issues of deception when assessing media reports about terrorism. Deception has been a potent weapon throughout the recorded history of warfare, and the fight against terrorism is a form of war. Often, it is necessary to deceive the public as a means of combating an enemy.

Deception is not necessarily shameful. To take an example from World War II, the D-Day landings of 1944 were preceded by one of the greatest deception schemes in history. As everyone now knows, the Allied plan was to land massive armies in Normandy, but it was essential to persuade the Germans that the main blow would come somewhere else, namely in the Pas de Calais region. The Allies planted false leads for German spies to find showing that the invasion target was Calais, not Normandy. They created huge fake "armies" of bogus tanks and trucks, constructed out of wood and canvas for German aircraft to photograph. When the invasion actually took place in Normandy, the Germans refused to believe that this was the main attack, and kept their forces in reserve in preparation for the "real" landings expected near Calais. Deception won the battle and, perhaps, the war.

Similar examples have occurred in recent years. During the Desert Storm war with Iraq in 1991, Allied forces spent months feeding false leads to the media suggesting that U.S. Marines would be launching frontal amphibious attacks against strong Iraqi coastal positions. As in the 1940s, this belief encouraged the enemy to keep large forces in readiness for those attacks that never came. Obviously, this strategy implied deceiving the media, since it was not possible to tell the truth to the American public without the Iraqis finding out. No newspapers headlined "Massive Allied Deception Operation Continues." Yet it is hard to believe that many people would complain about the use of lies or deception in such an instance, or would honestly expect the authorities to place all their cards on the table. In terrorist situations, likewise, there are many situations in which authorities are likely to issue false and deceptive statements, or at least to tell less than the whole truth, and it would be foolish to expect otherwise.

The obvious fact promoting deception is that law enforcement agencies do not wish to reveal crucial investigative techniques. Authorities will not reveal the existence of agents in place, since to do so would be to destroy their future effectiveness, and to risk the lives of those agents. We would not expect a news story to state that (say) a particular terrorist incident was ordered by the government of Iran—and we know this from information received from a highly placed member of the group, who is in the pay of the CIA. If we ever did read such a story, the one thing we could believe with certainty is that it was not true, and that some agency was using this carefully leaked news in order to create dissension within the group in question.

This fact makes it difficult to assess specific reports suggesting defections or current informants within terror groups. One example occurred in Britain during 2002, when a radical Muslim leader named Abu Qatada was publicly identified as a senior leader of al-Qaeda in Western Europe, and probably a major organizer close to Osama bin Laden personally. Facing intense investigation by police and media, he dropped from sight, and apparently went into hiding somewhere in England. Soon afterwards stories began surfacing that he was living in a safe house under the protection of the British Security Service, MI5, and that he was a double agent for British intelligence. Allegedly, his information had allowed the police to round up many suspected terrorists (Dodd 2002). At the time of writing, it is quite uncertain whether these accounts are true; if they are worthless journalistic speculation; or if they represent a scheme by British intelligence to discredit Abu Qatada within his network, and perhaps to get him killed. If in fact he was a double agent, it is very difficult to believe that the British government would publicize this fact so freely.

Other powerful weapons against terrorism include the techniques of electronic surveillance, of which U.S. authorities make enormous use. If the U.S. government received information about a particular terrorist group from intercepted communications, it would not reveal that fact publicly for fear that the group involved would, once warned, either tighten its security or change its means of communication altogether. If U.S. authorities intervened to prevent an attack discovered by such means, they would have to produce some false story to explain how they had come across the information in the first place.

Occasionally, too, cases illustrate other kinds of activity that governments do not wish to publicize. One remarkable incident followed the 1972 Munich Olympics massacre, discussed earlier. Following this bloody incident, which left nine hostages and five terrorists dead, the West German government found itself holding the three remaining Black September terrorists. Recent precedents made it absolutely certain that the organization would gain the release of the men, presumably by hijacking a German aircraft or raiding an embassy, and taking hostages to force a prisoner release. In order to avoid bloodshed, the German government reportedly made the astonishing decision to connive with Black September in staging a hijacking of an agreed airliner with only a few passengers aboard. The Germans would then have an excuse to release the prisoners, and this scenario was duly played out less than two months after the Olympic massacre, when a Lufthansa jet was hijacked leaving Beirut. The hijackers were duly freed, and none of the passengers were harmed. In other words, that particular hijacking was a charade designed to allow the German government an excuse to do something they could not admit publicly, to give them a kind of deniability. If their actual deal with the Palestinians had been announced at the time, it would have brought down the German government. At the time, though, the media printed nothing but the "official story," and the other interpretation remained hidden for thirty years (Reeve 2000).

SECRETS AND LIES

These remarks about not revealing sources of intelligence may seem obvious, but some aspects of this story are more complex. Keeping the public in the dark about electronic intercepts or agents in place may seem natural and understandable, but agencies also have a long track record of keeping secrets from other agencies, that is, from other elements of the same government. In the intelligence world, information is revealed on a "need to know" basis, but this doctrine is sometimes interpreted in such a way that greatly complicates the investigative process.

To take a historical example, one of the greatest intelligence triumphs of the last century was the so-called VENONA program of the 1940s and 1950s, by which the U.S. government intercepted top secret Soviet signals concerning the activities of spies in Western countries (Haynes and Klehr

1999). Through this, for example, we can state with confidence that some of those accused during the controversial espionage trials of the era genuinely were active Soviet agents, figures like the Rosenbergs, the so-called Atom Spies said to have revealed the secrets of the nuclear bomb to the USSR. Yet this priceless information was jealously hoarded by the FBI. Even the existence of the VENONA program was concealed from other agencies that would have had good reason to know, including the CIA. FBI Director J. Edgar Hoover justified excluding the CIA from these secrets because, as he wrote in 1952, "In view of loose methods in CIA and some of its questionable personnel we must be most circumspect." Until recently, it was thought that even the President and the White House were not told of the existence of this politically vital program, though it now appears that some limited information was allowed to reach the Commander in Chief ("Moynihan, VENONA and Truman" 1999). If such highly sensitive materials could be so controlled, obviously material of less significance was, and is, routinely held within particular agencies. Partly, this is a result of interagency competition and bureaucratic rivalry, but there is also a well-substantiated fear that the more widely any secret is shared, the more likely it is to leak (Riebling 1994).

In addition to the problems of dealing with informants, sharing what is discovered during investigations is doubly difficult in a country that claims to operate under the rule of law. The U.S. views terrorist acts as criminal violations, to be dealt with under due process. (Only after September 11 did the administration raise the possibility of treating captured fighters as illegal combatants, possibly subject to military tribunals.) This use of criminal process is important politically in helping to prevent captured terrorists being seen internationally as political martyrs, rather than criminal bombers and murderers. However, it means that information found by one part of an investigation cannot be passed to another agency without jeopardizing the prosecution. In the 1993 WTC bombing, promising leads about international dimensions surfaced during the grand jury hearings, but this material could not be passed to the CIA (Miller et al 2001). The apparent lack of evidence meant that neither government nor media paid proper attention to the wider threats the U.S. was facing from Islamist extremism, and perhaps from nations like Iran and Iraq.

LEFT HANDS AND RIGHT HANDS

Putting these elements together, we can understand some of the likely complications of investigating terrorism. For one thing, separate agencies pursue quite different agendas, possibly in ignorance of what other groups are doing. One agency might be pursuing or monitoring a group without even knowing that leading members within that group are in contact with some other federal agency. We recall the French bombing campaign of the 1980s, in which the domestic and foreign security agencies were following totally different investigative tracks, almost pursuing separate foreign policies.

As a case study of the failure to communicate, let us trace the different warnings that federal agencies had of the plot that would come to fruition on September 11. (The following account is based on a variety of journalistic sources, including Miller et al. 2001; Risen 2001; Johnston 2002a–b; Johnston and Becker 2002; Oliphant 2002; Eggen and Schmidt; Isikoff 2002b; Miller and Stone 2002.) To begin with, the FBI had some important clues in its possession. As early as 1998, intelligence sources were reporting concerns that the al-Qaeda network was planning air attacks on the United States: one plot reportedly involved flying a bomb-laden plane into the World Trade Center (Risen 2002f–g; Priest and Eggen 2002; Shenon 2002). Also in 1998, the chief pilot in the FBI's Oklahoma City division remarked on the number of Middle Eastern men receiving flight training in the state, and suggested a possible terrorist connection. Light aircraft, he warned, "would be an ideal means of spreading chemical or biological agents." In 2001, another FBI agent in Phoenix wrote a memorandum warning of the same pattern of Middle Eastern pupils at U.S. flight schools. The agent, Kenneth Williams, warned on July 10 of an "effort by Osama bin Laden to send students to the U.S. to attend civil aviation universities and colleges." One man who attracted Williams' special attention was an associate of Hani Hanjour, who would later pilot the American Airlines flight into the Pentagon (Risen 2002g).

In addition, the FBI had identified one specific individual as likely to be involved in terrorist attacks on U.S. soil, using aircraft. This was Zacarias Moussaoui, whose activities at a Minnesota flight school set off warning bells for his instructors. In brainstorming sessions trying to assess his motives, FBI agents suggested that he might be involved in various schemes, even planning to "fly something into the World Trade Center," while French intelligence confirmed his links with radical Islamic movements. (Though the CIA ran a trace on Moussaoui, it failed to discover any al-Qaeda links.) Moussaoui was arrested on technical immigration charges on August 15, 2001, possibly preventing him from becoming the 20th hijacker—though this issue remains controversial. By September 11, he was "the subject of a five-inch-thick file" in the FBI.

Meanwhile, the CIA also knew many things that might well have raised an alarm, if they had ever been collated with the FBI's findings. In January 2000, Malaysian authorities told the CIA about a meeting held in that country by al-Qaeda members, including Khalid al-Mihdhar and Nawaf al-Hazmi: both would later perish on the airliner that smashed into the

Pentagon (Isikoff 2002b). The two met with a bin Laden representative, who some months afterwards was involved in planning the attack on the U.S. destroyer *Cole* in Aden. Though al-Mihdhar and al-Hazmi were deadly dangerous militants, the CIA failed for several months to inform the FBI or State Department of their activities, even after they entered the United States. In June 2001, the State Department routinely renewed al-Mihdhar's expired visa. Nor did anyone notice that the two men were among those who had received flight training of the sort outlined in the FBI memos. Not until a couple of weeks before the WTC attack were they placed on any watch list. And while the FBI knew the pair were in southern California, they failed to take elementary steps to locate them: al-Hazmi was listed in the San Diego phone directory under his own name. The men were even rooming in the same house as a man who had served as a trusted FBI informant (Isikoff 2002c). Meanwhile, the CIA had also heard threats that bin Laden wished to strike at the U.S. homeland. According to one government source speaking after the event, "There was something specific in early August that said to us that he was determined in striking on U.S. soil. But there was nothing about who, when, where or how" (Solomon 2001). This "something" probably resulted from electronic surveillance, possibly acquired by the ECHELON intelligence gathering system.

In retrospect, these various pieces of information cry out for official action. Why was the plot not discovered, and prevented? Surely, closer interaction with the ongoing FBI investigations might have illuminated the question of "who, when, where or how." The FBI had the how, and the CIA had the why. Ideally, the agencies should by no later than August of 2001 have put the available information together. A powerful and experienced Islamist network wished to strike targets on U.S. soil; the terrorists were planning to use aircraft in some way; some of their members were already in the U.S.; and some had received training in flying large airliners. The possibility of crashing aircraft into strategic targets had been floating around the terrorist underworld since the mid-1990s, and so had the idea of a "spectacular" involving the simultaneous seizure of several aircraft. The logical response by federal agencies would have been to launch an urgent search of U.S. flight school records to find Arab or Middle Eastern men who had received training in the previous two or three years, and to find these men, to place them under surveillance. Under no circumstances should they have been allowed to board airliners, least of all in groups.

As it was, on September 11, "two people already identified by the government as suspected terrorists boarded separate American Airlines flights from Boston using their own names" (Miller et al. 2001). Nor were the terrorists exactly masterful at concealing their intentions. On the day of the attacks, no fewer than nine of the nineteen were selected for special security screening and searches, events that were much less common at that point than they would become shortly afterwards. Yet all were allowed to board. This record makes us look askance at the statement of FBI Director Robert Mueller on September 17, when he told the media that "there were no warning signs that I'm aware of that would indicate this type of operation in the country."

To some extent, our attempt at hindsight is misleading, because any agency receives thousands of such tidbits of information in any given year, and often it is not clear until after the event which ones had any substance. Yet having said this, the confluence of stories involving flight training and the world of al-Qaeda should have set off alarm bells, and the total lack of interagency communication does seem truly grievous (Gertz 2002).

Apart from the usual conflicts between agencies, both the main protagonists, FBI and CIA, were deeply affected by the dominant ideology of terrorism popular at that time, which underplayed the central role of Middle Eastern groups. This focus also raised the danger that any proactive investigation of Arabs or Middle Easterners would lead to political protests over anti-Arab bias or "ethnic profiling." This last phrase had come into common usage in 1998, and the practice was by 2001 an extremely sensitive issue with liberal and black leaders. By mid-2001, the Bush administration was nervous about raising any new issues that could further alienate minority constituencies. Neither the CIA nor the FBI wished to take the lead in launching a proactive investigation that could arouse such passions, and that could well have led to one or both of the agency's directors facing embarrassing questions on Capitol Hill.

We have to recall the partisan alignment at this time under a conservative president who had been very narrowly elected the previous year, and in a contest that was still controversial. President Bush was under regular attack from a hostile liberal media, suspicious of threats to civil liberties, and on the alert for any signs of aggressive "cowboy" international policies. Media hostility focused especially on Attorney General John Ashcroft, the ultimate overlord of the FBI. If the FBI and other federal agencies had announced a major terrorist plot in August 2001, or demanded a dramatic tightening of airline security standards, the media would have challenged the authenticity of the claims, and references to *Wag the Dog* would have proliferated. Not only would the agencies have received little credit for their work, but they would have been attacked for their paranoia, their racism, and their violations of civil liberties. In many ways, ideological and partisan considerations shaped and constrained the official response to the accumulating warnings of 9-11; and neither liberal nor conservative sides can take any comfort from observing the process.

Agencies investigating terrorism have multiple motives for being less than honest in their public statements, and some of these are structural to the world of intelligence and clandestine policing. While agencies have to use moles and electronic interception, they cannot reveal this fact. Also, the fact of having distinct intelligence forces and agencies—rather than one omnipotent Orwellian police state—means that there will always be failures of communication, and gaps in intelligence. These problems are always going to occur. On other occasions, statements about investigations are distorted or manipulated through reasons of bureaucratic self-interest, as agencies try to make themselves seem as efficient as possible, and to deflect criticism. As we observe the official response to terrorist attacks, we can often find some common patterns of averting blame, and self-justification.

7

Explaining Failure

> At any given moment, there is a sort of all-pervading orthodoxy, a general tacit agreement not to discuss large and uncomfortable facts.
>
> —George Orwell

For obvious reasons, no official agency likes to admit failure, and police and intelligence services are no exception to this rule. In the world of terrorism, though, success and failure are defined quite differently from what we find with normal criminality or social policy. In most crimes, official success is defined in terms of catching and convicting the offender. If a murder occurs, police are thought to have done well if they identify and arrest the culprit within a short time. In terrorist incidents, however, the fact that an attack occurs is itself a major failure, in that agencies have failed to detect and prevent what was going to happen. To quote FBI counter-terrorism expert Dale Watson, "We're like a soccer goalkeeper. We can block 99 shots, and nobody wants to talk about any of those. And the only thing anyone wants to talk about is the one that gets through" (Risen and Johnston 2002). In order to explain terrorist acts that do occur, agencies are likely to stress certain themes in any statements intended for public consumption, themes that may or may not reflect their actual interpretations of the event.

THE PROBLEMS OF SUCCESS

The greatest successes in antiterrorist campaigns consist of entirely preventing such deeds before they occur, and such triumphs occur more frequently than most people know or acknowledge. In 1995, for instance, U.S. agencies helped prevent a scheme to blow up eleven U.S. airliners simultaneously over the Pacific Ocean (Wallace 1995; "U.S. warned in 1995" 2001). Though the story is not well known, it represents a model anti-terrorist effort.

And there have been other examples. If someone were asked whether anything important had happened on September 11, 2001, the person would regard the question as a sick joke, since the horrors of that day are so widely known. But the same person would have no idea of the significant events of January 1, 2000. If matters had worked out slightly differently, this would have been the date of the Millennium Plot, a simultaneous series of horrific attacks in Jordan and the United States that would have killed hundreds and perhaps thousands of Americans and Israelis. Another disaster was averted in July 2001 when Islamists were plotting to kill the leaders of all the Western countries at the G-8 summit in Genoa, Italy, possibly using an airborne suicide attack.

More recently, U.S. intervention in Afghanistan, coupled with greater official vigilance, resulted in the disruption of several major terrorist attacks planned by al-Qaeda and its allies. Just in the year following September 11, planned schemes averted by law enforcement included the mass assassination of political leaders in the U.S.; attacks on the U.S. embassies in Rome and Paris, probably using lethal chemicals like cyanide; the use of a radioactive "dirty bomb" against a U.S. city; the bombing of French and German synagogues; a bomb attack on a Christmas market in Strasbourg, France; and attempts to sink British or U.S. warships in the Straits of Gibraltar (Erlanger, Stephen and Chris Hedges 2001; Sanger 2001; Hedges 2001; Neuffer 2002; Henneberger 2002; Andrews 2002). This is in addition to foiled schemes to hijack or bring down airliners. (The best publicized of these failed attacks involved a British man who tried to detonate explosives concealed in his shoes.) That represents an impressive catalogue of disasters prevented, and also indicates the continuing scale of the terrorist threat.

Yet terrorist spectaculars that are prevented scarcely register in the public consciousness. One of the great difficulties faced by police agencies is that so little attention is paid to successes. The more successful and vigilant a country is, the fewer the terrorist attacks, and the more the public comes to regard terrorism as a nonissue. Often, as in the U.S. in the late 1990s, the public becomes receptive to claims that counter-terrorism efforts are a waste of resources, an infringement on civil liberties, perhaps a political charade. Less than a year after the September 11 attacks, some liberals were already regarding official warnings of new terrorist dangers as hysterical manipulation by a government anxious to distract attention from internal problems and stock market woes (Silberstein 2002). Writing in the *New York Times*, columnist Frank Rich (2002) suggested, "Wagging the dog no longer cuts it. If the Bush administration wants to distract

Americans from watching their 401(k)'s go down the toilet, it will have to unleash the whole kennel. Maybe only unilateral annihilation of the entire axis of evil will do . . . . When John Ashcroft, in full quiver, told Congress that the country was dotted with al-Qaeda sleeper cells 'waiting to strike again,' he commanded less media attention than Ted Williams's corpse." (Baseball player Williams had requested to be cryogenically frozen after death.)

But if an attack does occur—if all the agencies fail in their protective efforts—suddenly, all attention focuses on law enforcement and its supposedly lackadaisical ways. What can the authorities do to make their situation less damaging? Ideally, agencies would probably like to deny the occurrence of terrorism altogether, and for many years that was the favored course in countries with closed media like the Soviet Union and China, which liked to believe that they had none of the conditions giving rise to terrorism. Incidents largely went unreported, and information leaked only through rumor. And there are more recent examples of attempted denial. Since 1999, Egyptian officials have resolutely resisted all U.S. efforts to link the crash of the Egyptair airliner to any criminal action by the suspected pilot, al-Batouti. They naturally have a powerful vested interest in portraying this act as happenstance rather than terrorism, since any such political violence would raise questions about that nation's stability, not to mention the safety of its airlines. Nevertheless U.S. officials have been forced to rely on official Egyptian analysts and interpreters to understand al-Batouti's actions, and his cryptic last words (Langewiesche 2001).

Another recent example occurred in Tunisia. In April 2002, an explosion destroyed a synagogue in the resort of Djerba, killing nineteen people, mostly European tourists. Local authorities declared the event a tragic accident and promised to help rebuild. Soon German and other sources discovered the explosion was the work of a suicide bomber. The deed was claimed by an al-Qaeda spokesman, who viewed it as revenge for Israeli atrocities against Palestinians (Williams 2002). Given that the Tunisian security police have a solid reputation, it is unlikely that they believed the initial dismissal of the act as accidental. However, they had excellent motives for supporting such a fiction, since it freed them from the burden of failing to prevent the crime, while at the same time protecting the nation's flourishing tourist industry. Tunisia was not the sort of country where this kind of thing was meant to happen.

FAILURES

When an attack does occur, whether in the U.S. or elsewhere, agencies are anxious to avoid blame for the failure. It is very much in their interests to emphasize certain aspects of the story rather than others, and this often means emphasizing individual motivations on the part of offenders, while playing down evidence of organized activity. In this sense, it can help to depoliticize terrorist actions.

In teaching classes about terrorism, I sometimes use a scenario that involves role-playing. Participants are asked to imagine that a high-ranked U.S. politician is mysteriously assassinated, and that they represent a senior FBI official testifying to a Congressional committee. The situation is all but impossible for the bureaucrat, since the only proper behavior the agency could have undertaken would have been to prevent the attack, and that is no longer possible. The official is asked the basic question of whether the agency knew about the act in advance, and has to produce the least damaging answer. If the official answers no, they knew nothing about this act in advance, then the obvious follow up question will be, why not? Why had FBI intelligence capacities not identified this particular group as a threat? An even worse answer, however, would be yes, the agency had in fact known of the plot, that they had an agent within the organization. The next question would be, so why did they let it happen? In either case, the FBI will be damned for its inefficiency, its reckless disregard for U.S. security.

One of the very few strategies that can work in this scenario is to argue that the crime could not have been predicted because it was the work of a tiny cell with no wider connections, or better still, a "lone nut." Because such unconnected activists have no contacts with organized networks or foreign countries, law enforcement could not have been expected to track them. Also, there would be no other conspirators to apprehend after the attack, no loose ends. The story began and ended with one man. Obviously, such a tactic could not work with what was evidently a vast organized conspiracy, like the attacks of September 11, but it does carry weight. We can expect official explanations of terrorist incidents to emphasize and perhaps exaggerate their isolated and irrational character.

AVOIDING CONSPIRACIES

This approach is by no means an American prerogative. In the nineteenth century, British governments always dismissed assassination attempts against Queen Victoria or prominent politicians as the work of "lone nuts," which helped to deny that anyone could have sane or legitimate grounds for protesting against official policies.

In modern times debates over the motivations of assassins and terrorists have been particularly influential in the United States. Perhaps the most famous example of a lone nut interpretation involves the notorious assassination of President John F. Kennedy in 1963, which was widely blamed on a lone assassin named Lee Harvey Oswald. This event is still, forty years later, deeply controversial, and many people believe that the killing was the work of organized conspiracies, perhaps connected with official agencies in the U.S. or some other country. According to one popular scenario, the use of Oswald was a classic example of stigmatization. In this view, right-wing forces within the U.S. government and intelligence, allied to anti-Castro fanatics, created a bogus Communist sympathizer to ensure that blame for the assassination would fall on the Soviets and Cubans. This was the story portrayed in Oliver Stone's celebrated (or notorious) epic, *JFK*. For the sake of argument though, let us assume the truth of the official analysis formulated by the investigative commission headed by Chief Justice Earl Warren. According to this view, the president was shot by Lee Harvey Oswald, who acted alone, probably as a result of personal feelings of anger and inadequacy. Oswald himself was then killed by Dallas businessman Jack Ruby, acting out of grief at the loss of the president.

From the point of view of law enforcement or intelligence agencies, that story is almost perfect, because it means that the assassination could have been neither foreseen nor, probably, prevented. The FBI could not be blamed for failing to keep a potential assassin under surveillance, or for failing to track subversive groups. The CIA could not be faulted for not detecting sinister foreign conspiracies. At worst, police could be blamed for not maintaining observation of buildings along a parade route, and for failing to protect Oswald while in custody. However, this explanation can only be sustained if at every point, alternative explanations can be ignored or discredited. Through the workings of the Warren Commission and of subsequent investigations, we therefore find systematic attempts to discredit claims that might indicate conspiracy, any stories that Oswald or Ruby might have been acquainted with figures in organized crime or paramilitary groups. Often, these claims seem quite plausible, which does not necessarily mean that these connections contributed to the assassination. However, the Warren Commission was relying for its information on the very federal law enforcement agencies that stood to lose so much if evidence of conspiracy came to light.

Looking at the Warren Commission, it seems much less an objective investigation than a determined attempt to prove a particular case by a selective use of evidence. So vigorous was this effort, in fact, that it may have proved counter-productive in the long term. The more the Commission tried to ignore or conceal evidence, the more it acted as if it had something to hide, as if it was engaging in a cover-up. This impression gave enormous ammunition for the conspiracy theories that would become such a lively industry in following decades. A pattern of concealment or media manipulation encourages speculation that official agencies themselves were involved in the act, even if they had no sinister activities whatever to hide.

The Warren Commission interpretation shaped responses to later acts of political violence. Whether or not the idea had its origins in the interests of law enforcement agencies, it soon acquired a momentum of its own, since it appealed to other influential interest groups at the time. During the 1960s, psychiatric and psychodynamic explanations of human behavior enjoyed enormous popularity, and the Oswald case seemed to offer a textbook example of individual motivation, and the need for a therapeutic response.

Over the next twenty years, several more assassinations would occur in the U.S., the victims including President Kennedy's brother Robert Kennedy, and Martin Luther King (Clarke 1982). Plausibly or not, the lone nut theory served as a template for understanding all these later crimes, even when (as in the King assassination) the evidence for an organized domestic conspiracy was quite powerful (US House of Representatives 1979). The emphasis on individual pathology reached quite bizarre extremes. In the death of Robert Kennedy, the evidence for a political motive was quite strong, even if no organized conspiracy was involved. The assassin was a Palestinian Arab, and the crime occurred a year to the day after the outbreak of the Middle Eastern war that had resulted in catastrophe for the Palestinian people. Kennedy himself had recently attracted controversy by his outspoken support for U.S. arms sales to Israel. When we put these elements together, the shooting probably was politically motivated, if not actually terrorism. Even in this case, though, the official interpretation was entirely in terms of the assassin's individual and family conflicts. It was a matter for psychiatrists rather than counterinsurgency experts.

Sometimes, this reluctance to explore conspiracies can have dreadful consequences. In 1990, ultraright-wing Jewish activist Rabbi Meir Kahane was assassinated in New York City. Kahane was a deeply controversial figure who called for the expulsion of Arabs from Israel, and whose supporters have on occasion been listed as subversives in that nation (Kahane 2000). In this context, it caused little surprise that Kahane's killer was an Arab Muslim named El Sayyid Nosair, whose militancy might have been intensified by the ongoing publicity about the imminent war with Iraq. While his motivation was presumably political, police and FBI soon let it be known that they saw no evidence of a wider conspiracy. If not a "nut," then Nosair clearly was a lone wolf.

This decision reflected the popular ideology of assassins, but it also fitted with contemporary political needs. Through the 1980s, the U.S. had been allied with radical Islamists in a common war against the Soviet occupying forces in Afghanistan. This meant that the U.S. tolerated the operation of fund-raising and recruitment on its soil, including through radical mosques, and Nosair was closely connected with one of these in Jersey City, *Masjid al-Salam*. Any investigation of Nosair's wider links might well have turned up embarrassing stories of intelligence operations, focused on Afghan-related refugee centers in Brooklyn. And while some groups were pressing for an investigation of conspiratorial links, public pressure was not great because Kahane had been so desperately unpopular even in the Jewish community. Meanwhile, given the lack of obvious conspiracy, any intense investigation would be viewed as an ethnically based assault on the region's Muslim and Middle Eastern communities, which had grown dramatically in recent years, and which were beginning to flex their political muscle. Far from accepting any suggestions of conspiracy, the court trying Nosair was unable even to convict him of murder, and he was sentenced only for a weapons violation. The assassination was left to rest with Nosair, and him alone.

If the authorities had launched a serious exploration of conspiracy, they would have found quite significant linkages. Nosair was closely connected with an Egyptian relative called Ibrahim El Gabrowny, who was a central figure in the plot that in 1993 culminated in the first World Trade Center bombing. Investigating El Gabrowny would have produced links to several others in this network, including the individual who actually rented the Rider truck used in the attack (and who had led pro-Nosair street demonstrations in 1991). Had the group been kept under surveillance, the bombing might have been prevented, and lives saved (US House of Representatives 1994; Reeve 1999; Mylroe 2000; Miller and Stone 2002). Once the activists had been identified, their other plans could be prevented. In 1995, network members were convicted of trying to destroy several major landmarks in the New York City area, including the New York FBI building, the Lincoln Tunnel, the Holland Tunnel, and the George Washington Bridge. One of the conspirators who escaped was probably a senior agent of the Iraqi secret service.

Also, the refusal to explore conspiracy meant that Nosair's abundant notes were not actually translated by authorities until after the attack. Had they been read, the authorities would have discovered extensive evidence about proposed targets, including the WTC itself. Incidentally, the translation that was done was so poor that even the word Qaeda was initially missed, since it was assumed to be a technical word for "basis." (Qaeda actually means "base.") Nothing better illustrates the very low priority assigned to this alleged loner.

The official preference for loners was again illustrated in 1996, following the bomb attack at Atlanta's Olympic Park. Despite early suspicions of terrorist action, the FBI worked consistently to defuse such ideas. The agency swiftly focused on a security guard as its most likely suspect, and massive media leaks implied that they had certainly found the right man. The guard himself was ultimately vindicated (US Senate 1997c). However, this story had a sequel when in 1998, the bombing of an abortion clinic in

Birmingham, Alabama, resulted in the death of a security guard and the maiming of a clinic nurse. The suspect in this attack was Eric Rudolph, who was also linked to the earlier Olympic bombing in Atlanta, and an attack on a gay nightclub in the same city (Bragg 1998a–b).

Rudolph's crimes were taken very seriously, and he earned a place on the FBI's most wanted list, though at the time of writing, he remains at liberty. Yet interpretations of his motives remain controversial, and the FBI still went to extraordinary lengths to deny a terrorist motive. Speaking shortly after the Birmingham attack, a senior FBI profiler commented that Rudolph should be seen as a nonideological offender who was a pathological case rather than an authentic terrorist. After all, the agent asked, what possible strand connected three such widely disparate targets? In contrast, many observers would look at the targets of this campaign and see an obvious logic, at least from the perspective of the ultraright or Patriot movement. In these circles, both abortion and homosexuality represent abominations that should not be tolerated, and if the government will not suppress them, then ordinary citizens should take the law into their own hands. The Olympic Games, meanwhile, represent the same kind of internationalism and attack on national sovereignty as the United Nations itself. In this way, the attacks follow a highly recognizable political pattern, and therefore fit into the category of terrorism. The attempt to deny such a linkage illustrates how deeply ingrained the lone nut concept has become in bureaucratic thinking.

FOREIGN ENTANGLEMENTS

In addition to bureaucratic self-protection, governments and law enforcement agencies have other reasons for wishing to avoid conspiratorial interpretations of sensational terrorist crimes. If a conspiracy proves to have international dimensions, if a foreign power had carried out attacks on U.S. soil, this could have vast policy consequences in forcing the government toward confrontation and war. In the case of President Kennedy, early suspicions focused on possible involvement by the Communist regimes of the Soviet Union or Cuba, and if these were proven true, the result could be a global thermonuclear war. When President Lyndon Johnson appointed Earl Warren to investigate the affair, he warned him from the outset about the importance of the affair, since the result might involve the deaths of millions of people. Clearly, the investigators were aware of a vast responsibility to avoid such a consequence.

There are many more recent examples of such reluctance to address foreign linkages. In June 1996, a bomb attack occurred at the U.S. military facility at Khobar Towers in Saudi Arabia, where nineteen U.S. personnel lost their lives. Attribution of this act has shifted over the years, though it is today often laid at the feet of Osama bin Laden. Many analysts, however, think it much more likely that the work was the act of guerrillas working directly for the Iranians, either Saudi nationals or foreigners, possibly organized through the Hizbullah network (Risen and Perlez 2001). Whether the question of blame can ever be answered is very unlikely because of the Saudi response. Despite promising full assistance to U.S. law enforcement, the Saudis soon identified three men as the chief culprits, and executed all in secret, before they had been fully interrogated. Critics charge that the Saudis were trying to prevent the exposure of any foreign leads that might have forced a confrontation with Iran, and the outbreak of a major regional war.

As often before and since, Osama bin Laden serves a valuable political function for many regimes, by allowing terrorist acts to be attributed to a rootless international organization not obviously connected to any single state. This process was particularly evident in lists of alleged al-Qaeda operations drawn up retroactively in the aftermath of September 11, and including many acts hitherto attributed to other organizations. Notably absent from the lists are attacks previously linked to Hizbullah, and thus to Iran. Many intelligence analysts feel that Hizbullah is at least as dangerous an organization as al-Qaeda, and probably has a far wider and better-rooted network of supporters and activists around the globe, including within the United States (Anti-Defamation League of B'nai B'rith 1993). We might describe al-Qaeda as "the Hizbullah we are allowed to hate."

Perhaps these new post-September 11 attributions of blame reflect significant new breakthroughs in intelligence gathering, but the U.S. and other states are also trying to avoid being forced into untimely confrontations with quite genuine state sponsors of terrorism, like Iran. The new stress on Osama leaves countries attacked by terrorism the discretion to follow embarrassing leads that might lead to state sponsors or, just as often, to ignore them.

UNDERSTANDING OKLAHOMA CITY

To illustrate some of these official approaches, we can look at a specific incident that occurred in 1995, when the federal building in Oklahoma City was destroyed in what was, at that point, the worst domestic terrorist incident in American history. The number of dead reached 168. Two men were convicted in connection with the crime, Timothy McVeigh and Terry Nichols, who were associated with the ultra-right-wing Patriot and militia movements that had become so active in the U.S. during the previous few years. Early news reports suggested that the two men had at least one accomplice, the "John Doe number two" described by some witnesses. Incontestably, some other people had advance knowledge of the attack and faced legal penalties for their failure to warn the authorities. In other words, the attack was the work of a conspiracy in that a number of people were involved in the attack, and for several weeks law enforcement agencies stated that other conspirators were on the loose (Hamm 1997; Jones and Israel 1998; Revel 1998; Serrano 1998; Michel and Herbeck 2001; Linenthal 2001).

Supporting this idea were various pieces of evidence that pointed to a wider conspiracy, which were available to federal agencies immediately after the attack. Journalistic investigators have stressed the role of Elohim City, an Oklahoma-based compound of believers in Christian Identity doctrine, which exalts the white race and loathes Blacks and Jews. (The following account is chiefly drawn from Evans-Pritchard 1997.) Compounds of this sort had been important organizational bases of the campaign by the neo-Nazi "Order" in the 1980s, when they tried to implement the ideas put forth in the book *The Turner Diaries.* While most people assume that the date of the bombing—April 19—was intended to commemorate the end of the Waco siege in 1993, other interpretations are possible. This was the date in 1985 that the Arkansas compound known as the Covenant, Sword, and Arm of the Lord (CSA) had surrendered to federal authorities. One veteran of the Order campaign was Richard Wayne Snell, who had visited Elohim City, as had the head of CSA. By 1995 Snell was on death row in Arkansas for murdering a police officer and a storekeeper he believed to be Jewish. Snell's execution was scheduled for the very day of the Murrah Building attack, leading some observers to suggest that the bombing was intended as a protest against his death. This would have been all the more appropriate since as far back as 1983, the CSA had been plotting to destroy that very building with a rocket launcher. The Oklahoma City bombing in 1995 was undertaken precisely according to a blueprint laid out in *Turner Diaries,* which had an enormous influence on McVeigh.

The head of security at Elohim City was a right-wing German militant named Andreas Strassmeir, who had previously met McVeigh. For reasons still unknown, McVeigh had telephoned the compound two weeks before the bombing, leaving a message for "Andy." According to an informant debriefed by the FBI two days after the bombing, Strassmeir "is trained in weaponry, and has discussed assassinations, bombings and mass shootings." (The memo is reproduced in Evans-Pritchard 1997, 397.) Sources in far right groups had already warned the FBI of possible attacks in Oklahoma City and elsewhere, involving very much this cast of characters. In addition, reputable European media have suggested a linkage between McVeigh and other terrorist organizations well known on the far right. One was the Aryan Republican Army, which carried out a series of bank robberies and violent attacks during the early 1990s. According to the Anti-Defamation League—normally a well-informed source—the ARA had used Elohim City as a "refuge" from police (http://www.adl.org/learn/ext_us/Elohim.asp?xpicked=3&item=13).

Nor does the obvious activity by domestic ultra-rightists rule out the kind of Middle Eastern connection that was proposed in the immediate aftermath of the attack. Since the time of the attack, informants of widely varying credibility have claimed links to Iraq or to Islamic fundamentalists, an idea that has spawned some luxuriant conspiracy theories (In 2002, some survivors of the disaster, together with victims' relatives, initiated a lawsuit charging Iraqi complicity: Ridgeway 2002). Yet however odd the association might appear, Middle Eastern extremists have a long record of collaboration with European ultrarightists, who for one thing share their visceral hatred of Israel. Since the 1980s, police have often been uncertain whether attacks on Jewish targets in several nations could be traced to Middle Easterners like Abu Nidal, to neo-Nazis, or to some tactical alliance between the two. In the U.S. too, the far right demonstrates a striking sympathy for Arab issues, and Palestinian causes receive a remarkably good press on rightist Web sites. Right-wing leader David Duke denounced America's post-September 11 war on terrorism as a plot by "the ultra-powerful Jewish lobby . . . Zionist warmongers in media and government." William Pierce criticized U.S. removal of the Taliban regime, which he claimed had brought "peace and stability" to Afghanistan ("ADL Says U.S. Based Anti-Semites" 2001). In turn, a Hizbullah-run web site offers links to this and other Pierce statements. At the climax of Pierce's *Turner Diaries*, Arabs swarm over the remains of Israel to massacre the last Jews in the region. It is quite conceivable that a Middle Eastern nation wishing to strike at the U.S. would subcontract through the local extreme right. Major terrorist acts often involve a range of participants and sponsors.

Despite all these possible connections, the FBI soon determined that there was no wider conspiracy beyond McVeigh and Nichols, who had no real connections in the terrorist underworld. The two men represented less a classic terrorist cell than a model example of psychological *folie a deux*. In fact, perhaps they represented a model of the phantom cell concept, the leaderless resistance that had recently been discussed on the far right. Though the act unquestionably constituted terrorism, the ramifications were as limited as they possibly could be without postulating a lone nut. The solution was, above all, neat.

For the purposes of this book, it does not matter whether the FBI interpretation is correct, or if the attack was the work of a cell connected to some larger movement. The debate over John Doe is nevertheless a classic illustration of the dilemmas involved in investigating and reporting any terrorist actions. Let us assume for the sake of argument that John Doe was in fact a third active participant. Perhaps the FBI genuinely does not believe this fact, and honestly states its opinion. Alternatively, there are many conceivable reasons why they would know of his guilt, and deny it. Perhaps the individual was a government infiltrator within the terrorist conspiracy, and the FBI wished to avoid the embarrassment of having failed to prevent the crime. Perhaps they know they can never find him, and wish to conceal their incompetence. Perhaps they know John Doe was an agent of a foreign power, and it was politically essential to avoid the diplomatic ramifications of having to confront this fact. Conceivably, the Bureau might have wanted to avoid yet another confrontation with a well-armed paramilitary compound, and a repetition of the Waco disaster of 1993. In any of these cases, a powerful bureaucratic dynamic would ensure that the FBI would put heavy influence on the news media to discredit the slightest suggestion that John Doe existed. Suggestions to the contrary would be dismissed as paranoid conspiracy theory—which is all the more plausible considering all the outrageous theories that genuinely did circulate following this attack.

One of the greatest fictional works on the world of intelligence is Eric Ambler's classic thriller *A Coffin for Dimitrios* (1939), in which a police officer explains that "The important thing to know about an assassination is not who fired the shot, but who paid for the bullet." This principle can also apply to acts of terrorism, in the sense that while the actual participants can often be identified, the underlying context is far harder to discern. It is discovered by a process of investigation undertaken by police and intelligence agencies, which are often constrained by diplomatic or bureaucratic factors. Ultimately, the account of an incident presented in the media represents not an objective evaluation of truth, but rather a negotiated consensus.

8

Terrorism and the Mass Media

Bureaucracy always seeks the path of least disclosure.
—Darrell Evans

Most informed people realize that they have to exercise care in accepting stories that are offered by the news media, but even the most cautious rarely take account of the special problems involved in dealing with stories about terrorism and intelligence. As a result, public discussions of these topics sometimes depend on inaccurate and tendentious news stories, which are shaped by the interests and needs of the bureaucratic agencies involved. When we read or watch media coverage of terrorism, we have to understand the limits of what the media know, what they can say, and how completely even the most critical journalists depend on the good will of federal law enforcement and intelligence agencies.

Yet the news media are not the only way that people form their images of terrorism. In order for a story to be widely credible, it has to mesh with existing assumptions and stereotypes. Any account of how the news media treat terrorism must therefore consider issues of audience, and that means treating popular culture and cinema alongside serious news. In both cases, truth and fiction, we can observe the interplay of interest groups, the balance of political and commercial interests.

INFORMED SOURCES

Studies of social problems generally focus on the individuals and groups who make claims about the scale and nature of a given issue, and who try to have their particular view accepted as correct and authoritative. Some claims makers start with a real advantage over others by virtue of their insider status, their position within government or bureaucracy, which makes it far more likely that their opinions will be taken seriously than, for instance, some upstart pressure group. Such insider claims makers play a central role in the definition of the terrorism problem, because most materials that appear in the media can be traced to a small number of official agencies and, indeed, subunits of those agencies, which enjoy a very high degree of credibility. Only a little exposure to reporting of terrorism allows a reader to determine almost immediately what these "informed sources" are, when for instance a journalist is drawing on the FBI as opposed to the CIA, State Department, or Defense Department. Outside this charmed circle only a very few other sources enjoy anything like this status, though Israeli diplomats and intelligence agencies often fulfill such a role.

Though U.S. government sources are on occasion criticized seriously, as in the aftermath of September 11, the news media generally treat this kind of official information as authoritative, and it is rare for a journalist to discuss the flaws and biases that it might seem to contain. Nor is this faith in officialdom shaken by any number of errors or inconsistencies that emerge over time. As in the media response to other kinds of crime problem, such as illicit drugs, the media often seem content to serve as the mouthpieces of the law enforcement bureaucracy.

Media reliance on law enforcement sources is not difficult to understand because, for all their flaws, agencies like the FBI should in fact be the best-informed group in the country, with access to abundant evidence from moles, infiltrators, and surveillance materials. And official agencies can deploy carrot-and-stick tactics to maintain the friendship of the media. Outlets that are considered friendly can reap rich rewards. They can be granted access to defectors from terrorist organizations, who can be the subject of interviews and major news stories. Friendly journalists can also be given the kind of extensive background materials on terrorist incidents that allow journalists to make their investigative reports look like intelligence dossiers, with all kinds of insider information like weapons, surveillance photos, airline tickets, and so on (see for example Miller 1987). If investigations culminate in arrests, friendly journalists are on the scene to cover the dramatic moments that make headlines in newspapers or television news. At every stage, journalists considered hostile can be denied these same perks and privileges.

Official agencies are most valued for what they can provide in terms of leaks and off-the-record briefings, information that is supplied to the media without direct attribution. These are the sort of statements that appear in news stories under vague introductions like "Law enforcement sources say X" or "Intelligence sources say Y." For most readers, these items carry weight since they seem to reflect what government or law enforcement really thinks about a given issue, information that a well-connected journalist has obtained through skillful investigation. Such stories are considered to be much more authoritative than the official statements put out by agencies, which are more carefully tailored for public consumption. Even thirty years after the event, popular concepts of investigative journalism are still profoundly shaped by the exposure of Watergate, and the role of *Washington Post* journalists Bob Woodward and Carl Bernstein.

In fact, news leaks involve a rather more complex dynamic than this approach would suggest. Leaks are planned just as carefully as public statements and are issued in order to achieve desired political goals, usually benefiting the particular agency or administrative department. Several possible purposes come to mind. A leak might be issued to float a balloon, to test the public reaction to some scheme or idea prior to announcing it officially: if reaction is overwhelmingly hostile then the scheme can be dropped without embarrassment. An agency might leak information to discredit a rival or to support its own political position against some other. Over the last two years, the news media have often reported what "official sources say" about Iraqi involvement in terrorism, with stories variously claiming or rejecting such activity. Virtually all such leaks can be traced to the ongoing war within the Bush administration, with the Defense Department pushing to make Iraq seem as dangerous as possible, and the State Department trying to defuse charges concerning Iraqi terrorism. Such partisan motives are scarcely hard to deduce, but journalists continue to present these leaks as if they represent pure unadulterated truth. Journalists must know better, and most of them do. The problem is that if they report these statements with the qualifications they deserve, taking full account of their biases and limitations, then these media outlets will not be favored with future leaks, which often do constitute significant news stories. We never read, for instance, that "the CIA believes this view, but it is natural that they would say this, because it directly serves their interests."

In addition to the general relationship between media and bureaucracy, an important interpersonal dynamic is at work. Journalists form personal relationships with specific informants in government or official agencies to whom they know they can turn for material, and in turn, those officials know that these journalists will treat their information with proper discretion. The longer these relationships exist, the more the journalist is likely to treat the informant as a friend, and share his or her perspectives on interagency rivalries, sharing the stereotypes and in-jokes of one bureaucratic body as opposed to another. Consciously or otherwise, journalists can become active partisans of (say) the FBI or the CIA, and they increasingly gain the reputation within that agency of being a friendly and reliable conduit for information. In some cases, the degree of co-optation can become so notorious as to earn such favored journalists the description of "groupies" for a particular agency—though professional jealousy provokes rival writers into applying this language.

The process of official leaking is well illustrated by the attempts of federal agencies to exercise damage control after the September 11 attacks. In the immediate aftermath of the events, the consensus was that nobody could have predicted them, at least in anything like the form they took. Though intelligence sources had warned generally of an al-Qaeda strike at the U.S., these concerns were too general to serve as the basis for action. As we have seen, though, this account was misleading to the extent that both the CIA and FBI separately knew things that—properly collated—should have raised the alarm, that something like the proposed attacks was in the making. News of these warning signs appeared in the media during the spring of 2002, as Congress began considering a formal inquiry and the issue became something of a national scandal. The crucial question was, who was chiefly to blame?

Through these months, we can trace a pattern of leaks that can be directly traced to the two major agencies, respectively the FBI and CIA, who both had a huge amount to lose in the conflict. Apart from the obvious dangers to the agencies' leaderships, the administration was at this time considering a fundamental restructuring of the internal security and intelligence apparatus that might in theory result in one or both of the organizations losing its independence. The leaks followed something like a tit-for-tat sequence, in which a statement casting blame on one agency was rapidly followed by a counterpart pointing to blunders by the rival (Johnston 2002a-b; Johnston and Becker 2002; Oliphant 2002; Risen 2002e; Miniter 2002; Eggen and Schmidt; Isikoff 2002b). In May a news story, assuredly stemming from the CIA, claimed that the agency had in August 2001 warned the President of a likely hijacking on U.S. territory. This led to extravagant news headlines: *Newsweek's* cover on May 27 offered the horrible picture of the aircraft striking the South Tower of the WTC, and in large letters over the explosion are the words asking "What Bush Knew." This leak was followed almost immediately by a lengthy report attributed to "government officials," which revealed the CIA's disastrous blunder in failing to respond appropriately to al-Mihdhar and al-Hazmi, the two al-Qaeda members present at the Malaysian meeting who subsequently entered the United States. These stories, with their implied absolution of the FBI, can confidently be traced to that agency. The FBI also used leaks to discredit an agent who had criticized the agency's handling of the investigation. Leaks and counter-leaks continued apace for several weeks until the two agencies reached an informal pact to end this particular clandestine war. Throughout the process, the news media largely served as bulletin boards for the uncritical publication of *parti pris* official statements, with little obvious effort to criticize the agencies offering these materials.

CONSPIRACY THEORIES

Contributing to the media's reliance on officialdom is the fear that a journalist might be discredited for adopting crank theories. In religious terms, relying on official statements means that the media cleave to orthodoxy without being tempted to stray into heresy. This can be a serious danger. For decades, the whole clandestine world of intelligence, terrorism, and assassinations has attracted a luxuriant undergrowth of conspiracy theories, some of which may have substance, most of which are absurd or pernicious. The fact that some terrorist groups engage in provocation and deception has led many writers to argue that virtually all terrorist movements are bogus, false fronts, that nothing is what it initially seems. The unregulated information market of the Internet has vastly enhanced the number of such theories, many of which beggar belief. Grazing the Internet conspiracy sites, we can find lengthy and convincing-looking proofs that the U.S. government itself launched the September 11 attacks in order to justify the occupation of Afghanistan on behalf of American oil interests. Other theories claim that the attacks were launched by the Israeli intelligence agency Mossad; and that the the Pentagon was not even struck by an aircraft, but was rather the target for a U.S.-launched missile or a demolition device (Brisard and Dasquie 2002). The Oklahoma City bombing has produced just as much nonsense. Summarizing the Oklahoma theories, author Gore Vidal has claimed, "Evidence . . . is overwhelming that there was a plot involving militia types and government infiltrators as prime movers to create panic to get Clinton to sign that infamous Anti-Terrorism Act" (Bone n.d.).

Most such tales seem so outrageously false that no responsible observer is likely to be deceived by them, but some horror stories suggest otherwise. In 1996, for instance, TWA flight 800 crashed off Long Island in a still unexplained catastrophe that as we have seen, was initially cited as a likely terrorist incident. Shortly afterwards, a retired pilot sent a letter claiming that the aircraft had been shot down by the accidental launch of an Aegis missile fired from a U.S. Navy ship carrying out exercises nearby, and that the FBI was suppressing investigation of that fact. The letter soon appeared on the Internet, where it circulated freely. Some months later, highly respected journalist Pierre Salinger publicized the missile theory as authentic, generating international headlines ("Salinger Totally Sure" 1997). Though he reportedly received the information from sources in French intelligence, he produced nothing that had not previously circulated in the conspiracy factories of the Internet. After some initial interest, Salinger's theory was rejected by all mainstream media, and his reputation suffered. Conspiracy-mongering is a prime sin for a journalist. Cases like this provide stern object lessons for journalists tempted to stray from the orthodoxies preached by the FBI and other agencies within the charmed circle.

MAKING TELEVISION NEWS

Special concerns apply when dealing with the visual coverage that does so much to condition our views of the realities of terrorism, and which is so dependent on official attitudes. The importance of visual treatments can hardly be exaggerated. While everyone knows that the Pentagon was attacked on September 11, the event registered little on the public consciousness when set beside the far more spectacular WTC disaster. Contributing to this neglect is the absence of any news footage of the Pentagon event, no memorable videos of the aircraft about to strike. Undoubtedly, if such visual materials were available, they would have contributed to making the Washington events far more central, and more traumatic, to recollections of that day.

In the Middle East, similarly, one reason for U.S. sympathy toward Israel is that coverage of terrorist attacks usually portrays people who look like average Americans, and who usually speak English. In contrast, an attack in Afghanistan or Kashmir involves victims who are visibly foreign in dress and speech, and who must generally speak through interpreters. The degree of identification, and of sympathy, is all the smaller. Most Americans neither knew nor cared about the horrific terrorist war in Algeria during the 1990s because that nation is not part of the usual U.S. media circuit, so we literally saw nothing of the crisis, no mutilated bodies, no terrified children.

The ability to televise events depends in large measure on official favor. This remark may sound strange to an audience that is accustomed to think of the television camera as an objective roving eye, but cameras are of course operated by human beings, who are subject to arrest or violence, and who also have their own attitudes and prejudices. When a *60 Minutes* crew interviews a terrorist prisoner in a Peruvian or Pakistani jail, they are doing so with the permission of the respective authorities, who have their own agendas in permitting this access.

The politics of television news are illustrated by the Middle East crisis of spring 2002, when Israeli forces invaded the Palestinian areas of the West Bank. Because Palestinian fury at the West made it impossible for Western news crews to enter the areas under attack, the CNN network made use of Arab and Palestinian personnel, who presented the story in a manner completely different from what had been commonplace hitherto. Now, television screens around the world were depicting Arab civilians as victims, showing hospitalized children and frightened women, while the Israelis were appearing as an army of occupation. This made it far more difficult to portray the conflict as simply one of Israeli democracy versus Arab terrorism. These images contributed mightily to the negative worldwide reaction to Israeli actions, and naturally infuriated the Israelis themselves. Matters deteriorated when CNN devoted a lengthy segment to interviewing the family of an Arab suicide bomber, while paying little attention to the victims or their families. At the same time, CNN founder Ted Turner made public statements about the "terrorism" of the Israeli armed forces.

CNN's status in Israel plummeted. Israeli media wrote freely of the station as PNN, the Palestinian News Network, and threatened retaliation. CNN was faced with removal from the regional satellite system YES, and its replacement by the far more pro-Israel Fox Network (Hirschberg 2002). Lacking official support or sanction, CNN would be deprived of interviews with prominent Israelis, access to breaking news stories, and could conceivably be excluded from any scenes of military action or counterinsurgency. In addition to the commercial consequences in Israel itself, the network would be virtually destroyed as a media presence in a region pivotal to world politics. CNN very soon made amends, offering a series of substantial interviews with the families of Israeli terror victims, and promising to be more vigilant in future about any possible pro-Arab bias. Advertising the new pro-Israel slant, the network promised, "A special CNN series will take you inside everyday life in Israel and introduce you to the people whose lives are turned around by the fear and the violence. In part one—living the nightmare of losing a loved one."

The CNN case is noteworthy because a conflict with a host government became so widely publicized. Normally, such disputes do not occur overtly, because networks and journalists acknowledge the limitations they must observe in particular countries, and know how far they can go in offending the sensibilities of local officialdom. To that extent, a great deal of television coverage of terrorist events and personalities is filtered through the concerns and interests of particular police agencies and security forces.

EVALUATION

Having raised all these problems about news coverage, is it possible to believe any statement about terrorism or intelligence? I would argue that we need not be reduced to despair or total skepticism, but rather we need to apply common sense when reading any news story. This is especially true with stories that try and place terrorist acts in a wider context, which connect attack X to group Y and country Z. Some obvious questions would include:

- What is the source for the story? Is the group or individual in a position to know about the topics discussed?
- Can we trace the story to a particular agency or even individual? Do we know anything about the track record of that particular source?

- Do the claims seem plausible? Does the story rely on improbable stereotypes?
- Do the claims makers have any obvious agenda in making these statements? How do the interpretations offered relate to current debates or controversies?
- Is there any evidence of conflicting claims by rival bodies? Why is one account given precedence over another?
- If official agencies or intelligence services are quoted in the accounts, can we tell why they should be making public statements on these matters? If, for example, an American journalist is quoting some foreign police or intelligence service, why should that organization bother to speak to the U.S. media? What do they think they have to gain or lose?
- Does the current interpretation represent a change or revision from earlier accounts? If so, does the new interpretation try to explain that discrepancy, or just ignore it?

To illustrate these themes, we can examine one of the conspiracy stories that surfaced following September 11, and which is still widely believed around the world, namely the charge that the Israeli Mossad was responsible for the attacks in New York and Washington (Gee 2001). For multiple reasons, I believe this story is worthless, and that it is horrifying that anyone could come up with such a fairy tale. But why do I feel this, apart from a gut reaction? Is there anything more than a subjective sense that makes me believe that this story is bogus, while other claims about surreptitious involvement by intelligence agencies seem plausible? Obviously, I do have reasons for my beliefs, which it is useful to spell out here. This story in itself is scarcely worth debunking, because it is so wildly improbable, but it offers a basis to describe the criteria for evidence that can be used in another more plausible case.

The Mossad story originally surfaced in Pakistani newspapers days after the attacks, and soon gained credence across the Muslim world. Allegedly, no Muslim group or power would have had the technical or organizational skill to carry out the attacks, but the Mossad certainly would. It also had the motive, in that the Israelis wished to create irreparable divisions between Americans and the Arab powers, and to establish complete sympathy for the Israeli cause. This was all the more important in 2001, since the Palestinians were launching their popular rising against Israeli control, the second *Intifada.* American attitudes would be critical in influencing Israeli policy, and the Republican Party of newly elected President George W. Bush was traditionally less uncritically sympathetic to Israel than were the Democrats. Also, Israel hoped to stir a war between the U.S. and some of the most radical Muslim nations, including Afghanistan and Iraq. Mossad thus launched the September plot, but the

Israelis were careful to pass a warning to American Jews. On the morning of the attacks—so the legend goes—four thousand Jews stayed away from their normal place of work in the World Trade Center. The story gained support among American radicals and black nationalists. In 2002, New Jersey's new Poet Laureate Amiri Baraka created controversy when he read a poem giving credence to the tale (Purdy 2002). In his poem "Somebody Blew Up America," Baraka asked,

> Who knew the World Trade Center was gonna get bombed
> Who told 4000 Israeli workers at the Twin Towers
> To stay home that day
> Why did Sharon stay away?

Responding to critics, Baraka claimed that "Everything said about Israel in the poem is easily researched."

The most important point in analyzing the Mossad story is that it is no more than that, a story, which derives from no source or authority that has proved to be reliable in the past. In fact, it is far from clear what the source is, apart from the wishful thinking of some Muslims who wanted to divert the blame from their own people. That fact alone should remove the theory from serious consideration.

But at so many points, the story runs flat contrary to what we know of the alleged participants. One does not have to believe that Israeli intelligence officers are saints in order to dismiss the tale. What we need to know is that the agency is very reluctant to operate against Western powers, for fear of losing the critical friends on which the nation of Israel ultimately depends for its very existence. A number of defectors and hostile critics have offered unflattering accounts of Mossad's history, yet nothing vaguely like this act has ever surfaced. It is completely out of character for the agency and the government involved. To the contrary, if Israeli involvement in a scheme like this ever came to light, the American reaction might, quite literally, bring an end to the Israeli state. And we are asked to believe that this deadly secret was entrusted to four thousand Jews, who were told to stay away from work that day. Has one of these Jews ever testified to such an event? Apart from its other flaws, the story also depends on an ancient stereotype, namely that all Jews are faithful members of a global conspiracy, directed from the state of Israel.

At every point where the story can be tested, it proves to be not only unsubstantiated, but also wholly improbable. At no stage does it have any strengths that come close to challenging the commonly accepted belief that the attacks were the work of radical Islamists. The story is so blatantly bogus as to discredit any media outlet that ever reported it seriously. It belongs in the disreputable realm of the urban legend.

Much more difficult to dismiss is a theory that surfaced within days after the September 11 attacks, which the U.S. government blamed almost immediately on al-Qaeda. Nevertheless, stories began to appear on the Internet that the attacks might instead be the work of Imad Mughniyeh, the chief of operations for the Lebanese based Shi'ite organization Hizbullah (Safire 2001b; Risen 2002). The stories claimed that Mughniyeh was responsible for a catalog of crimes that made Osama bin Laden look like an American ally. Reportedly, Mughniyeh was directly involved in every major attack on U.S. interests in Lebanon through the 1980s, as well as the 1996 attack on Khobar Towers in Saudi Arabia. As the Israeli newspaper *Ha'Aretz* reported, "Israeli officials say Mugniyah, who conveys instructions and transfers finances between Tehran and Hezbollah's operations base in Lebanon, is the most senior figure behind the group's terror activities. The officials claim he was responsible for the bombings in Buenos Aires of the Israel Embassy in 1992 and the AMIA Jewish center in 1994. He was also involved in attacks against U.S. Marines and French troops in Beirut in 1983 and in the 1985 hijacking of a TWA plane to Beirut" (Harel 2001).

What gave the stories credibility was the thorough background provided on recent Middle Eastern history, and what seemed to be intelligence data. The broad outlines of the account were confirmed by CIA sources. Initially, though, the material probably derived from Israeli sources, and probably from the intelligence service, Mossad, an extremely capable and well-informed organization. The Mughniyeh theory was attractive because it gave those who heard it a sense of access to highly valuable insider information not available to the mainstream media, and the idea circulated for some months afterwards. It may also have influenced the U.S. government since, in October 2001, Mughniyeh was on the list of 39 leaders and organizations whose assets were frozen because of their suspected involvement with terrorism. Unlike the theory blaming Mossad, this particular idea had substantial roots in a source with an excellent track record.

At the time of writing, we cannot say whether in fact Mughniyeh had anything to do with the attacks, though no later evidence of a possible role has emerged, while al-Qaeda's guilt seems certain. This is beyond doubt given the videos that have appeared showing bin Laden boasting of the event. On the other hand, we can see excellent reasons why the leak would surface at the time it did, and the Israelis had strong motives for issuing a story of this kind, other than a simple desire to promote objective truth.

In the immediate aftermath of September 11, furious Americans were ready for draconian steps against any outside force that could plausibly be tied to the atrocities, but the initial government response was strictly focused on groups directly linked to al-Qaeda. The U.S. did not initially seek to penalize other radical Islamic nations that were not believed to be involved with the attacks, and which might indeed be persuaded to help counter-terrorism efforts: this chiefly meant Iran and Syria. Though these nations were not perceived as enemies of the U.S., they remained bitter foes of Israel, and supporters of the anti-Israel campaign directed by Hamas and Hizbullah. From an Israeli perspective, then, it would be hugely beneficial if the U.S. could be persuaded to view these nations as enemies. If the claim were believed, the idea that Hizbullah was involved with the New York attacks would turn the U.S. against Iran and Syria, and vastly strengthen the Israeli position in the Middle East. It would also remind Americans of other Hizbullah attacks, and prevent this organization being forgotten in the surge of anger against al-Qaeda. (Later Israeli stories claimed that the Syrians had permitted fleeing al-Qaeda fighters to take refuge in areas under their control, in both Syria and Lebanon: Schiff 2002.)

The Mughniyeh leak should therefore be seen as a partisan effort to influence U.S. policy, and this element of self-interest must be taken into account when we consider whether the story is plausible. Any news outlet that failed to pay attention to this context would be either naïve or cynical.

AUDIENCES

People make claims, which others then accept or reject. In order to analyze a social problem, we have to understand the nature of the audience that will make the decision about whether claims are plausible or not. Normally, the pronouncements of governments and bureaucratic agencies are likely to carry particular weight on the assumption that they have the best access to information and intelligence. However, matters may change quite dramatically on occasion, when the authority of officialdom is challenged, opening the way to claims makers who might hitherto have been ignored.

Official pronouncements are more likely to be disbelieved in the aftermath of a conspicuous failure or a public scandal, which has demonstrated corruption or incompetence on the part of agencies. The most obvious recent example would be the September 11 attacks that U.S. agencies failed to predict or prevent, and which also indicated vast gaps in intelligence, even in matters as basic as translating Middle Eastern languages. Almost as damaging, in a rather different way, was the crisis of the intelligence agencies in the Watergate era when Congressional investigations revealed widespread official misbehavior.

Also in the 1970s, political struggles raised questions about exactly who were the "inside" claims makers. In these years, agencies were riven by deep ideological and personal conflicts, which were especially damaging within the CIA. Between 1973 and 1978, many conservative officers and administrators who espoused hard-line anti-Communist views were driven out by more liberal forces, and those expelled found refuge in think-tanks and consultancies (Mangold 1991; Wise 1992; Corn 1994; Olmsted 1996; Cahn 1998). The conservatives staged a comeback under the Reagan administration, while the liberals now found themselves in opposition. Through the 1970s and 1980s, official statements on terrorism or intelligence problems were likely to be countered by radically different opinions deriving from other people who appeared to enjoy exactly the same insider status, and comparable access to intelligence information. This division was reflected in the ideological battle of these years about the nature of external terrorism, and the idea of the Moscow-backed terror network.

Another factor affecting the credibility of claims is what might be called the horizon of memory, namely that both media and public are more influenced by recent events than by more distant occurrences. Some events in particular have a sharp impact on the public consciousness, and serve to define terrorism for a period of several years. Between 1985 and 1990, the terrorist events that registered most clearly on the American consciousness were all connected with Middle Eastern groups. These included, most notoriously, several airport massacres and airliner hijackings, the Lockerbie bombing, the Beirut hostage situation, and the *Achille Lauro* ship hijacking, which led to the savage murder of disabled American Leon Klinghoffer. Though the pace of Middle Eastern related activity slowed somewhat, the stereotype of terrorism as a purely Arab/Muslim phenomenon was kept alive by the first World Trade Center bombing of 1993. Through the 1980s and early 1990s, the media regularly began stories on this subject with a question like "Could terrorism come to the United States?"—a ludicrous comment if we consider the nation's lengthy experience with political violence of this type. The question about "coming to America" was nevertheless important in indicating the strong feeling that terrorism was foreign, ethnically, and religiously

Yet this ethnic equation changed substantially in the Clinton years with the establishment of a new liberal consensus about the nature of terrorism. Also critical was the Oklahoma City bombing of 1995, which to general amazement proved to be truly domestic in origin, an act perpetrated not by foreign Muslims, but by men named Tim and Terry. For several years, memories of Oklahoma City helped reshape American notions of terrorism, placing a new emphasis on domestic ultraright movements.

The post-Oklahoma City reluctance to condemn Arabs or Muslims continued despite a plethora of major Arab-linked attacks on U.S. targets overseas through the late 1990s. Matters only changed with the apocalypse of September 2001, after which domestic terrorism was virtually forgotten, and the emphasis shifted once again to the Islamist danger. The "obvious realities" of terrorism in 2003 are thus quite different from what they had been in 1996, which were in turn radically at variance with the orthodoxies of 1992. These shifts conditioned what people were prepared to accept in official statements, in the news media, and in popular culture.

POPULAR CULTURE AND TERRORISM

Whether we are looking at films or television movies, reading novels or true crime accounts of terrorism, popular culture plays a critical political role in shaping American attitudes toward terrorism. Even if popular films and books are primarily interested in offering entertainment and making money, the images and stereotypes they offer are nevertheless influential. If films about terrorism are always portraying terrorists as Arab or Middle Easterners, who are moreover depicted as savage fanatics, that cannot fail to affect public opinion (and this was very much the situation through much of the 1980s). Such images confirm the belief that "real" terrorism is automatically connected to the Middle East, while violent activities elsewhere in the world somehow fall short of this category (Dobkin 1992).

This image affects law enforcement priorities, in encouraging politicians and law enforcement agencies to exercise surveillance over Middle Eastern groups rather than others. In such a setting, law enforcement bureaucrats know that the announcement of an arrest of Middle Eastern suspects is likely to be much more newsworthy than a similar action against (say) Sri Lankan or Spanish guerrillas. A Middle Eastern investigation is more likely to be seen as a sign of police efficiency. Conversely, if the media are nightly depicting terrorism as deriving from red-necked neo-Nazi extremists in fortified compounds in Idaho or Arkansas, that perception may make agencies chary about exploring Middle Eastern connections for fear of being denounced as xenophobic and anti-immigrant.

Terrorism has frequently served as a popular culture theme, inevitably given the potential for spectacular violence and demonic villains, all loosely related to actual events in the news headlines. Since this book concerns the shaping of American images of terrorism, my account of popular culture focuses entirely on U.S.-made films, with the exception of a few foreign productions like *Battle of Algiers* that had a vast impact on shaping both terrorism and counter-terrorism in the real world. This point needs stressing because such rich materials exist for a global or cross-cultural study of these topics. As far back as 1936, Alfred Hitchcock's British film *Sabotage* told a story of urban terrorist bombing adapted from Joseph Conrad's novel *The Secret Agent.* In recent years, themes of terrorism and repression have often attracted filmmakers in Britain and Ireland (*Hidden Agenda, Some Mother's Son, Defence of the Realm, The Crying Game*), in continental Europe (*Z, State of Siege, Deutschland in Herbst, The Lost Honor of*

Katherine Blum), in the Arab Middle East (*West Beirut*), in Latin America (*Four Days in September, The Official Story)* and in India (*The Terrorist*). The popular culture treatments of each individual society naturally reflect the different concerns and political interaction of the nation in question. Not surprisingly, the most sophisticated productions tend to come from nations with the longest exposure to terrorism, and some observers feel that the Israeli *Streets of Yesterday* (*Rehovot Ha'Etmol*) is one of the finest films ever made on the topic. (This story was also adapted from a Conrad novel, *Under Western Eyes*.)

In American cinema, terrorists have provided thriller villains rivaled only by "drug lords." In many ways, though, the realities of the terrorism issue have been systematically distorted by commercial and political pressures on writers and filmmakers. Above all, the terrorists themselves tend to be thoroughly depoliticized. There is little space in a film or novel for anything more than the sketchiest reflection of the authentic background of a terrorist movement, the issues and grievances driving it. Placing any emphasis on such social or political factors would undermine the simplistic struggle of good versus evil that so often provides the narrative framework of these stories. Even when Arab terrorists were most in vogue during the 1980s, films devoted no attention to exploring the political conflicts in Palestine or elsewhere that might have motivated the screen villains. Equally, terrorist fiction usually places a disproportionate emphasis on individuals, super-villains like the fictional megalomaniacs of the James Bond world, or the real-life Carlos the Jackal, whose exploits were vastly exaggerated in countless films, books, and news segments (Dobson 1977; Follain 1998).

This individual focus can be seen as a kind of popular therapy for a public alarmed at waves of authentic terrorist incidents, for which there seems no imaginable solution. The message from popular culture is that the problem is chiefly the work of a handful of very evil individuals, and understanding this menace is perhaps less difficult than comprehending the diverse factors (political, social, economic, spiritual) which drive the faceless terrorists of real life. Terrorism can thus be personalized in the form of Carlos, Colonel Qaddafi, or Osama bin Laden. Once such an individual has been identified, he can be fought, defeated, and captured, by whatever means are appropriate.

Clearly, Osama makes a much more plausible candidate for such super-villain status, but even there, the notion of a global terrorist mastermind is vastly exaggerated. His al-Qaeda movement was after all composed from the union of three or more preexisting terrorist movements, each with vast experience and resources in its own right, and any of the unified movement's twenty or so senior leaders could probably provide leadership comparable to his. Moreover, it is far from clear how centralized the operation is, or whether many acts claimed by the network might be the work of decentralized units exercising local initiative. Nevertheless, in both news accounts and popular fiction, Osama alone has since the mid-1990s represented the abhorred face of world terrorism, the absolute head of a uniquely evil empire.

WHICH TERRORISTS?

The choice of movements and conflicts covered has been very patchy. No correlation exists between the actual seriousness or potential harm of a terrorist movement and the attention it receives in popular media, mainly because there is little interest in covering groups not seen as relevant to U.S. conditions. To take a fairly recent example, any consideration of the world's most dangerous and destructive terrorist wars would give a high place to the Algerian struggle of the 1990s in which a hundred thousand may have perished. To put that figure in perspective, that is far more than the total number of casualties suffered by all North American and European nations in all terrorist incidents since 1960—provided we omit the victims of the Balkan wars of the past decade. Yet the savage Algerian conflict made next to no impression in popular culture, nor even in the U.S. news media. Almost as lethal has been the violence in the Indian region of Kashmir, which is also claimed by neighboring Pakistan. During the 1990s, guerrilla campaigns by Muslim separatist forces led to perhaps sixty thousand dead, including many civilians. Yet in the West, Kashmir has been ignored as thoroughly as Algeria—at least until the point in 2001 that news reports linked local Islamic militants to al-Qaeda. Also absent from such treatment have been most of the world's most lethally efficient terrorist organizations, especially those based in the Indian subcontinent: how many Americans have even heard of the Sri Lankan-based Tamil Tigers, who have carried out the world's longest and deadliest suicide bombing campaign? Nor have long-running terrorist crises like that in Spain's Basque country attracted the attention of US filmmakers.

At the same time, other groups that clearly do arouse interest in the U.S. have been excluded because they might be too controversial. This was not problematic before the modern upsurge of international terrorism and the sense that Americans themselves might be victims. Before the late 1960s, a number of Hollywood films depicted classic guerrilla and terrorist struggles, and showed unashamed sympathy for the fighters. Irish guerrillas are treated heroically in films like *The Informer* and *Shake Hands with the Devil*. The Jewish war of resistance in Palestine is depicted in epic terms in *Exodus* and *Cast a Giant Shadow*, and as in the Irish studies, these films show no awareness of possible moral ambiguities in this struggle. In *Exodus*, the guerrillas are fighting not just British authorities but also German ex-Nazis, who have inexplicably found themselves leading the Palestinian Arab forces.

From about 1968, though, news coverage of terrorist warfare around the globe made films about terrorism a much more sensitive issue. How, for instance, could one treat the activities of the IRA or (before its victory) the South African ANC? Both movements had substantial followings in the U.S., respectively among Irish-Americans and African-Americans, yet the prospect of depicting events like bombings as heroic was disturbing at a time when Americans were being targeted by other terrorist groups in many countries. While Irish violence did receive some coverage in U.S. films, the most important productions were located safely in the past, in films like *Michael Collins* (1996). When treating current topics, it was easier to address cases in which Irish patriots were quite falsely accused of terrorism by ruthless British police, as with *In the Name of the Father* (1993). Though dealing with a terrorist crisis, such films evade the problem of how to portray actual terrorists.

Portraits of modern-day Irish guerrillas have thus been rare. One exception was the 1997 film *The Devil's Own*, which does indeed depict an IRA militant on U.S. soil, but the characters are portrayed in tones far subtler than the conventional demonization of Arab villains. IRA man Frankie MacGuire is played heroically, by Brad Pitt, and the audience is meant to view him as, at worst, a flawed idealist—and a very good-looking one. Also, the IRA activity described in the film is clearly not terrorism, in the sense of attacks against civilians: MacGuire is trying to obtain Stinger missiles to shoot down British helicopters, that is, purely military targets. Adding to the ambiguities of the situation, the police hero of the film who has to fight the terrorists (and to save Frankie) is himself an Irish-American named Tom O'Meara, who views Frankie as a substitute son. In *Patriot Games*, an evil IRA man is combated by the staunchly Irish-American hero, Jack Ryan.

THE TERRORISTS WE DO NOT SEE

Within the United States itself, the coverage of domestic terrorist groups is still less systematic, and the choice of subjects seems almost random. A great many American films deal centrally with terrorist-related issues, including the activities of terrorist groups, and their effects on their victims, though these works are not usually seen as a free-standing genre. Often, civil rights struggles and racial conflicts have provided the material for filmmakers, and some of these works properly belong in any discussion of terrorism. Examples would include *Ghosts of Mississippi*, *Mississippi Burning* and Spike Lee's documentary *Four Little Girls*, none of which would commonly be thought of as studies of terrorism.

Other films touch on what we conventionally regard as terrorist groups and organizations, though the choice of subjects is capricious. Groups and events virtually absent from popular culture include the anti-Castro Cubans and the Puerto Rican independence movements, which we have already noted as highly active and often dangerous groups. With few exceptions, both are absent from the Hollywood view of terrorism. One rare treatment of Puerto Rican conflicts is the 1989 reality-based film *A Show of Force*, which describes the illegal killing of several militants by the island's police in 1978. The film follows a classic Watergate-era format, in which heroic journalists expose the crimes and cover-ups of repressive government and police agencies. The terrorists, in other words, appear solely as victimized dissidents, and the audience has no sense of the very extensive range of actions that Puerto Rican groups have carried out over the years.

This kind of depiction might lead us to believe that filmmakers are avoiding the Puerto Rican theme because of liberal political prejudices, and a reluctance to portray violence by leftist anti-imperialists, and this might be part of the story. Yet equally rare are depictions of anti-Castro Cubans, who stand on the political far right. The best-known appearance by such groups in recent film is in Oliver Stone's *JFK*, but otherwise, they scarcely feature. Chiefly, the media's reluctance reflected a desire to avoid offending domestic constituencies from those groups, provoking boycotts and controversy. But the result is that highly active groups like the FALN or *Macheteros* simply never existed in the American popular consciousness in anything like the same way as Black September or even the IRA.

Equally surprising is the lack of films portraying the radical anti-Vietnam war violence associated with names like the Weathermen. This is all the more curious when we think of the ethnic composition of the groups. While Hollywood might be tempted to dismiss Latino movements as of little interest to "mainstream" white audiences, the Weather Underground and other campus radicals were generally white and middle class. Yet these themes received strikingly little attention at the height of the movement, about 1970. Campus radicals received a little nervous attention, but Weathermen and bombers hardly at all. The 1970 film *The Revolutionary* depicts a college radical turned terrorist, but in a film stripped of any specifically contemporary or American context. Radical domestic bombers appear briefly in another 1970 film, *Fritz the Cat*, where they literally are cartoon characters. In *Zabriskie Point*, a terrorist act on campus features only incidentally in a phantasmagoric setting. While the 1975 documentary *Underground* offers serious political analysis of the Weather movement, the film received little commercial exposure.

In other films that did include radical characters, like Clint Eastwood's *The Enforcer* (1976), the terrorists are clichéd villains, with no convincing political motivation. The group's leader is appalled at the "power to the people" rhetoric of his followers, which in his view only gets in the way of his serious criminal goals. This approach fits with the conservatism of director Eastwood, who depicts the political establishment caving in to the demands of gangsters posing as guerrillas. A group loosely based on the Symbionese Liberation Army appears in the 1976 film *Network,* but their function in the work is largely comic, and symbolic. They are mostly meant to demonstrate the media's fabrication of reality for commercial purposes. (In one wonderful scene, the terrorists' lawyers demand the best possible deal for syndication and ancillary rights arising from the televising of any of their attacks that the network will show.) A similar focus on media misdeeds emerges from *The Lost Honor of Kathryn Beck* (1988), in which gutter journalists maliciously transform an innocent woman into a terrorist villain.

Black revolutionaries are even scarcer in the cinema, though *Network* depicted a racially mixed militant group. One rare attempt to examine the armed violence of the early 1970s was *Badge of the Assassin*, about the 1971 killing of police officers by B.L.A. militants: significantly, though, this film was not made until 1985, many years after the event. Not until 1995 did *Panther* portray the key black revolutionary group of the 1960s, and then in a highly idealized view, with the movement largely stripped of its violent and revolutionary implications. Even when treating a radical figure like Malcolm X, Spike Lee's film *X* concludes with an attempt to present a message of cooperation and reconciliation. Little remains to suggest the advocate of revolutionary warfare.

Equally romanticized in many ways was the media coverage of the armed Native American activists like AIM (American Indian Movement) who had seemed to pose a real threat of guerrilla warfare during the 1970s. AIM's clashes with the authorities culminated in the Wounded Knee siege of 1973, and a 1975 shootout that left two FBI agents dead (Matthiessen 1983). This latter incident has been the subject of two films, namely *Thunderheart* and the documentary *Incident at Oglala:* both present the story entirely from AIM's point of view, so that federal agents emerge as bullies and oppressors. *Thunderheart* adds a spurious justification for the 1975 violence, offering a fictitious subplot in which the FBI are scheming to mine uranium illegally on the Indian reservation. Both films depict the guerrillas heroically, and if any terrorists were involved in the conflicts, they are to be found in the ranks of the federal government. Like *Show of Force, Thunderheart* is basically a Watergate movie out of its time.

Two separate reasons help explain the neglect of America's domestic terrorist movements. First, extremism is a difficult product to market commercially. The domestic movements were often very controversial at the time, and the violent protest of the late 1960s was so divisive that fictional treatments would not have been commercially viable. Also, it is difficult to imagine how the characters could have been treated. If the radicals were portrayed as anything short of mad bombers, the films would probably have alienated mainstream audiences. On the other hand, if they were presented as crazy or evil, such a simplistic portrayal would have deterred many potential young adult viewers.

Second, portrayals of terrorist movements tend to alienate ethnic or political groups who might not sympathize with the actual violence, but who see themselves as part of the same ideological spectrum as the militants. Such considerations constrained the media in their response to violent Puerto Rican and Cuban activities in the United States. This approach may help explain the relative absence of leftist terrorists and Weathermen, and the favorable depiction of black and Native American guerrillas. Since Hollywood has a strong left-liberal slant, it is natural that filmmakers would tread very cautiously when dealing with individuals that are seen as broadly sympathetic in political terms. As we have seen, one of the rare treatments of a Weather-style activist group is Eastwood's *The Enforcer*, by a director noted for his political conservatism.

Liberal attitudes to these radical groups are better reflected by the film *Running on Empty* (1988), written by Naomi Foner. The story portrays two Weather-era activists who by the mid-1980s find themselves on the run with their young family, living clandestine lives. The militants themselves, Arthur and Annie, are meant to be highly sympathetic characters, parents of an idyllic middle class family: they are played by Judd Hirsch and Christine Lahti, and their son is heartthrob River Phoenix. Also the crimes for which they are on the run fall far short of deliberate terrorism. At the height of the Vietnam protest movement, they carried out a bombing that accidentally killed an innocent victim, and the film portrays their deep regret for this event. The larger radical network only features when mysterious figures appear to deliver messages and offer assistance. This portrait looks curious when we consider the very real terrorist operations of the Weather Underground, B.L.A., and other groups that continued through the early 1980s. To take an obvious example, we never see Hirsch or Lahti plotting a bank robbery or a jailbreak. The radicals are the real heroes, victims of their misguided quest for peace and justice, and the audience is meant to applaud their narrow escapes from the sinister FBI. In this rose-tinted view, the Weather Underground has merged imperceptibly into the Brady Bunch.

OTHER ABSENCES

Shifting media stereotypes of terrorists are conditioned by interest-group politics. The highly selective nature of terrorism depictions is illustrated by the very intense antiabortion violence that raged across much of the U.S. through the early 1990s, but which was virtually never portrayed in films or television movies. This may seem odd given the heavily female composition of the audience for such productions, but the media clearly felt that to portray even outrageous acts of violence in this area would be seen as an attack on mainstream pro-life supporters, who could respond with protests and boycotts. When antiabortion terrorism eventually appeared in television movies, as late as 1996, such a portrayal was still too daring for the networks with their sensitive advertisers. The films *If These Walls Could Talk* and *Critical Choices* were both broadcast on pay cable channels, respectively HBO and Showtime (James 1996).

Why did the antiabortion theme not attract the same media fascination as other forms of terrorism? Certainly it was not for lack of intrinsic interest and one can easily construct the sort of fictional themes that might have been employed. Imagine the obvious film that could have been made about a determined female investigator rooting out a network of fanatical clinic bombers and assassins. In so doing, she uncovers highly placed sympathizers for the terrorists within her own organization, perhaps among her superiors at the FBI or the Justice Department. One would have thought the subject overwhelmingly attractive, offering as it does the adaptation of familiar genres such as the antiterrorist film, the lone investigator, and the conspiracy story. The hypothetical film would present a superb opportunity for a strong female lead, and might have had enormous demographic appeal to younger women. Of course, there never was such a feminist *Mississippi Burning*, and the issue has been as absent from cinema screens as from TV movies.

The lack of attention is far more than a historical curiosity because the media serve such a critical role in constructing an issue for public consumption, and thereby in establishing both public and official priorities for responding to it. Some degree of interpretation is inevitable: if the media are to report on any question, they must attempt to give it some meaning, to place it in a frame of reference that will be familiar to the assumed audience. If however the abortion violence issue is simply absent—while other forms of terrorism receive intense attention—the message is clearly that this form of violence either does not exist or has no real significance. In turn, this lack ensures that there is no public pressure on elected and appointed officials, no cry for a "war on terror" in this particular form; and no rewards for the bureaucratic agencies that achieve success in such a struggle. Until the mid-1990s, the phenomenon remained unconstructed, and thus did not exist as a social problem.

ARABIAN NIGHTMARES

Political sensitivities were also evident in the portrayal of terrorist movements linked to particular ethnic groups. The whole issue of ethnic stereotyping in popular culture has been extraordinarily sensitive since the black civil rights movement of the 1960s. As social or ethnic groups grow in number and influence, they make their public presence felt by gaining the right to be free from offense by the media. Asian-Americans and Latinos both made it clear that the once-familiar stereotypes would no longer be tolerated, and newer communities have tried to send the same message.

Over the past quarter century, media stereotypes of Middle Easterners have changed radically, as fundamentally perhaps as black images changed from the era of Walt Disney to that of Denzel Washington (McAlister 2001; Said 1997). The image of the Arab terrorist was at its height in the late 1970s and 1980s, when numerous films portrayed American agents or soldiers avenging terrorist atrocities by massacring Arab commandos. Arabs emerge in this unsubtle form in the films about the Israeli commando mission at Entebbe, *Victory at Entebbe* (1976) and *Raid on Entebbe* (1977). In both films the Arabs are doubly tainted by their association with European terrorists, who are painted as Nazis and anti-Semites. *Black Sunday* (1977) portrays Arab Black September fanatics planning to use the Goodyear blimp to cause massive carnage at the Super Bowl. Any Arab character in a suspense film or thriller from this period was almost certain to be a terrorist, however sympathetically he or she is portrayed in the early part of the work: see for instance a film like Sigourney Weaver's *Half Moon Street* (1986). Depictions proliferated with the revival of international terrorism in the mid-1980s, which was the era of the savage Arab terrorists in films like *Delta Force*.

One crude portrayal occurred in the 1985 film *To Live and Die in LA*, which describes a struggle between U.S. Secret Service agents and criminal counterfeiters. Near the beginning of the film, though, the agents are on protective detail guarding a senior politician when they find that a suicide bomber is planning an imminent attack. When the agent confronts the would-be bomber on a hotel roof, the terrorist is clearly Arab in origin, and his speech fits every known cliché of Middle Eastern fanaticism. He declares, "I am a martyr! Death to America and all the enemies of Islam!" The presentation thus includes religious as well as ethnic stereotypes. (A Secret Serviceman ultimately pulls the terrorist off the roof so that his bomb explodes in mid-air, killing only himself.) This particular sequence is only tenuously linked to the main plot, and could easily have been omitted, suggesting that the filmmakers felt no qualms about angering any section of the audience. Similar themes emerge in the best-selling fiction of the 1980s, in which novels on Middle Eastern terrorists vary only in the degree of psychopathic evil attributed to the Arab or Islamic militants. These books can often be identified from their titles alone, by the use of words or names implying Arab fanaticism and violence—such as Jihad or Saladin.

During the 1980s and 1990s, as people of Middle Eastern origins became more numerous in the United States, they organized to combat damaging stereotypes, which above all meant the terrorist image. An early source of conflict was the 1994 Arnold Schwarzenegger film *True Lies,* though the comic book character of this film made it difficult to take too seriously. Still, the campaign made its impact, and served notice on Hollywood's highly liberal community that henceforward, Arab and Middle Eastern issues had to be treated as respectfully any other civil rights cause (Shaheen 2001).

Effective protest became vastly easier following the Oklahoma City debacle, and the sense that Arabs had been subjected to ethnic prejudice. When, in 1998, the film *The Siege* offered a (prescient) view of New York City under assault by Arab terrorists, the producers thought it politic to work closely with Arab-American and Muslim groups in order to minimize charges of stereotyping and negative portrayals. It was thought imperative to have a sympathetic Arab character among the heroic investigators. Moreover, the film itself reflects the liberal approaches to terrorism characteristic of the mid-1990s, since it focuses as much on the plight of ordinary Muslims caught up in a ferocious government repression as it does on the evil terrorists who launch the initial attacks. In this way, it is much like conspiracy films such as *Show of Force.* Nevertheless, Arab-American activists thought that any film depicting how "Arab terrorists methodically lay waste to Manhattan" was not only clearly fantastic in its own right, but also "reinforces historically damaging stereotypes." Hollywood had a public responsibility not to encourage such labeling, which had the potential to harm innocent Americans of Middle Eastern origins (Mandel 2001). Aiding this campaign was the issue of specifically anti-Muslim prejudice, since religious stereotyping arouses concerns even more acute than ethnic labeling. It is inconceivable that a sequence like that in *To Live and Die in LA* could have been released at any point after the mid-1990s. (One of the last films in this classic mode was Stephen Seagal's 1996 *Executive Decision.*)

One important media controversy of these years concerned the 1997 film *Path to Paradise,* which described the first World Trade Center attack and the blunders of the subsequent FBI investigation. The film ends with a moment that in retrospect is thoroughly chilling, as captured terrorist Ramzi Youssef looks at the twin towers and declares that "Next time, we will bring them both down." Though the film's prophetic quality could not have been known at the time, there was no doubt that it was a searching and generally accurate portrait of a historical event. Nevertheless, *Path to Paradise* was attacked by Arab-American groups as a vicious slander on Arabs and on

Islam. One pressure group complained, "Leaving behind all concerns for social responsibility, producers at HBO are preparing to air the made-for-stereotyping movie *Path to Paradise*. . . . This film and the image of Islam that it presents demands a full and vocal response from the American Muslim community and all those who share a love for religious tolerance. HBO, and all other film producers, must know that the public finds this kind of irresponsible film-making totally unacceptable" ("HBO Slanders Islam in *Path to Paradise*" 1997). The film was shown not on a commercial channel, but on HBO, which was less subject to pressure from advertisers.

IF NOT ARABS, WHO?

Filmmakers learned important lessons from the struggles over both *The Siege* and *Path to Paradise*. After Oklahoma City especially, it was vital to choose terrorist villains who would not attract the ire of active interest groups within the U.S. and by that point, that was a major challenge. One safe course was to choose groups with no obvious ideology or ethnic affiliation, generic "mad bombers" like in *Speed*, or the hijackers in *Passenger 57*. In the 1996 film *Independence Day*, we see scenes of mass destruction in New York and Washington that, in retrospect, uncomfortably foreshadowed September 11; but these fictional attacks were launched by aliens from another planet.

Some domestic villains conformed with the liberal stereotype that evil was likely to stem from authoritarian and military sources, perhaps from "rogue elements" in the CIA or other domestic intelligence agencies. This was a strong tradition in Hollywood that had reached a height during the years of political paranoia and conspiracy mania during the mid-1970s. If anything, evil spies and government agents had during those years surpassed Arabs as movie demon figures: we think of films like *The Parallax View*, *Executive Action*, *Three Days of the Condor*, *Killer Elite*, or *Winter Kills*. A similar repertory of villainous authority figures resurfaced in the terrorism thrillers of the 1990s. Rogue CIA officers are the villains in *Under Siege* (1992). In films like *The Rock* and *Broken Arrow* (both 1996), it is renegade U.S. generals and army officers who are seeking weapons of mass destruction. In the movie version of *The X Files* (1998) we witness the destruction of a federal office building in Dallas in scenes that recall the Oklahoma City disaster; but the culprits, insofar as the plot bothers to identify them, are faceless representatives of an amorphous conspiracy that manipulates the U.S. government.

One promising source of acceptable stereotyping was the far right, which had virtually no defenders in mainstream media, either liberal or conservative. Militias, skinheads and neo-Nazis became staple villains in

1980s films like *Talk Radio* and *Betrayed,* and much more frequently in the Clinton years, in productions like *American History X.* The same themes became obligatory in television series, where countless police and detective shows found themselves dealing with ultraright villains. Nazis, militias, and skinheads also featured in some widely seen documentary exposés, such as *Blood in the Face* (1990) and some specials on HBO's *America Under Cover* series (such as *Skinheads USA: Soldiers of the Race War*).

The high water mark of far right villainy in the cinema occurred in the 1999 film *Arlington Road,* which tells how a terrorism expert comes to suspect that his too-perfect neighbors are in fact the masterminds of a massive conspiracy. The film culminates in the destruction of the FBI headquarters in Washington D.C., on lines very similar to the description in *The Turner Diaries. Arlington Road* has impeccably liberal political credentials, in its depiction of a heroic government fighting monstrously evil antigovernment forces, which are clearly a pressing danger to democracy. As the leading character states, growing numbers of Americans are joining a far-right resistance: "How long are we going to call these numbers insignificant?" Despite this liberal bent, the film is strongly reminiscent of the highly conservative productions of the 1950s, the height of cold war paranoia, when Hollywood made a rash of conspiracy films warning of Communist subversion: most were so overblown that they are now regarded as camp classics. Allowing for the change of ideology, *Arlington Road* fits exactly into this mode. The audience is told that subversives can be anywhere, and even your pleasant next door neighbors might turn out to be deadly enemies of national security. As in the McCarthy era, the subversives specialize in seducing the young, in this instance through a network of pseudo-boy scouts called the Discoverers. And then as now, only the FBI could protect us from these fearsome outsiders. As the film's publicity warns, "Your paranoia is real!"

It was still more difficult to find noncontroversial foreign villains, given the increasing difficulties of depicting Arabs. Generically Latin American terrorists appeared in *Toy Soldiers* (1991), and Colombians in *Collateral Damage* (2002), but Latin themes were sensitive. One possible strategy was to use terrorist themes and images without linking the villains to a specific cause or ethnic identity—in other words, to depoliticize international terrorism just as earlier films had treated the domestic variety. This was in fact the course taken in the three *Die Hard* films released between 1988 and 1995, which use all the familiar images of terrorism—cosmopolitan villains, bombing, hostage-taking, and the destruction of airliners—but situated in a strictly nonpolitical context. In the first and third films, the apparent terrorists are in fact renegades from a militant political organization, and they are interested only in the profits from massive robberies. "Terrorist" mastermind Hans Gruber mocks the FBI's expectations about terrorist organizations by demanding the release of obscure Third World militants he has read about only in *Newsweek*. In *Die Hard II*, the terrorist operation is masterminded by characters closely modeled on the real-life Panamanian General Manuel Noriega, allied to sinister forces from the U.S. far right, and a renegade Army officer clearly based on Oliver North.

Another solution was to find foreign villains who commanded next to no sympathy within the United States. In *Air Force One*, the mayhem is caused by the servants of a dictator from somewhere within the former Soviet Union, who are furious with the United States for its human rights stands. In the 1997 film *The Peacemaker*, a plot to destroy New York City with nuclear weapons is directed by another Slav, a Serb, from a nation that had earned the unanimous condemnation of the U.S. media during the recent Balkan wars. A similar plot draws Yugoslavs to attack New York in the 2002 film *Bad Company*. Also in 2002, *The Sum of All Fears* used the theme of a nuclear threat but deliberately shied away from any Middle Eastern references. As critic Michael Medved remarks, "Its producers changed the identity of the nuclear terrorists specifically to avoid any imagery that might show Muslims in an unflattering light. In Tom Clancy's best-selling novel, on which this film is based, Palestinian fanatics lead an elaborate conspiracy; but the movie version's laughably caricatured Nazis, complete with accents and overacting reminiscent of *Hogan's Heroes*, take over the plot and make it look ridiculous" (Medved 2002).

This chapter has focused on issues of belief, of how claims and stories shift in a very short time from being highly credible, indeed social orthodoxy, to slipping into the realm of the absurd, the far-fetched, and the actively offensive. While this process partly depends on reactions to specific events, it also depends greatly on the interplay of interest groups, in government and the media. This observation applies not only to the definition of particular types of terrorism but also to the critical political issue of how individual groups relate to nation-states. In some periods, the concept of state sponsorship of terrorism is seen as highly credible, while in others it is implausible conspiracy theory. And attitudes change with remarkable speed.

9

Iraq and State Terrorism

> The hand of the revolution can reach out to its enemies wherever they are found.
>
> —Saddam Hussein

The notion of state sponsorship is a well-established part of the history of terrorism. At least since the 1880s, states have repeatedly given covert support to terrorist groups, which have served as their deployable agents overseas, pursuing tasks that the state could not achieve publicly. Some of the worst culprits included tsarist Russia in the early twentieth century, Nazi Germany and the Soviet Union in the 1930s. Prior to modern times, the state most deeply involved in this kind of activity was probably Fascist Italy, which during the 1920s and 1930s used terrorist surrogates to attack and destabilize rival nations across both central Europe and the Mediterranean world. Foreshadowing modern conditions, the Italian secret service OVRA operated through nationalist and separatist fronts, working closely with armed Croatian, Macedonian and Palestinian groups. These historical activities are well documented, and the reality of the state sponsorship phenomenon is beyond question. In modern times, states like Iran and Syria have made extensive use of such violent surrogates.

As we have seen, the sponsorship issue lay at the heart of the whole terror network theory of the 1980s. In this view, the U.S. and other Western powers had a right and a duty to retaliate against the states that sponsored terrorist attacks. Imagine that a terrorist group carries out an attack against American targets in Europe and claims the credit in the name of some group like Islamic Jihad. Many terrorism experts believe that often such acts are not the work of some free-standing terrorist organization, but should rather be linked to a particular country. If so, then trying to track down the particular group concerned is irrelevant. In order to deter future terrorism, we need to punish the state or nation that has sponsored the crime, either diplomatically or militarily. In extreme cases, such a counterstrike can involve a major air raid or even an invasion, which can detonate a full-scale war. It is not a prospect that any government views lightly.

During the mid-1980s, however, both the volume of international terrorism and the evidence for state sponsorship had become so intolerable that some countries began a policy of counterstrikes against sponsor states. The Israelis began the trend toward retaliation and deterrence, forced by the necessity of trying to defend a tiny state only minutes away from hostile neighbors, and their view became widely influential. In 1986, the U.S. ordered air strikes against Libya for its support of a bomb attack against American targets in Germany. In 1998, the Clinton administration launched missile attacks on Afghanistan and Sudan.

The belief in state sponsorship has been highly contentious, and not just for those reluctant to use military power outside the context of a declared war. The assignment of blame requires faith in the expert opinions of intelligence agencies and, sometimes, political activists, so that again, we face the critical issue of how do we know? Western governments may indeed know that a particular state has ordered a terrorist attack, perhaps through electronic surveillance, or else through spies in that nation's government. However, a great deal of recent evidence suggests that even if they possess this knowledge, they will not necessarily share it with the media, or with the wider public. Some obvious factors decide whether a given state will or will not be blamed for its terrorist connections. It might be too strong militarily, or else an attack on that country might be too dangerous in its potential of igniting a wider war. So why do authorities decide to focus on the terrorist activities of one nation rather than another? In the language of criminology, why should writers on terrorism choose to label one actor as deviant rather than another, if there is as much evidence easily available for the unlawful activities of both parties?

BANDIT STATES

From time to time, the U.S. and other governments issue lists of the states that are the leading sponsors of terrorism. During the 1980s, the main culprits usually involved three names, Libya, Iran and Syria, occasionally with the addition of others, such as the Sudan and North Korea; while more recently, Iraq has come to the fore. In the aftermath of the September 11 attacks, President Bush used a striking phrase to characterize the three major outlaw states of Iran, Iraq, and North Korea, which he described as an Axis of Evil. Suggesting the weighty policy implications of such labeling, it was around the same time that the main international bandits were listed among the nations that the U.S. was prepared to hit with nuclear weapons, if the need arose.

All such lists, though, can be criticized as much for what they omit as for what they include. These labels do not necessarily reflect the objective danger posed by a particular state. They are very much politically determined, and must be understood in terms of the relationship between diplomacy, national security, and media interests. Few would deny that the regime of Iraq is a ruthless dictatorship that brutally represses its own citizens, and has frequently employed terrorist tactics at home and abroad: it has long been a major source of international terrorism. Yet exactly the same could be said of nearly all the major powers in the region including Algeria, Iran, Libya, Syria, and Saudi Arabia. Of these five countries, the U.S. regards Saudi Arabia as perhaps its most important international ally, while at the time of writing, Iran and Syria are both treated as "on probation" as potential U.S. allies. Iraq and Libya are still viewed as bandits, and as always, Algeria is largely ignored. If historical experience is anything to go by, in five years' time, the assignation of status among this grouping—outlaws or allies—will be quite different, regardless of any change in their actual conduct.

Perhaps the most egregious gap between perception and reality involves Saudi Arabia, which has over the years fully realized the importance of good public relations in the U.S. media. Yet if one wished to portray a terrorist sponsor state, this nation would fit the bill quite well. Over the years, the Saudi regime has lavishly distributed its money to support Islamic causes, in the hope of persuading radical fundamentalists to divert their attentions elsewhere, instead of trying to confront the conservative monarchies of the Gulf (Adams 1986, Miller 1996). The regime had a particular shock in 1979, when fundamentalists overthrew the monarchy in Iran, and activists tried to repeat this feat in Saudi Arabia itself. Ever since that date, Saudi largesse has funded countless radical causes. Palestinian guerrilla movements would have had nothing like the success they have enjoyed had it not been for Saudi support from the 1960s onward. Since the 1980s, the Saudis have been the major sponsors of the shift to Islamist terrorism and suicide bombing campaigns against Israel. The Saudis were the chief sponsors of the nightmarish Taliban regime in Afghanistan, which provided the critical base for al-Qaeda. The regime's other supporter through the 1990s was Pakistan, which was also, ostensibly, another key U.S. ally (Kux 2001). Much of the recent Muslim-Christian bloodshed in West Africa is a direct consequence of Saudi pressure on local Muslim officials to impose Islamic law in their territories, a policy that is generously funded by Saudi authorities. Against this background, the condemnations poured upon such relatively minor players as Sudan look disproportionate.

In this chapter, I will explore the concept of state sponsorship as it applies to one country, namely Iraq, which at least since the 1970s has been deeply involved in the support of international terrorism. Despite this, it has only sporadically been recognized as a terrorist sponsor by the U.S. and its allies. Since about 1980, U.S. attitudes toward Iraqi terrorism have varied enormously, not in response to actual changes in Iraqi behavior, but rather reflecting shifts in Western interests and policies. The changes can be summarized as follows:

Late 1970s	Iraq listed by the U.S. government as a terrorist sponsor
1982–1990	US ceases to refer to Iraq as a terrorist sponsor state
1990–1991	Iraq cited as most dangerous and active supporter of global terrorism
1991–2001	Intense internal debates within U.S. administrations over Iraqi connection to terrorism
2001–present	Debates within U.S. government and intelligence community over possible Iraqi connections to September 11 attacks

The fluctuations in attitudes toward Iraq have been incredibly wide, and over very short periods. To use an analogy from conventional crime, it is almost as if police in one year identified a man as a serial killer suspect, then stated for some years that he was an upstanding citizen, and then later declared that he was probably a Mafia overlord. In 1988, say, Iraq was cited in the terrorism literature chiefly as an innocent victim. By late 1990, though, there was widespread panic about the allegedly vast terrorist network gathered around Saddam Hussein, and fear that this weapon would soon be turned against the U.S. and its allies. The lack of comment on Iraqi activities in the 1980s is almost as amazing as the sharp focus of 1990 and 1991. Also, during the peak of concern during this period, the media systematically rewrote recent history to suggest not only that Iraq was a terrorist sponsor, but also that everyone had always known this fact. At the time of writing, these debates are of renewed importance because of widespread charges, presently unsubstantiated, that Iraq was directly implicated in the attacks of September 11. If these charges proved true—or if they were widely believed—the result would likely be a war in the Middle East, an event with enormous implications for global politics.

Based on this example, we have to ask whether the labeling of a particular country as a terrorist state reflects its true activities, or merely suits the political convenience of those nations with the power to undertake such labeling, with all their diplomatic authority, and their vast media establishments. Like so much in terrorism, state sponsorship is very much a socially constructed phenomenon. In describing the changing construction of Iraqi-linked terrorism, we will observe all the major themes that have emerged in this study so far: the extensive use of deception and false flags;

the selective and politicized nature of terrorist investigation; and the reluctance of the mass media to challenge officially-sanctioned interpretations.

THE POLITICS OF OIL

In the Middle Eastern context, the process of labeling a group or nation as terrorist has everything to do with economics and politics, and specifically the politics of oil. Though these connections are too complex to be described in detail here, some general points need to be made.

It is oil that gives the Middle East its importance, and which shapes the political outlook of the U.S. and Europe. Of the world's fifteen largest producers today, five are Arab (Saudi Arabia, Kuwait, Iraq, the United Arab Emirates, and Libya) and two more (Iran and Indonesia) are non-Arab Muslim states. The most important oil-producing region is the Arabian peninsula, together with the regions of Iran and Iraq located north of it. This Gulf region is critical in the long term future, since it has very deep reserves of easily producible oil that will still be flowing when other regions have run dry. Of the twenty largest known oil fields in the world, the "elephants," Saudi Arabia, Iran, and the Gulf states account for fourteen, including what are far and away the biggest two fields on the planet, Ghawar (Saudi Arabia) and Burgan (Kuwait) (Table 9: 1). The reserves of Ghawar alone are six times greater than the likely production of the largest U.S. field, Alaska's Prudhoe Bay. Any nation that hopes still to be importing oil in the 2030s will have to have good relations with the countries bordering the Arab Gulf.

The extent of global dependence on oil was suggested by the catastrophic shock caused by the massive price rises of the early 1970s, orchestrated by Middle Eastern suppliers. The U.S. itself is nothing like as dependent on this region's oil as it once was, since it presently draws much of its supplies from Western Hemisphere nations. However, Europe still relies heavily on the Middle East, which goes far towards explaining the much more pro-Arab slant of European politics. An oil cutback anywhere in the world would ultimately put pressure on the U.S., and perhaps cause a global depression. Moreover, the U.S. needs to consider its long term supplies, and has to preserve a good working relationship with that region.

Both for present and future needs, it is vital for any U.S. government to consider the control of the Arab gulf, and especially the wealthy but militarily weak Arab nations, like Saudi Arabia, Kuwait, and the United Arab Emirates (U.A.E.). During the 1980s, Iran seemed to be the major threat to this region, and accordingly the U.S. supported Iraq in its war against that nation. American forces offered material aid to Iraq, and political support continued even after it was clear that the Iraqis were using chemical

Table 9.1 The World's Largest Oil Fields

Field	Country	*Size Estimate* (billion barrels)
1. Ghawar	Saudi Arabia	75–83
2. Burgan	Kuwait	66–72
3. Bolivar Coastal	Venezuela	30–32
4. Safaniya-Khafji	Saudi Arabia/Neutral Zone	30
5. Rumaila	Iraq	20
6. Tengiz	Kazakhstan	15–26
7. Ahwaz	Iran	17
8. Kirkuk	Iraq	16
9. Marun	Iran	16
10. Gachsaran	Iran	15
11. Aghajari	Iran	14
12. Samotlor	West Siberia, Russia	14–16
13. Abqaiq	Saudi Arabia	12
14. Romashkino	Volga-Ural, Russia	12–14
15. Chicontepec	Mexico	12
16. Berri	Saudi Arabia	12
17. Zakum	Abu Dhabi, U.A.E.	12
18. Manifa	Saudi Arabia	11
19. Faroozan-Marjan	Saudi Arabia/Iran	10
20. Marlim, Campos	Brazil	10–14

Adapted from: "Some interesting oil industry statistics," http://www.gravmag.com/oil.html

weapons against their enemies. (For the regional background of this struggle, see Hiro 1991, 2001; Pelletiere 1992; Tarock 1998.) In 1990, though, Iraq seized the nation of Kuwait and threatened the Gulf, raising the prospect that Iraq would dominate the world's largest oil fields. At this stage, the West found it essential to defeat and contain Iraq. During the 1990s, meanwhile, the continued economic power of Saudi Arabia both shaped and constrained possible U.S. responses to Iraqi behavior. While on several occasions, the U.S. might well have wished to intervene militarily against Iraq, any such effort faced massive Saudi opposition. A Western attack might well provoke Arab nationalist and Muslim sentiment across the region, endangering the stability of the oil states. At every stage, therefore, U.S. action against terrorism—and the application of the terrorist label—was ultimately shaped by economic needs.

A TERRORIST REGIME

With this background in mind, we can examine the specific case of Iraq. The nation has been governed since 1968 by the Arab *Ba'ath* (Renaissance)

Socialist Party, ABSP, in which Saddam Hussein has long been the most powerful member. (The following account is based on CARDRI 1986; al-Khalil 1990; Miller and Mylroie 1990; Sciolino 1991; Karsh and Rautsi 1991; Darwish and Alexander 1991; Mackey 2002.) However, it is only since 1979 that his rule became overt and publicly known. The ABSP is a classic totalitarian party modeled on European fascist and Nazi parties of the 1930s, and has exercised its rule through a vast apparatus of army, police, party militia and secret services. The latter include the *Estikhbarat* (military intelligence) and *Mukhabarat* (party intelligence). All major institutions are in the hands not merely of the party, but of the narrow family clique close to Hussein, the al-Takritis.

The *Ba'ath* regime has stayed in power because it has systematically removed all political rivals. Through intimidation and political repression, the regime killed or subdued any potential competitors within Iraq itself, including Communists and Islamic militants. Foreign exiles were dealt with by assassination or kidnapping, carried out by agents or representatives of the Iraqi state. Saddam himself was no stranger to these methods, since he had personal experience as an assassin for the *Ba'ath* party in the 1950s (al-Khalil 1990, 14). Many of these killings were the work of the military intelligence agency, the *Estikhbarat*.

Iraqi state terrorism was not however confined to such exalted figures. There were several assassinations or attempts against dissidents and exiles in Lebanon and France; and even in the United States. Iraqi death squads have been blamed for the murders of a journalist in Detroit and three other killings in the Detroit area between 1977 and 1980 (al-Khalil 1990, 12–16). In 1990, FBI wiretaps on the Iraqi mission to the United Nations found evidence of assassination plots within the United States (Emerson and Del Sesto 1991, 208–209). Anti-*Ba'ath*, Assyrian and Kurdish activists have been the chief targets. An Iraqi activist was also implicated in bombing attempts against Israeli-linked banks in New York city in 1973 ("Iraqi wanted in U.S. for eighteen years is seized"). Iraqi death squads were active in foreign countries, including Great Britain. At least since the 1970s, Iraq has a massive record of international terrorism, which was well known to the U.S. government and other Western countries.

ABU NIDAL 1973–1986

Such actions have rarely been carried out overtly with a public claim of responsibility by the Iraqi state or intelligence. Usually, they have been undertaken anonymously, sometimes through false front groups, acting under a variety of guises and pseudonyms (Jenkins 1988a). One of these, at least—Abu Nidal—became synonymous with international terrorism and extremism in the 1970s and 1980s. At the time, this name was as notorious as Osama bin Laden would be in later years (Melman 1987; Miller 1987; Seale 1992). It seems though that the whole Abu Nidal phenomenon was very much an Iraqi creation, a way of deflecting blame for violence and terrorism.

The Abu Nidal movement began as one radical offshoot of the Palestinian guerrilla movements that proliferated in the decade after 1967. At first, most of these groups were independent of direct control from any one Arab country, though they received money and support from several governments. Some states, however, established Palestinian groups as wholly-owned subsidiaries or front organizations. From 1973, Iraq developed what would become their most notorious front group, which was led by the PLO representative in Baghdad, Sabri al-Banna. Under the name Abu Nidal, he now formed the dissident terrorist group that would become so notorious.

Acting through the Abu Nidal group, the Iraqis launched a global wave of terrorist attacks, some aimed against Western and Israeli targets, but many directed against rivals in the Arab world. Major targets included Arab political forces, above all the Palestine Liberation Organization, and nations such as Syria, Saudi Arabia, and the Gulf states. To understand the Abu Nidal group and its counterparts, we have to see it chiefly as a factor in inter-Arab politics, and as a surrogate for the Iraqi state and the *Estikhbarat*. (Abu Nidal would die in Baghdad in 2002, in mysterious circumstances: Whitaker 2002; Ledeen 2002b; Rubinstein and Melman 2002.)

This clandestine terrorist war escalated during the 1980s when Iraq became engaged in a long and bloody war with Iran, and Saddam Hussein repeatedly used his terrorist allies against his enemies. Sometimes, these operations had as much in common with criminal extortion as with politically motivated terrorism. Through the war years, the Iraqis stressed that they were defending the Arab oil states, and should accordingly be paid for their efforts by the governments of Saudi Arabia and the Gulf. However, there were frequent disputes about the amount and promptness of payments, and the issue of whether the money involved was a loan or an outright gift. Interestingly, in 1982, "Abu Nidal" attacks began to occur in the Gulf, and against international targets associated with wealthy Gulf states like Abu Dhabi, the United Arab Emirates, and Kuwait itself (Melman 1987). In 1983, an airliner of the U.A.E.'s Gulf Air was blown up, with 120 fatalities; and several Kuwaiti and U.A.E. diplomats were targeted. It looks as if these acts were forms of pressure on those governments to meet their obligations to the Iraqi state.

At the same time, other Iraqi-sponsored groups escalated their clandestine war against the West, in an attempt to prove Saddam's credentials as a leader of anti-Israel resistance. These acts included attempts to blow up a Pan Am airliner over Honolulu in 1982, a similar attack on a TWA aircraft over the Mediterranean in 1986, and numerous aborted strikes at airliners and hotels. This time, the attacks were connected not with Abu Nidal, but with another Palestinian terrorist called Abu Ibrahim, who ran an international network skilled in the techniques of destroying aircraft. Some of Abu Ibrahim's followers and pupils would later join the ranks of al-Qaeda.

THE DECADE OF SILENCE 1980–1990

But if Iraqi activities were so wide-ranging and egregious, it remains mysterious why Iraq is so resoundingly absent from virtually all the accounts of terrorism written during the 1980s. This may appear a sweeping statement, but Iraq is scarcely mentioned even in most books that attempt to delineate an international terror network. All the attention is directed at the unholy trinity of Syria, Iran, and Libya, behind which were believed to stand the Communist bogeymen of the USSR, Bulgaria, and East Germany. Even Claire Sterling's 1981 book *Terror Network,* which describes all these familiar villains, has next to nothing to say about Iraqi activity. Sterling seems to accept Saddam's claims to have renounced his ties to terror no later than about 1980 (Sterling 1981, 264). Another sweeping denunciation of the global terror network appeared in 1986 from a group of international experts who portrayed the *Hydra of Carnage*. These find space for only one incidental reference to Iraq, but again not as a perpetrator of terrorism (Ra'anan 1986, 269). Even when Iraq was sponsoring some of the bloodiest acts of violence, it remained invisible in the books and television documentaries available to the Western public.

Most of these books cite Iraq, if at all, as a victim rather than a perpetrator of international terrorism. Sterling for example discusses the illegal Communist party of Iraq as part of the international network, which was preparing to attack the Saddam Hussein regime (Sterling 1981, 52). Taheri's account of Islamic terrorism includes several references to the victimization of Iraq by international networks such as Hizbullah (Taheri 1987, 121–122, 161–164). Dobson and Payne (1986) list some attacks by Abu Nidal and Iraqi secret service groups, but also focus on the "victim" theme, describing Islamic militant groups active against Saddam Hussein (Dobson and Payne 1986, 227). This is not to suggest that Iraqi involvement in terrorism remained unknown to the media and the public (Melman 1987; Pluchinsky 1982). Even the *New York Times,* which would remain so firm an advocate of the crimes of Syria, Iran, and Libya, published in 1986 a detailed account of Iraq's Abu Ibrahim network, which it linked to bomb attacks in western Europe (Miller 1986). The story was remarkable because it depicted a situation at odds with the normal stereotypes of international villainy; and yet its implications went largely unexplored.

Given the availability of so much information, why did Iraq appear so relatively "clean" throughout the decade? The specific decision to remove Iraq from the list of sponsor states was made in 1982, and must be understood in terms of diplomatic exigencies. There was at the time an overwhelming fear that the war Saddam provoked in 1980 would go disastrously wrong, and result in radical Iranian Islam sweeping first across southern Iraq, and then into the Shi'ite areas of the Gulf, especially Kuwait. The danger to Gulf oil was therefore seen as stemming from Iran, and the need to aid and bolster Iraq governed much U.S. and Western policy until 1988. In order to supply arms and intelligence, the removal of Iraq's terrorist status was a prime necessity to circumvent Congressional restrictions.

What is more surprising is the apparent media consensus that followed this decision, which accepted Saddam's apparent retirement from terrorism. Obviously, no simple conspiracy or coverup can be suggested here, since so much damning material on Iraq continued to be available (Melman 1987; Seale 1992). Still, the vast bulk of evidence emerging from official and intelligence sources, Western or Israeli, had as a prime goal the denunciation of Syria, Iran, and Libya, while Iraqi activities were underplayed. Official, media and fictional accounts combined to create a self-sustaining myth of three, and only three, members of the "terror cartel," the prototype of today's Axis of Evil.

KUWAIT AND AFTERWARDS

Conversely, when Iraq became a prime enemy after the Kuwait invasion, the abundant evidence of Iraqi terrorism was made available to such an extent that the Ba'athists now appeared virtually the only significant lords of terror. In constructing Saddam as a major enemy in the months leading up to the 1991 war, it became as necessary to magnify his past activities as systematically as they had been played down in previous years. By late 1990, there was widespread panic about the allegedly vast terrorist network gathered around Saddam Hussein, and fear that this weapon would soon be turned against the USA and its allies ("Iraq's terrorist allies" 1990; Hoffman 1990; Johnston 1991; Seger 1991; Wines 1991; Bulloch and Morris 1991). It was widely noted that Saddam Hussein had a long track record in using terror as a political device. There even began a kind of retroactive demonization, attributing to Iraq guilt for earlier incidents that had hitherto been associated with other nations or culprits like Syria and Iran.

The new view of Iraq is epitomized by a book published in 1991 by Steven Emerson and Cristina del Sesto, under the title *Terrorist: the Inside Story of the Highest Ranking Iraqi Terrorist Ever to Defect to the West.* The book describes the career of Adnan Awad, who became associated with Palestinian terrorist cells based in Baghdad, and later with the Abu Ibrahim network. The authors also present abundant evidence of Iraqi links with other militants, including the group that undertook the *Achille Lauro* hijacking of 1985.

For the authors of *Terrorist*, Iraq's alliance with terrorism is obvious. In 1990, they claim, Baghdad was the scene of a "terrorist summit" that involved some weighty names from the Palestinian guerrilla groups, including groups normally thought to be connected with Syria and other nations. Those present included Abu Abbas, George Habash, Nayef Hawatmeh, Samir Gousha, Salim Abu Salem, and Abu Ibrahim, "men responsible for the death of thousands of people in bloody attacks over the previous twenty-five years" (Emerson and del Sesto 1991, 213). The authors also charge that Iraq's terrorist sponsorship went far beyond the Arab world, involving as it did ties to the IRA, the Basque ETA, the German Red Army Fraction, the Japanese Red Army, and Italian Red Brigades (211–213). Iraqis supposedly worked for and with the East German state security apparatus, the *Stasi*. Even the legendary "Carlos" was brought into this picture of "the Iraqi Terror Network." As Bruce Hoffman (1990) wrote, Saddam mobilized an "ultimate fifth column."

For about two years, the whole terror network rhetoric was brought to bear on this one country, to the exclusion of all others; not only were there no other candidates for the role of Terror Overlord, but it suddenly seemed that there never had been.

THE IRAQI CONNECTION 1991–2001

In 1991, the U.S. had led a broadly based coalition against Iraq to end that nation's occupation of Kuwait. However, the U.S. had at that point refrained from a decisive military action that would end the Saddam Hussein regime. Subsequent U.S. administrations came to regret that decision, and there were repeated calls for a new invasion. Others opposed this idea just as strenuously, because they thought a new war would poison U.S. relations with Arab nations like Saudi Arabia, and would moreover cause chaos in oil markets. This policy split profoundly affected views of terrorism worldwide, and specifically in the United States (Freedman and Karsh 1995).

It is only in this context that we can understand official and media reactions to two of the most notorious crimes in American history, the first attack on the World Trade Center in 1993, and the events of September 11. In both cases, strong evidence pointed to an Iraqi role; yet on both occasions, government and law enforcement devoted a great deal of effort to discouraging such speculations. Whatever the real story of these incidents (and that may be unknowable) it looks as if the investigations were shaped by political and diplomatic factors, rather than by any objective quest for truth.

The first attack on the WTC occurred on February 26, 1993, a significant date since it marked the second anniversary of the height of the U.S.-led ground war against Iraq, in Operation Desert Storm. This timing would be appropriate if indeed the attack was intended as a form of revenge against the U.S. That interpretation would fit well with other actions undertaken around that same time, especially the April 1993 plot to assassinate former President George Bush on a visit to Kuwait. Bush was regarded as a special enemy of Iraq because he had led the international coalition during the 1991 war. In the Kuwait case, there is no doubt that the plot was organized and directed by Iraqi intelligence, and President Clinton retaliated by launching a missile strike against the headquarters of that agency. To put these other events in context, the attempted plot in Kuwait would have occurred just six weeks after the actual bombing in New York City.

Moreover, it has been widely reported that the man chiefly responsible for organizing the WTC attack, Ramzi Youssef, was an agent of Iraq's *Mukhabarat*. Telephone records suggest that Ramzi remained in contact with Iraqi authorities throughout the months that the WTC plot was being developed. In addition, the man who made the actual bomb, Abdul Yasin, was an Iraqi who subsequently escaped to that nation. Terrorism expert Laurie Mylroie (2001) has argued that "there is considerable evidence that the Trade Center bombing was a case of Iraqi intelligence directing a major terrorist operation and leaving behind a few minor figures to be arrested and take the blame" (compare Dwyer 1995; Reeve 2001; Katz 2002). In that case, Ramzi and Yasin would have been working directly for the *Ba'ath* party, and specifically for members of Saddam's family, the al-Takritis.

Ramzi Youssef escaped the investigators of the first WTC attack, but he was in the news again in 1995 when he developed a plot for the simultaneous mass bombings of eleven or twelve U.S. jumbo jets over the Pacific (the *Bojinka* scheme). Under interrogation, Ramzi's deputy also reported that the group was planning to hijack a commercial airliner and crash it into CIA headquarters in Langley, Virginia (Wallace 1995; Brzezinski 2001; "U.S. warned in 1995," 2001). Though Ramzi was arrested, his career indicates that at least by 1995, a group with probable Iraqi connections was plotting attacks that involved the WTC, a simultaneous attack against airliners, and the use of airliners as guided missiles on American soil. Presumably, some of his friends and allies used Ramzi's scheme as the foundation for what actually occurred on September 11, 2001. U.S. authorities have now named one of Ramzi's relatives as the likely mastermind of the first WTC attack (Risen 2002b).

At least by 1993, there was evidence that Iraq was involved in planning serious terrorist attacks against the United States. Even so, U.S. law enforcement did not investigate these foreign linkages in detail, and the U.S. media were discouraged from pursuing these connections. The political reasons for such an approach were very strong. The Clinton administration had taken office only a month before the first WTC attack, and was expecting to be involved in major domestic policy controversies, such as health care and gay rights. Internationally, the "big issues" in the president's first term were planned to be "Russia, Eastern Bloc, Middle East peace, human rights, rogue nations, and then terrorism" (Miller et al. 2001). The last thing the new president wanted was a war that could disrupt his administration, and blight economic recovery. The administration was justifiably worried about a backlash against people of Middle Eastern descent within the U.S., which would be all the more dangerous if the plot was seen as part of a major network on U.S. soil.

The government therefore stressed that the 1993 WTC attack was the work of "a few stupid people" without any ties to organized terrorism, still less to any outside nation or intelligence service. The FBI's National Security Division attributed the attack to International Radical Terrorism, or IRT, that is to anonymous transnational terrorists unconnected to any single nation. This notion was closely related to the "leaderless resistance" theory then gaining popularity within the U.S. far right, an idea that fascinated investigators. While not exactly a lone nut designation, this concept came close, since it provided an excellent means of limiting the possible reaches of a conspiracy. Investigators who wanted to pursue an Iraqi connection—like leading FBI agent Jim Fox, and the Bureau's New York office—were prevented from doing so (Mylroie 2000, 2001).

ANTHRAX

The 1993 WTC investigation indicates the enormous political stakes at risk in any terrorist attack that might possess an international dimension. This is not necessarily to say that federal law enforcement agencies knew about an Iraqi dimension and concealed it. Rather, it means that certain directions in the investigation were pursued enthusiastically, while others were discouraged.

Very much the same pattern can be observed in the second and far larger WTC attack in 2001, when once again, potent evidence seemed to link the crimes to other states or intelligence agencies, and specifically Iraq. For present purposes, it does not matter whether these leads were in fact correct, or if the Iraqis had anything to do with the crimes. The point is that the investigators chose to stress certain angles rather than others, and that the media faithfully reflected these changing official approaches.

This selective pattern of investigation can be observed from the controversies surrounding two of the critical events in the recent story, namely the response to the anthrax attacks in late 2001; and the charge that accused hijacker Mohammed Atta had met with Iraqi intelligence agents.

While the United States was still reeling from the attacks of September 11, officials soon had to deal with another nightmare apparently linked to terrorism, namely the use of anthrax against targets representing government and media. Anthrax-laden letters were dispatched only days after September 11, though not until early October did evidence of the attacks come to light. The first signs of this new menace came in Florida, when anthrax was detected at a newspaper office, and shortly afterwards, lethal spores were found in letters addressed to Congressional leaders like Senators Tom Daschle and Patrick J. Leahy. (The letters were postmarked from New Jersey, which now became the center of investigations.) Prominent media figures like news anchor Tom Brokaw were also targeted, as was the *New York Post*. Several people, including post office workers, died through contact with the letters, or through cross-contamination. Not surprisingly, these widely publicized attacks spawned much fear, and many false reports began to appear. Only at the end of November did public fears begin to subside (see table 9.2).

At the time of writing, authorities have no clear suspect in the sending of the anthrax letters. We do not know whether the attack was the work of a group or an individual, or if the biological warfare campaign had its roots within the United States or in some other country. Technically, we do not even know if the crimes can properly be described as terrorism. If the anthrax was dispatched by one lone person who was mentally deranged or who had some kind of personal grudge, then the mailings would lack the political motive essential to qualify as terrorism. For present purposes, though, the actual culprit is less important than the different theories advanced as the investigation proceeded.

At first glance, the anthrax campaign seemed overwhelmingly likely to be associated with Middle Eastern terrorism, and with the groups involved with the September 11 attacks. The chronology alone suggested that a campaign had been prepared before that grim date, and that militants were only waiting for the opportunity to launch a coordinated assault. The first anthrax letter was mailed only a week after the fall of the WTC. Observers were struck by the handwriting on the envelopes used to deliver the anthrax spores, since it slanted in a way that is very common for people who originally learned to write in a language that flows from right to left—such as Arabic.

We also know that the al-Qaeda leadership was interested in using biological or chemical weapons. If anthrax was to be used, then several likely sources come to mind, but by far the most likely would be the government

Table 9.2 Chronology of Anthrax Investigation in U.S., 2001–2002

	2001
June	Ahmed al-Haznawi and Ziad al-Jarrah report to Fort Lauderdale hospital: al-Haznawi complains of symptoms later identified as possible cutaneous anthrax
September 18	First anthrax-laden letter mailed in Trenton, New Jersey
September 30	News media report that planned U.S. attack on Afghanistan is delayed due to objections by U.S. allies in Middle East
October 5:	Photo editor at *National Enquirer* in Florida dies of inhalation anthrax
October 7	Beginning of U.S./British attack on Afghanistan
October 9	Second anthrax letter mailed
October 12	NBC assistant to Tom Brokaw gets cutaneous anthrax from letter
October 15	Anthrax confirmed on letter sent to Sen. Tom Daschle
October 21–23	Two Washington, D.C. postal workers die of inhalation anthrax
October 31	New York woman dies of inhalation anthrax
November 2	FBI Director Mueller says FBI has no idea who is launching the attacks
November 9	FBI profile describes anthrax attacker as an American "loner"
November 16	Anthrax letter to Sen. Patrick Leahy found
November 21	Elderly Connecticut woman dies of inhalation anthrax
	2002
January	FBI approaches members of American Society for Microbiology for assistance in locating American rogue scientist who might have been involved in attacks
June	FBI searches homes of Stephen Hatfill and other American scientists with possible backgrounds in anthrax and biological warfare
August	FBI suggests that Stephen Hatfill is their principal suspect in the anthrax investigation.

Adapted from Albert R. Hunt, "Anthrax: A Botched Investigation?" *Wall Street Journal*, May 9, 2002.

of Iraq, which had had a vigorous biological warfare program since the 1980s. Through the 1990s, the regime played a cat-and-mouse game to try and conceal its weapons development policies from United Nations inspectors, and devoted the most attention to concealing those programs on which it placed most importance (Hamzah and Stein 2000; Miller et al. 2001). Above all, this meant its fledgling nuclear program, and its attempt to deploy anthrax as a military weapon. "Prior to the Gulf War, according to the Iraqi government, Baghdad produced 8,400 liters of anthrax, 19,000 liters of botulinum and 2,000 liters each of aflatoxin and clostridium. A single gram of anthrax—roughly 1/30 oz.—contains 1 trillion spores, or enough for 100 million fatal doses if properly dispersed" (Tyrangiel 2002). In 1999, a U.S. government report on terrorist dangers warned that "If Iran's mullahs or Iraq's Saddam Hussein decide to use terrorists to attack the continental United States, they would likely turn to bin Laden's al Qaeda. Al Qaeda is among the Islamic groups recruiting increasingly skilled professionals [including] Iraqi chemical weapons experts and others capable of helping to develop [Weapons of Mass Destruction]" ("Early Warnings" 2002).

Evidence for some kind of governmental link grew as the months went on (This account is based on Rose and Vulliamy 2001; Hunt 2002; Broad and Johnston 2002a-b). As U.S. investigators looked at the anthrax used in the attacks, they were ever more impressed with the high degree of sophistication needed to produce such high grade weaponized material, which would have required work in a major laboratory, probably belonging to a government facility. It was far more complex than could have been obtained by amateur biochemists. This reduced the likely sources for the anthrax to labs in the United States, the former Soviet Union—or Iraq.

Tending to confirm that the U.S. anthrax had a Middle Eastern origin, on several occasions, investigators noted suggestive linkages with the individuals involved in the hijacking (Broad and Johnston 2002a). This included the strange outbreaks of anthrax in south Florida, which did not involve what most people would consider significant diplomatic or military targets. One of the first occurrences was at the Boca Raton offices of American Media Inc., publisher of tabloid newspapers such as *The Sun, National Enquirer*, and *Weekly World News*: the offices were found to be thoroughly contaminated with anthrax. One anthrax fatality was a middle-aged photo editor who lived in the town of Lantana. The geographical setting is interesting, because we know that during August 2001, hijacker Mohammed Atta had rented planes at a flight school near Palm Beach County Park Airport, just one mile from the editor's home (Atta was probably the pilot who flew the first airliner into the WTC.) Several other hijackers lived in an apartment complex just ten miles away. It was while living in this area that Atta had been exploring the possibility of obtaining crop-duster aircraft, presumably with a view to attacking U.S. population centers with chemical or biological weapons. And the coincidences kept mounting: a real-estate agent who worked (quite innocently) with two of the hijackers was married to the publisher of the tabloid newspaper involved. One terrorism expert has suggested that the seemingly random target of American Media was chosen as a kind of dry run for later attacks: "This most likely was an experiment to see if some of the stuff was high quality and potentially lethal anthrax." Also, the terrorists may have been practicing the best means of infecting a major office building, as a precursor to hitting a major political target, like the Capitol. If the Florida cases were not connected in some way to the hijackers, then the degree of coincidence becomes astonishing (Hunt 2002).

A still more convincing linkage came to light when a Florida doctor reported that in June 2001, he had examined Ahmed al-Haznawi, who then lived near Boca Raton (Broad and Johnston. 2002a). Al-Haznawi was complaining of a puzzling dark lesion on his leg. In retrospect, the doctor concluded that the most likely explanation of the man's symptoms was cutaneous anthrax, and this diagnosis has been supported by other medical experts. (Al-Haznawi was accompanied to the hospital by Ziad al-Jarrah: the two men would perish together on United flight 93.) This story was reinforced by the evidence of a pharmacist who reported examining mysterious burns on the hands of Mohammed Atta, injuries that again seemed to be anthrax-related. If the hijackers were operating in an environment in which anthrax was being used or distributed, it makes it immensely more likely that their friends or allies were responsible for the later attacks.

Despite these suspicious connections, investigators were reluctant to draw any direct connection with the hijackings or with al-Qaeda, or even with the Middle East. Initially, this might appear to be an example of cautious restraint, a refusal to make ungrounded charges, and there were particular reasons to doubt the obvious linkage between the presumed users of anthrax—al-Qaeda—and the likely suppliers, in Iraq. Osama bin Laden had in the early 1990s been a deadly enemy of Saddam Hussein, who represented a much more secular kind of radicalism than his own, and Osama had condemned the Iraqi invasion of Kuwait. Many observers felt that Osama-linked terrorists would not have worked together with the old enemy. Others felt that the hostility might have been overcome by a common hatred for the U.S. and Israel. A number of writers have claimed to trace specific connections and tactical alliances between Iraq and al-Qaeda from at least the mid-1990s, so perhaps the spat between the two over the Kuwait invasion did not create an irreparable breach. One suggestive recent linkage involves a shadowy group named *Ansar al-Islam* that operates in northern Iraq, and which on its surface appears to be a Taliban-style Islamist group tied to al-Qaeda. In reality, though, it is apparently controlled by the Iraqi regime, which makes it all the more interesting that *Ansar al-Islam* has been implicated in making and testing biological weapons. Whatever the true relationship between Saddam and Osama, evidence linking Iraq to the Middle Eastern terrorist networks did in fact exist, and deserved consideration.

HUNTING THE LONE WOLF

Yet the anthrax investigation soon took a quite surprising turn (Woodward and Eggen 2001). In November 2001, federal authorities stated that they believed the anthrax used in the recent attacks had been produced in the U.S., and that the crimes were the work of an American without Middle Eastern connections. A major argument for this was that the anthrax used belonged to the so-called Ames strain, which was not known to be in Iraqi hands (though this does not mean that they did not have access to it, unknown to the Americans). In addition, evidence available at the time suggested that the anthrax used was of relatively low quality as a weapon, and so could plausibly have been made in an amateur laboratory: as we have seen, though, later investigation would indicate the need for much higher technical capacities. Finally, the FBI felt that the letters that accompanied the spores were far more likely to have been written by a non-Muslim American than by a Middle Easterner, despite their use of words like "jihad." Federal agents felt that some American was pretending to be a Middle Eastern terrorist, probably to divert attention from his real identity or goals.

Over the following months, investigators developed this picture of a rogue scientist or laboratory worker, possibly connected with some right-wing extremist or racist group within the United States (Ripley 2001; Schmidt 2001; Bendavid and Davey 2001; Kristof 2002a–b; "FBI profile says anthrax mailer" 2001; "Killer's Trail" 2001). In this view, the perpetrator was "A reclusive, science-minded criminal who sends murder through the mail and frustrates investigators. That's the behavioral profile of the anthrax perpetrator released Friday by the Federal Bureau of Investigation. It's also strikingly similar to Theodore Kaczynski, the infamous Unabomber who killed or injured more than a dozen people with mail bombs" (Schoofs 2001). The FBI found "no direct or clear linkage between this series of incidents or any terrorist cell or network." If in fact such an individual was responsible for the biological attacks of that autumn, then the fact that the Arab hijackers had also been dabbling in similar weapons becomes no more than a coincidence, albeit an enormously puzzling one. Also casting doubt on this theory was the evidence that mounted over coming months that the anthrax used was of high military grade, nothing even a brilliant amateur could have produced in a back room.

Yet the new theory achieved instant media credibility. The press consistently reported the FBI's findings as likely to be definitive, and maintained this solid support over the coming months. The *Associated Press* story was headed "FBI profile says anthrax mailer is a male loner with a grudge." The *Washington Post* reported, "Anthrax Letter Suspect Profiled; FBI Says Author Likely Is Male Loner; Ties to Bin Laden Are Doubted"; the *Chicago Tribune* agreed that "FBI suspects tainted letters were sent by lone American; Profile indicates sole perpetrator; link to terrorist groups unlikely" (Schmidt 2001; Bendavid and Davey 2001). The *Wall Street Journal* headlined "Killer's Trail: Why Anthrax Probe Is Increasingly Hunting Domestic 'Lone Wolf.' (Schoofs 2001). Respected media sources like *Time* magazine now began referring not to terrorism but to a serial killer and drew comparisons with the Unabomber case. After the end of 2001, few media outlets discussed any possible Middle Eastern connections for the anthrax attacks, which were effectively removed from the whole debate over terrorism—and Iraq.

Liberal media outlets greeted the new interpretation with particular relief. Ever since September 11, the dominant interpretation of terrorism had overwhelmingly been the conservative model, which required firm military intervention overseas, and a harsh crackdown on foreign subversive groups at home. Now, however, the focus on a domestic perpetrator permitted a revival of concerns about ultraright-wing activism, connected to racist and Christian Identity sects. This seemed to be confirmed by the attackers' choice of Leahy and Daschle, who had in the past attracted the ire of moral conservatives. National Public Radio speculated about possible involvement by the Traditional Values Coalition, trying to map this strictly legal political organization together with terrorist violence (NPR later issued a groveling apology for this story). Liberal and left-wing magazines contextualized the real anthrax cases with numerous instances in which antiabortion activists had sent clinics packages of harmless materials that were labeled as biological warfare materials (Otis 2001). The ideological message was that even after September 11, the liberal view of terrorism was not extinct.

In the summer of 2002, the media gave the impression that the "mad scientist" had actually been identified. The suspect was an American biowarfare expert named Stephen Hatfill, who worked at the U.S. research center at Fort Detrick, Maryland, and who appeared to be the sinister "Mr. Z" identified in law enforcement leaks to the media over the previous months. Not only did Dr. Hatfill have expertise in anthrax but, according to the leaked stories, he was believed to hold right-wing extremist views. Perhaps he was even tangentially connected to some kind of racist terror network? He had reportedly served in the armed forces of the white supremacist governments of South Africa and Rhodesia. *New York Times* columnist Nicholas Kristof asked the FBI, "Have you examined whether Mr. Z has connections to the biggest anthrax outbreak among humans ever recorded, the one that sickened more than 10,000 black farmers in Zimbabwe in 1978–80? . . . . Could rogue elements of the American military have backed the Rhodesian Army in anthrax and cholera attacks against blacks?" (Kristof 2002a–d). As the ultimate proof of his misdeeds, Hatfill was said to have written an unpublished novel that described a biological attack on the United States very much like that which actually occurred in 2001. With a search of his property attracting front-page headlines, the media virtually proclaimed him guilty: the lone wolf was caged (Johnston 2002c).

At that point, however, the official case started to fall apart. No worthwhile evidence against Stephen Hatfill came to light, and many of the associations of time and place that seemed to connect him to the crimes proved false or misleading. Even the vaunted novel that supposedly foretold the attacks proved to be irrelevant, except to the extent that, like a hundred other thrillers from the 1990s, it dealt with the general theme of biological warfare against the United States. Hatfill repeatedly offered to take medical tests that would measure his exposure to anthrax, and basically did everything he reasonably could to prove he had nothing to do with the attacks. At the time of writing, Hatfill has been neither arrested nor charged; though the resulting publicity has effectively destroyed his career (Jackman 2002; Miller and Klaidman 2002; Schmidt 2002; Eggen 2002).

EXPLAINING THE SHIFT

By the time this book appears in print, it might be that the question of who sent the anthrax will be entirely settled, through new forensic evidence, or even a confession. Let us for the sake of argument assume that the culprit was indeed a domestic "mad scientist" as portrayed in the FBI profile, and that all the suggestive Middle Eastern linkages prove to be bogus. Even so, we still need to explain why one set of realities was firmly accepted until one dramatic day when another package of orthodoxy was believed with equal certainty. Much more was involved than merely the liberal desire to revive the focus on domestic extremists.

To understand this massive shift of emphasis, we need to appreciate the policy consequences of the rival interpretations, and the continuing debate among policy-makers over the appropriate response to Iraq. When President George W. Bush took office in early 2001, he received radically conflicting advice from different advisors about how to proceed with Saddam. Some advocated invasion and removal, others supported diplomatic means like containment and sanctions. This dispute flared anew after September 11, when highly placed officials in the Defense Department advocated war with Iraq, while the State Department favored nonmilitary solutions. The argument was personified by Secretary of State Colin Powell, for the State Department, while the hawkish anti-Iraq faction was symbolized by Defense Secretary Donald Rumsfeld, and his deputy, Paul Wolfowitz. The CIA was commonly reported to favor the State Department line, and had a powerful vested interest in minimizing the likely danger from Iraq.

The investigation of the anthrax attacks was intimately related to that policy debate. For the sake of argument, let us assume that investigators in the fall of 2001 had stated clearly that the anthrax attacks were directly related to September 11. These allegations were certainly being heard among U.S. policymakers, and were being leaked to the media in the U.S. and overseas. Throughout October, authoritative European newspapers were crediting these charges to "leading U.S. intelligence sources, involved with both the CIA and the Defense Department." The *New York Times* published an op-ed piece by Richard Butler, who had headed the U.N. arms inspection teams in Iraq during the 1990s. He wrote that "If the scientific path leads to Iraq as the supplier of the anthrax used by the terrorist mailers in the United States, no one should be surprised" (Butler 2001a–b).

However, these charges were not stated explicitly to the already enraged American public. If they had been, there would have been massive demands for retaliation, and in the circumstances of the time, that would mean a U.S. attack on Iraq. In terms of international law, there is no question that a state launching a biological attack against another would have committed an egregious act of war, and the other nation would be fully justified in responding militarily. Apart from the usual concerns about Arab sentiments, the U.S. administration was at that exact time trying to calm the nerves of friendly Arab states over the war then raging in Afghanistan. Arab nations were worried that popular opposition to U.S. actions could spill over into a new revolutionary movement across the Middle East, and spawn widespread support for Osama bin Laden and his followers. Such outrage would likely become uncontainable if the U.S. also attacked another Muslim power. The State Department in particular had an enormous investment in discouraging stories that placed anthrax in any Middle Eastern context whatever: so did the CIA.

In the context of the Fall of 2001, an American admission that Iraq might be involved in the biological warfare campaign would be politically intolerable. On diplomatic grounds alone, it made wonderful sense to hypothesize an American lone nut: and perhaps this view was even true. But once this idea came to dominate the investigation, any rival interpretations were basically ignored, or else condemned to the world of cranks and conspiracy theorists. The subsequent investigation was shaped by this political imperative. The FBI's well-publicized search of Stephen Hatfill's apartment occurred on the precise day in August 2002 that the US Congress was holding hearings on a possible US invasion of Iraq, in which numerous experts were giving their reasons not to act militarily, not to rock the boat of Middle Eastern diplomacy. Whatever Hatfill's possible role in the case—if any—the leaks surrounding the investigation should be seen in the light of the government's absolute need to avoid pursuing Middle Eastern connections.

ATTA AND THE IRAQIS

Public perceptions of terrorism are formed by the mass media, which are in turn shaped by bureaucratic agencies, which clearly have their distinctive needs and interests. This political context is most evident when different agencies, which are normally assumed to speak with equal authority, differ on important policy matters. At such times, we can see each agency striving to present its particular view in the media, leaking information that promotes that view, and seeking to discredit its rivals. Ultimately, one faction generally secures victory for its point of view, so that alternative realities are dismissed. Such a conflict provides a classic model of the rhetorical processes so often described by theorists of social problems.

In the aftermath of September 11, one of the most intense such conflicts developed over one straightforward question. Had hijacker Mohammed Atta traveled to Prague, in the Czech Republic, to meet with an Iraqi spy? The other man in the alleged meeting was Ahmed Khalil Ibrahim Samir al-Ani, who was formally the second secretary at the Iraqi embassy in Prague, but who was commonly regarded as a leading figure in that nation's European intelligence network. This charge first surfaced within weeks of the WTC attack, as the head of the Czech Security Information Service declared that Atta had been identified together with al-Ani on surveillance photographs taken in Prague between April 8 and 11, 2001. Atta had also traveled to Prague the previous year, in June 2000. The claim about the Iraqi contact gained credibility from its source, since Czech intelligence was highly regarded in the Communist era, and has retained much of its reputation. The specific meeting was confirmed directly by the Czech Prime Minister, suggesting the confidence of the intelligence service in its sources. This was much more than the rumor-mongering that is the standard currency of the intelligence underworld (Tyler and Tagliabue 2001; Safire 2001a, 2002; Whitmore 2001a–b; Longworth 2002).

If it is true, this story has enormous consequences. We have already seen that intelligence agencies often work alongside terrorist groups without necessarily controlling them, but this particular connection would have been far more significant. At the time of the supposed visit, Atta was living in the United States, and was presumably devoting his life to preparing for the September attacks, the greatest spectacular in the history of terrorism. His itinerary would then have proceeded as follows: "On April 4 he was in Virginia Beach. He flew to the Czech Republic on April 8 and met with the Iraqi intelligence officer, who was identified as Ahmed Khalil Ibrahim Samir al-Ani. By April 11, Mr. Atta was back in Florida renting a car" (Safire 2001a). Why should he interrupt his schedule in order to make a difficult and time-consuming voyage to Europe specifically to meet with someone, unless that meeting was of enormous significance? He was not there to chat about sports.

Several obvious answers come to mind. Most alarmingly, the meeting could prove that Iraqi intelligence was playing a key role in planning and directing the September attacks (Elliott 2001; Neiwert 2001). Alternatively, perhaps Atta was meeting to discuss or obtain something that could only be found through Iraqi sources, and one explanation that naturally came to mind involved supplies of anthrax from Iraq's government laboratories. The meeting also made nonsense of claims that Iraq remained hostile to Osama bin Laden's movement, since in this instance at least, the two sides seemed to be working together enthusiastically. Though a simple meeting would not constitute proof beyond a reasonable doubt in a U.S. courtroom, in intelligence terms it would provide very strong evidence that Iraq was directly linked to September 11 and/or the anthrax campaign.

Perhaps the most important aspect of the Prague story was not what it told in itself, but how it fitted into a lengthy story of terrorist sponsorship, from Abu Nidal through the first WTC attack, to the anthrax campaign ("Gunning for Saddam" 2002). Its significance was reinforced by other intelligence that came to light about this time. One Iraqi defector reported the existence of training camps in that country in which Islamist extremists received all sorts of instruction and training, "on assassinations, kidnapping, hijacking of airplanes, hijacking of buses, hijacking of trains, and all other kinds of operations related to terrorism" (Interview with Sabah Khodada 2001). The camp included a Boeing 707 that was used for hijacking simulations (Safire 2001c). Another defector told of Iraqi plans to sink U.S. warships in the Arab Gulf, plans very similar to the actual attack on the USS *Cole* in 2000, an incident that was commonly blamed on al-Qaeda. The more such evidence comes to light, the more the lines between Iraq and al-Qaeda blur. These incidents also cast doubt on the statements made by the director of CIA in early 2002, claiming, "Iraq has not engaged in terrorist operations against the United States in nearly a decade" (Risen 2002d).

The story of the "Prague Connection" is noteworthy because within a few months, it passed from the realm of commonly accepted fact to discredited conspiracy myth, and the change occurred on the basis of shifting political alignments rather than of any change in the interpretation of evidence.

Initially, the Atta meeting was universally accepted, even by those groups for whom it was enormously embarrassing because they opposed any intervention in Iraq. Within days of the attack, the meeting was being reported by mainstream media. As early as September 19, the *Boston Globe* headlined how "US probes a possible Iraq link: Hijacking suspect said to have met with agent," though "The officials cautioned that the information did not conclusively link Iraq to the attacks." By October, *Time* reported starkly, "We know that Mohamed Atta, thought to be the ringleader of the Sept. 11 terrorists, met in Prague with an Iraqi spy" (Elliott 2001). In November, the Reuters news agency reported as a matter of common knowledge that "Mr. Atta. . . . met an Iraqi intelligence officer,

Ahmed Khalil Ibrahim Samir al-Ani, when he visited Prague in April." Even a journalist reporting on CIA perceptions could state, "senior American intelligence officials have concluded that the meeting between Mr. Atta and the Iraqi officer . . . did take place" (Risen 2002d).

Reviewing recent investigations, journalist William Safire could report in November that the Atta meeting was "the undisputed fact connecting Iraq's Saddam Hussein to the September 11 attacks." For "hawks" like Safire, Richard Perle, and R. James Woolsey (a former CIA director), the Prague affair became the centerpiece of their campaigns for military action against Baghdad. Politically, this approach very much benefited the Defense Department hawks, and was dreadful news for the doves in the State Department and CIA.

Interestingly, for several months, the doves themselves found the Prague meeting so convincing that they made no attempt to deny it, but focused instead on trying to minimize the dangerous consequences. Anti-intervention writers stressed that although Atta assuredly had made the trip, the assignation had nothing to do with September 11. From this point of view, Atta must have had some other intention for his trip, specifically a plan to destroy the headquarters of Radio Free Europe based in that city, which had angered Saddam by its propaganda campaign against him.

In May 2002, however, attitudes toward the Prague meeting were largely reversed following the publication of a story in *Newsweek* that was viewed as killing the Iraq connection altogether. Pointing to confusions in the Czech version of the story, journalist Michael Isikoff argued that the meeting simply had not occurred, and that that fact was now commonly accepted in U.S. intelligence circles. In conclusion, "the much touted 'Prague connection' appears to be an intriguing, but embarrassing, mistake." The tone of Isikoff's story suggested further that the original tale grew out of conspiracy theories, the stuff of sensationalist fiction: the story itself was entitled "A Spy Story Tying Saddam to 9-11 is Looking Very Flimsy." Isikoff considered the whole affair "an illuminating window into the murky world of intelligence in the war on terrorism—and how easily facts can become distorted for political purposes." Rhetorically, the *Newsweek* story not only presented a new interpretation of events, but offered a stark condemnation of those who might doubt it: they were fantasists, conspiracy mongers, devotees of the world of spy fiction as contrasted with the objective experts of the intelligence agencies. The story was only believed because it fitted the interests of "hawks" and "hard-liners."

This potent account was deeply influential. Shortly afterwards, the *New York Times* reported that "a senior Bush administration official appeared to close the matter, saying FBI and CIA analysts had firmly concluded that no meeting had occurred." The liberal Internet magazine *Salon* crowed, "With its admission that an alleged link between Saddam Hussein and the

September 11 attacks doesn't exist, the Bush administration has lost its most compelling argument for invading Iraq. . . . Bush's foreign policy is based on a fairy tale, the persistent if childish hope that all of our problems can be solved by one solid blow to the latest Evil Empire, now found in Baghdad." (Scheer 2002). The story claimed that the Bush administration's focus on the Prague meeting had been part of a *Wag the Dog* strategy to generate a war with Iraq for internal political purposes, to secure re-election.

Yet the Atta story was, and remains, as plausible as many stories that have come to be accepted unquestioningly as providing critical connections in the terrorist underworld, and the evidence produced to discredit it scarcely amounts to dramatic new revelations. The grounds for not believing the story are, in short, that expert authorities had changed their mind about interpreting the events. Yet in fact, Czech officials stand firm in their original claims (see the discussion at http://edwardjayepstein.com/2002question/prague.htm). Writing after the *Newsweek* report, William Safire (2002) quoted a "senior Bush administration official" as saying that "You cannot say the Czech report about a meeting in 2001 between Atta and the Iraqi is discredited or disproven in any way. The Czechs stand by it and we're still in the process of pursuing it and sorting out the timing and venue. There's no doubt Atta was in Prague in 2000, and a subsequent meeting is at least plausible."

Contrary to Isikoff's account, it may well be the withdrawal of the Prague allegation that shows "how easily facts can become distorted for political purposes." We can find excellent reasons why U.S. agencies should have announced a change of mind at exactly this time, whether or not they actually believed it. Rather than reaching a new consensus about the story, based upon objective evidence, it seems more likely that elements within the administration, headed by the State Department and the CIA, had formed a united front on the need to kill or discredit the story.

Looking at the political circumstances of 2002, we can understand why such a change was necessary. Already in late 2001, Arab nations like Saudi Arabia and the Gulf states were nervous about a popular anti-American reaction if the U.S. struck at Iraq, but by the spring of 2002, the stakes were massively higher. The key change occurred in March and April when hundreds of Israelis perished in suicide bombings. In response, Israeli forces moved into the Palestinian controlled-areas of the West Bank, in a tough attempt to root out terrorism. Accurately or not, the ensuing violence was widely reported as a manifestation of Israeli repression and militarism. Especially controversial was a battle that occurred in the city of Jenin in early April, which pro-Palestinian activists characterized as a brutal massacre. Edward Said asked, "Are Palestinian civilian men, women and children no more than rats or cockroaches that can be attacked and killed in the thousands without so much as a word of compassion or in their defense?" (Said 2002). The crisis generated massive pro-Palestinian sympathy across the Muslim world (and across much of Europe), which threatened to turn into anti-American militancy. Saudi leaders demanded that the U.S. show more understanding of Arab sensitivities, and assist the Palestinians.

At such a time, it was politically essential to discredit something like the Prague connection, which threatened to ignite an immediate war with Iraq. This new political context goes far to explaining the relief with which the *Newsweek* interpretation was received in May 2002, and why "authoritative sources" came round to the new consensus that Atta had never set foot in Prague. The April 2001 visit became an un-fact.

Looking at the changing interpretations of Iraqi behavior through the last thirty years, we see that the stigma associated with a terrorist state cannot be explained either in terms of the nature and extent of its illegal activities, nor the degree to which its crimes are known to law enforcement agencies or the media. In large part, it reflects the diplomatic position of that nation, and its usefulness or danger to other countries with powerful diplomatic establishments and media. In the context of Western perceptions, this inevitably means that the changing attitudes of particular American administrations will decide whether one state rather than another will be categorized as deviant. And throughout this process, official sources and documents from each era must be evaluated in terms of the ideology and attitudes of the administration that compiled them and made them available.

10

A Critical Consumer's Guide to Understanding Terrorism

He who knows does not speak. He who speaks does not know.

—The *Tao Te Ching*

The greatest advantage of the approach to social problems we have employed in this book is that it denies the obviousness of the obvious. By tracing the long-term development of a given problem, we see that perceptions that at one time enjoy the status of absolute social orthodoxy have not always occupied that privileged position. Understanding how problems develop in this way forces us to ask why we regard a particular issue as such a grave social threat at a given time, when other themes appear to be just as potentially harmful. We must analyze the means by which particular groups choose to present a problem in a way that acquires widespread assent. We need to appreciate the interests that groups have in presenting a particular image, and the rhetorical means by which they establish this picture as the correct one, how in fact the issue achieves the status of social reality.

Terrorism offers a model case study for what I have called the constructionist approach to social problems. Above all, we see how very flexible the problem has been over time, and how useful to a striking variety of political causes and interest groups. In looking at the terrorism problem, then, we can employ the same methods and analytical tools that have proved useful when applied to familiar domestic problems of crime and social dysfunction. The same questions prove fruitful. When we look at the terrorism issue in this way, we see the process by which bureaucratic interests create and sustain the image presented in the mass media and popular culture.

MAKING THE TERRORISM PROBLEM

In the aftermath of September 11, 2001, the question of why terrorism comes to be seen as a significant problem scarcely seems worth asking. Raising as it does the basic question of national survival, such a catastrophe throws every other social concern into the deepest shadow. A historical perspective, though, suggests that the scope of the terrorism problem has fluctuated quite dramatically. Within just the past twenty years, we can find eras in which antiabortion violence has been constructed as terrorism, and others when it has not; and periods when domestic ultraright activism has been seen as a grave threat to public security, and others when it is viewed as a marginal annoyance. At different times too, stressing the threat posed by Middle Eastern militants has been presented either as a rational assessment of a pervasive threat, or a manifestation of anti-Arab bigotry and "Islamophobia."

In each instance, we can trace the familiar elements of problem construction, especially the work of interest groups seeking to gain credence for their particular needs and perspectives. Some of these groups are domestic—feminists trying to stigmatize antiabortion violence, Arab-Americans fighting against the terrorist stigma, Jews trying to buttress support for Israel—while others are foreign states. Apart from its immediate concern, each group tries to expand the domain of the terrorism problem to condemn other matters or issues that would not normally be regarded as terrorism. So, for instance, feminists might try and use the terrorism label to discredit all protests against abortion clinics; Jewish groups might expand the label to invalidate the whole Palestinian cause. These are familiar rhetorical processes.

Other claims makers in the construction process include bureaucratic agencies, which like police forces or bureaucracies everywhere, try to advance their particular agendas. They seek to win notice for the issues and responsibilities that fall under their particular ambit, and try to stress their own successes. Though they work for the cause of government and people, it would be naïve to pretend that they are not also motivated by their own self-interest, in terms of winning resources for their own agencies, and perhaps their own pet projects. Always critical to policy agendas is the defense of bureaucratic turf, preventing one's own responsibilities being ceded to some other aggressive agency, and information is regularly tailored to reduce such dangers.

Attitudes towards terrorism are formed by a process of negotiation, dependent on broader social and political attitudes, which ensure that certain avenues of interpretation are open at some times, but not others. Agencies and interest groups both seek to establish their views through the use of the mass media.

Also familiar from the constructionist literature is the concept of obligatory amnesia. Any claims makers seeking to establish a problem as urgent and dramatic tends to overstate its novelty, to make it something for which there is no real precedent. This means that accounts of terrorism must of necessity stress the unprecedented quality of the violence today, and the complexity or scale of the groups waging the underground war. The United States may be unique in the degree to which it achieved this denial, with the regular questions about "Can terrorism come to America?" This phrase is usually heard a few years after the previous great wave of violent domestic subversion has subsided. The question is an American perennial, much like the other recurring lament that some tragic event has caused America to "lose its innocence." Yet in other countries too, a surprising point about the response to terrorism has been the sense of surprise itself. Any historical study indicates that, technological developments apart, the modern world faces precisely no issues in terrorism that would have surprised an observer in 1900 or 1950. There is no excuse for modern agencies or media failing to appreciate the complexities of the clandestine world, the significance of deceptive tactics and clandestine state sponsorship, and the difficulties of assigning blame for specific incidents. If we understand the claims of "unprecedented" violence for the rhetorical devices they are, we are better able to see current events in a proper historical context, and perhaps even learn from past experience.

Yet while demonstrating the usefulness of constructionist methods, this particular study also suggests their limitations. Above all, because the issues involved are so closely connected with major political and economic concerns, the interest groups involved in shaping the problem are far more numerous, and the policy implications are much wider. To take some examples of "normal" issues, social problems like drunk driving, child abuse, and serial murder all touch on significant areas of social policy, but in no case are they likely to provoke war. Terrorism debates, however, literally do involve issues of war and peace, life and death, and these high stakes are reflected in the complexity of the politics we have to understand. In how many other contemporary problems must we seek to understand not just the politics of U.S. law enforcement, but also the diplomatic interests of a dozen separate nations, each with its own police and intelligence bureaucracy? A successful analysis of terrorism-related problems must therefore use not only familiar social science methods, but has of necessity to draw on other disciplines like economics, history, and political science.

A SECRET WORLD

Another key difference involves the clandestine nature of the activity we need to understand, which in some ways makes it all but impossible to evaluate the behavior of agencies. We can illustrate this by comparison with the work of a regular law enforcement organization charged with some more conventional crime problem. If an agency claims that a particular drug is "sweeping the nation," then that claim may well be accepted, and will carry credibility for some time, perhaps years. Ultimately, though, the claim can be tested and disproved in various ways, normally involving a critical examination of official statistics. Scholars might use arrest figures or emergency room admissions to show that the impact of the drug is far less than was claimed, or that it was confined to certain strictly limited areas. In my own work, I tried to disprove the exaggerated claims made for the incidence of serial murder activity in the United States, showing that the statistics employed to make the original case were tendentious (Jenkins 1994, 1999a). Statistics existed for analysis, and an impartial audience can judge the merits of the case being made. To that extent at least, the truth is out there.

Some specific claims about terrorism can be disproven in this way. Any agency, for instance, which argued in August 2001 that the threat of international terrorism was substantially ended would be utterly discredited within a few weeks. Other claims, though, can be neither tested nor falsified. As we have seen, statistics in this whole area are next to worthless, since they are so subject to vagaries in the definition of terrorism, and in the interpretation of individual motive. Without quantitative evaluation, any claims ultimately depend on assessing the claims of rival agencies, none of which is likely to release anything more than a tiny fraction of the evidence from which they are speaking. If some federal agency argues that Libya is the primary sponsor of international terrorism, and is the secret force behind a number of prominent incidents, then that belief is largely immune from testing. If challenged, then the agency can resort to asserting that it cannot release the substantiating evidence. The claim can only be challenged by some other agency or government with similar access to confidential intelligence, which has a competing interest in making its own claim.

As an example, we can return to a specific issue raised in an earlier chapter. Was Mohammed Atta in Prague in April 2001, and did he meet there with an Iraqi representative? Ultimately, those are simple questions subject to yes/no answers, but a case can be made that the true facts are not just unknown, but unknowable. The visit and meeting are so fraught with political implications and partisan agendas that it is probably impossible for any government, any agency, to discuss the affair with any kind of objectivity. Any new data that emerged on the question, any flight records or surveillance tapes, would be enthusiastically welcomed by one set of partisans, and equally thoroughly challenged by opponents. The only possible resolution might conceivably be if the Iraqi regime were destroyed, and documents emerged to settle the case once and for all, just as the collapse of German Nazism revealed the full inner workings of that state.

Atta was in Prague, or he was not: but as ordinary nonspecialist observers, we may never know for certain. If such specific facts are so open to interpretation, the difficulties involved in establishing more complex chains linking organizations or movements will be obvious.

THE CRITICAL CONSUMER

With these limitations, understanding the construction of the terrorism problem should help us to assess future claims in this area. Whether as elected officials, media representatives, or ordinary consumers of the mass media, the main lesson seems to be that we need to be much more demanding when presented with official claims about terrorism. I would suggest three major avenues that should be explored when confronted with official statements or media reports.

1. Above all, we need to ask the simple question, "How do we know this?" In doing so, we would not realistically expect an agency like the FBI to tell us the inner workings of its electronic surveillance or its network of informants, but they might well go on record with a number of specific pieces of evidence, perhaps deriving from criminal convictions. Once these claims are reported in the public domain, they can be tested against evidence that comes to light subsequently.

Some issues are especially subject to distortion or manipulation, and it is in these areas that consumers need to ask questions that generally the mass media do not raise. The details of a terrorist attack can usually be traced with fair accuracy, subject to a popular tendency to surround dramatic events with various myths and urban legends. Yet claims of responsibility and attributions of wider connections are much more suspect. Any reading of such claims must of necessity start with a consideration of the source involved, and the particular interests at stake.

2. We have to realize that claims have consequences. In all but the simplest statements, writers generally have agendas that may or may not be apparent from a superficial reading. Sometimes the policy advantages may be obvious enough. Israeli spokesmen will tend to stress, and perhaps exaggerate, the threat posed by Arab and Muslim groups and states. State Department representatives will emphasize the evils of certain countries with which the U.S. is currently at odds, while glossing over the misdeeds of friendly countries. Meanwhile, agencies like the FBI have powerful vested interests in explaining why a given attack was allowed to occur:

this may well involve understating any degree of terrorist organization, or trying to depoliticize the attack.

But some agendas go far beyond these immediate issues. Approaches to terrorism often involve ideological packages, in which the response to a particular incident will be inextricably bound up with other matters reflecting one's world view. Depending on the circumstances, these might involve attitudes to foreign policy and the use of military force, as well as domestic debates over race, ethnicity and gender, over civil liberties and the public right to seek official information. Statements about terrorism must be situated in the social and political concerns of the particular society in which they are made. Such statements need to be "unpacked" as far as possible, to understand the underlying agendas and debates.

3. Perhaps the greatest weapon for the critical consumer of terrorism claims is memory, an attribute that is reinforced by modern means of gathering and retrieving information. As we have seen on numerous occasions, law enforcement agencies regularly engage in sweeping reconstructions of the history of terrorism. In 1989, everyone knew that the Syrians and Iranians blew up Pan Am flight 103; in 1992, all reputable sources knew something totally different. In December 2001, everyone knew that Mohammed Atta had met with Iraqi spies in Prague; in June 2002, such a belief was supposedly held only by fanatical conspiracy theorists. I have argued that in many cases, these reconstructions do not represent re-evaluations based on new evidence, but are rather newly renegotiated versions of reality, reflecting new political alignments. Though the media generally ignore such shifts in basic orthodoxy, it should always be legitimate to question these tectonic changes. The obvious question to an agency should be, if you were so absolutely convinced about one reality in one year, why should we believe you when you claim to be absolutely certain about this totally different version today?

Ever since the late 1960s, understanding terrorism has been critical for appreciating so much of international politics, but also the domestic affairs of the individual nations that have had to encounter this issue. It is scarcely a matter on which one can be neutral. Since 2001, though, terrorism and counter-terrorism have become *the* critical issues in U.S. affairs. Now more than ever, we need to understand just what can and cannot be known with any certainty about terrorism, and why so much of what we are told with such certainty, in fact, rests on shaky foundations.

References

Abanes, Richard. 1996. *American Militias*. Downers Grove, IL: Inter Varsity Press.

Abu Gheith, Suleiman. 2002. "Why We Fight America." Available from:http://www.memri.org/bin/latestnews.cgi?ID=SD38802.

Adamic, Louis. 1963. *Dynamite*. rev. ed. Gloucester, MA: P. Smith.

Adams, James. 1986. *The Financing of Terror*. New York: Simon and Schuster.

"ADL Says U.S. Based Anti-Semites Are Feeding Sept. 11 Rumor Mill." 2001. Available from: http://www.adl.org/presrele/Mise_00/3959_00.asp.

Advisory Panel. 1999–2001. *Report to the President and the Congress of the Advisory Panel to Assess Domestic Response Capabilities for Terrorism Involving Weapons of Mass Destruction. I. Assessing the Threat; II. Toward a National Strategy for Combating Terrorism.* Arlington, VA: RAND Corporation.

Alexander, Yonah., ed. 2002. *Combating Terrorism.* Ann Arbor, MI: University of Michigan Press.

Alexander, Yonah, and Dennis A. Pluchinsky., eds. 1992. *European Terrorism Today and Tomorrow.* Washington DC: Brassey's US.

Alexander, Yonah, Michael S. Swetman, and Herbert M. Levine. 2001. *ETA: Profile of a Terrorist Group.* Ardsley, NY: Transnational Publishers.

Alexander, Yonah, and Kenneth A. Myers., ed. 1982. *Terrorism in Europe.* New York: St Martin's Press.

Alexander, Yonah, and Robert G. Picard., eds. 1991. *In the Camera's Eye.* Washington, DC: Brassey's.

Alexander, Yonah, and Michael S. Swetnam. 2001. *Usama Bin Laden's Al-Qaida.* New York: Transnational Books.

Al-Gama'a al-Islamiyya (n.d.) *Al-Gama'a al-Islamiyya.* Available from: http://www.ict.org.il/inter_ter/orgdet.cfm?orgid=12.

Ali, Tariq. 2002. *The Clash of Fundamentalisms.* New York: Verso Books.

Al-Khalil, Samir. 1990. *Republic of Fear.* New York: Pantheon.

Al-Skafi, Ayman. 2001, "Because I Am a Palestinian." Available from: http://www.memri.org/bin/articles.cgi?Page=archivesandArea=sdandID=SP31801.

Ambler, Eric. 1996. *A Coffin for Dimitrios.* New York: Carroll and Graf Publishers.

Anderson, Scott, and Jon Lee Anderson. 1986. *Inside the League.* New York: Dodd Mead.

Andrew, Christopher M., and Oleg Gordievsky. 1990. *KGB: The Inside Story.* New York: Harper Collins.

Andrew, Christopher M., and Vasili Mitrokhin, 1999. *The Sword and the Shield.* New York: Basic Books.

Andrews, Edmund L. 2002. In Rich Detail, Algerian Describes Plot to Blow Up French Synagogue. *New York Times*, April 24.

Anti-Defamation League of B'nai B'rith. 1993. *Hamas, Islamic Jihad and the Muslim Brotherhood.* New York: Anti-Defamation League of B'nai B'rith.

Anti-Defamation League of B'nai B'rith. 2002. *Countering Suicide Terrorism.* New York: iUniverse, Incorporated.

Arab Convention. 2000. "Arab Convention for the Suppression of Terrorism." Available from: http://www.leagueofarabstates.org/E_News_Antiterrorism.asp.

Aust, Stefan. 1987. *Baader-Meinhof Group*. London: Bodley Head.

Ayers, Bill. 2001. *Fugitive Days*. Boston: Beacon Press.

Baer, Robert. 2002. *See No Evil*. New York: Crown.

Baird-Windle, Patricia, and Eleanor J. Bader. 2001. *Targets of Hatred*. New York: St. Martin's Press.

Balz, Dan, and Bob Woodward. 2002. The Road to War. *Washington Post*, five-part series, January 27–31.

Bari, Judi. 1994. *Timber Wars.* Monroe, ME: Common Courage Press.

Barkun, Michael. 1997. *Religion and the Racist Right.* rev. ed. Chapel Hill: University of North Carolina Press.

Bates, Tom. 1993. *Rads*. New York: Harper Perennial Library.

"BBC's Double Standard." 2001. Available from: http://www.honestreporting.com/Followup/07_bbcterror.asp.

Beal, Mary F. 1976. *Safe House*. Eugene, OR: Northwest Matrix.

Beam, Louis. n.d. "Leaderless Resistance." Available from: http://users.mo-net.com/mlindste/ledrless.html.

Beaumont Peter. 2002. It Is Nice to Be Killed While Killing. *Guardian* (London), June 20.

Bearman, Jonathan. 1986. *Qadhafi's Libya.* London: Zed Books.

Bell, J. Bowyer. 1996. *Terror Out of Zion.* New Brunswick. NJ: Transaction Publishers.

Bell, J. Bowyer. 2000. *The IRA 1968-2000*. London: Frank Cass.

Bendavid, Naftali, and Monica Davey. 2001. FBI Suspects Tainted Letters Were Sent by Lone American. *Chicago Tribune*, November 11.

Bennett, David. 1995. *Party of Fear*. 2d ed. rev., and updated. New York: Vintage Books.

Bennett, James. 2002. The New Suicide Bombers. *New York Times*, June 21.

Bennett, James. 2001. A New Mideast Battle: Arafat vs. Hamas. *New York Times,* December 6.

Bennett, Vanora. 2001. *Crying Wolf*. London: Pan.

Bennett, William J. 2002. *Why We Fight: Moral Clarity and the War on Terrorism*. New York: Doubleday.

Beresford, David. 1997. *Ten Men Dead*. New York: Atlantic Monthly Press.

Bergen, Peter L. 2001. *Holy War, Inc.* New York: Free Press.

Berlet, Chip. 1995. *Eyes Right! Challenging the Right Wing Backlash*. Boston: South End Press.

Berlet, Chip, and Matthew N. Lyons. 2000. *Right-wing Populism in America*. New York: Guilford Press.

Bernstein, Richard. 1986. Chirac Remarks on El Al Plot Irk Israel. *New York Times,* November 8.

Bishop, Patrick, and Eamonn Mallie. 1989. *The Provisional IRA.* London: Corgi.

Bjorgo, Tore, ed. 1995. *Terror from the Extreme Right.* London: Frank Cass and Co.

Blackstock, Nelson. 1975. *Cointelpro: the FBI's Secret War on Political Freedom.* New York: Vintage Books.

Blanchard, Dallas A. 1994. *The Anti-Abortion Movement and the Rise of the Religious Right.* New York: Twayne.

Blanchard, Dallas A., and Terry J. Prewitt. 1993. *Religious Violence and Abortion.* Gainesville: University Press of Florida.

Bloom, Robert M. 2002. *Ratting: The Use and Abuse of Informants in the American Justice System*. Westport, CT: Praeger.

Blundy, David, and Andrew Lycett. 1987. *Qaddafi and the Libyan Revolution*. Boston: Little, Brown.

Bodansky, Yossef. 2001. *Bin Laden: The Man Who Declared War on America.* Rocklin, CA: Forum.

Bodansky, Yossef. *Target America and the West.* New York: Shapolsky Publishers, Inc.

Bone, James. n.d. "Gore Vidal Casts McVeigh as a hero." Available from: http://home.earthlink.net/~jamiranda/vidal.html.

Bonner, Raymond, and Douglas Frantz. 2002. French Suspect Moussaoui in Post-9/11 Plot. *New York Times,* July 28.

Bragg, Rick. 1998a. Bomb Kills Policeman at Alabama Abortion Clinic. *New York Times,* January 30.

Bragg, Rick. 1998b. Group Tied to Two Bombings Says it Set Off Clinic Blast. *New York Times,* February 3.

Brisard, Jean-Charles, and Guillaume Dasquie. 2002. *Forbidden Truth.* New York: Thunder's Mouth Press/Nation Books.

Broad, William J., and David Johnston. 2002a. Report Linking Anthrax and Hijackers Is Investigated. *New York Times,* March 23.

Broad, William J., and David Johnston. 2002b. Anthrax Sent Through Mail Gained Potency by the Letter. *New York Times,* May 7.

Bruce, Steve. 1992. *The Red Hand*. New York: Oxford University Press.

Bryan, John. 1975. *This Soldier Still at War*. New York: Harcourt Brace Jovanovich.

Brzezinski Matthew. 2001. Bust and Boom. *Washington Post,* December 30.

Bulloch, John, and Harvey Morris. 1991. *Saddam's War*. London: Faber.

Bushart, Howard, John R. Craig, and Myra Barnes. 1998. *Soldiers of God: White Supremacists and Their Holy War for America.* New York: Kensington Books.

Butler, Richard. 2001a. *The Greatest Threat*. New York: Public Affairs.

Butler, Richard. 2001b. Who Made the Anthrax? *New York Times,* October 18.

Cahn, Anne H. 1998. *Killing Détente*. University Park, PA: Pennsylvania State University Press.

CARDRI (Committee Against Repression and for Democratic Rights in Iraq). 1986. *Saddam's Iraq: Revolution or Reaction?* London: Zed Books.

Carey, Roane, ed. 2001. *The New Intifada: Resisting Israel's Apartheid*. London: Verso.

Carlson, John Roy. 1943. *Under Cover*. New York: The World Publishing Co.
Carr, Caleb. 2002. *Lessons of Terror.* New York: Random House.
Carroll, Thomas Patrick. 2002. "The CIA and the War on Terror," *Middle East Intelligence Bulletin* 4(9), available at http://www.meib.org/articles/0209_me2.htm
Castellucci, John. 1986. *The Big Dance*. New York: Dodd, Mead.
Catanzaro, Raimondo., ed. 1991. *The Red Brigades and Left-Wing Terrorism in Italy.* New York: St. Martin's Press.
Chalk, Peter. 1996. *West European Terrorism and Counter-Terrorism*. New York: St. Martin's Press.
Childs, David, and Richard Popplewell. 1996. *The Stasi*. New York: New York University Press.
Chomsky, Noam. 1988. *Culture of Terrorism.* Boston: South End Press.
Chomsky, Noam. 2000. *Rogue States*. Boston: South End Press.
Chomsky, Noam. 2001. *9-11*. New York: Seven Stories Press.
Churchill, Ward, and Jim Vander Wall. 1990. *COINTELPRO Papers*. Boston: South End Press.
Churchill, Ward, and Jim Vander Wall. 1988. *Agents of Repression*. Boston, MA: South End Press.
Clarke, James W. 1982. *American Assassins*. Princeton, NJ: Princeton University Press.
Clarke, Thurston. 1981. *By Blood and Fire*. London: Hutchinson.
Clarkson, Frederick. 1999. *Profiles in Terrorism*. Monroe, ME: Common Courage Press.
Cline, Ray, and Yonah Alexander. 1985. *State Sponsored Terrorism. Report Prepared for the Subcommittee on Security and Terrorism of the US Senate Judiciary Committee.* 99th Congress, 1st Session. Washington, DC: G.P.O.
Cline, Ray S., and Yonah Alexander. 1984. *Terrorism: the Soviet Connection*. New York: Crane Russak.
"A Closer Look." 2002. Available from: http://www.ocregister.com/news/expert200508cci6.shtml.
Clutterbuck, Richard L. 1980. *Guerrillas and Terrorists.* Chicago: Ohio University Press.
Clutterbuck, Richard. 1975. *Living With Terrorism.* New York: Arlington House Publishers.
Clutterbuck, Richard. 1990. *Terrorism and Guerrilla Warfare.* New York: Routledge.
Clutterbuck, Richard L. 1983. *Media and Political Violence.* 2d ed. London: MacMillan.
Cohn, Norman. 1996. *Warrant for Genocide*. New ed. London: Serif.
Collin, Richard, and Gordon L. Freedman. 1990. *Winter of Fire*. New York: Dutton.
Collins, Aukai. 2002. *My Jihad*. New York: Lyons Press.
Cooley, John K. 2000. *Unholy Wars*. London: Pluto.
Coppola, Vincent. 1997. *Dragons of God*. Atlanta: Longstreet Press.
Corbin, Jane. 2002. *Al Qaeda: In Search of the Terror Network that Shook the World*. New York: Thunder's Mouth Press/Nation Books.
Corcoran, James. 1995. *Bitter Harvest: The Birth of Paramilitary Terrorism in the Heartland*. New ed. New York: Penguin Books.

Cordesman, Anthony H. 1999. *Transnational Threats from the Middle East: Crying Wolf or Crying Havoc?* Carlisle Barracks, PA: Strategic Studies Institute, U.S. Army War College.

Corn, David. 1994. *Blond Ghost*. New York: Simon and Schuster.

Corn, David. 1998. "Did Bill Wag The Dog?" *Salon*. Available from: http://www.salon.com/news/1998/08/21newsc.html.

Coup Plot. 1990. Coup Plot Allegations. *Terror Update* 15, July 4.

Coutin, Susan Bibler. 1993. *The Culture of Protest*. Boulder: Westview Press.

Crankshaw, Joe. 1976. Did Chilean Agents Seek Exiles as Assassins? *Miami Herald*, November 9.

Crankshaw, Joe, and Gloria Marina. 1976. Miami a Hotbed for Terrorism. *Miami Herald*, November 29.

Crenshaw, Martha, ed. 1995. *Terrorism in Context*. University Park, PA: Pennsylvania State University Press.

Crenshaw, Martha. 1983. *Terrorism, Legitimacy and Power*. Middletown, CT: Wesleyan University Press.

Crock, Stan. 2000. The Terrorist Threat in America Is . . . Overblown? *Business Week*, December 7.

Cuban Information Archives. n.d. "Cuban Information Archives." Available from: http://cuban-exile.com/menu1/!menu.html.

Danner, Mark. 1994. *The Massacre at El Mozote*. New York: Vintage.

Darrow, Clarence. 1957. *Attorney for the Damned*. New York: Simon and Schuster.

Dartnell, Michael Y. 1995. *Action Directe*. London: Frank Cass

Darwish, Adel, and Gregory Alexander. 1991. *Unholy Babylon*. London: Gollancz.

Davis, Brian L. 1990. *Qaddafi,Terrorism, and the Origins of the U.S. Attack on Libya*. New York: Praeger.

Davis, Stephen M. 1987. *Apartheid's Rebels: Inside South Africa's Hidden War*. New Haven, CT: Yale University Press.

De Borchgrave, Arnauld, and Robert Moss. 1980. *The Spike*. New York: Avon.

Dees, Morris, and James Corcoran. 1996. *Gathering Storm: America's Militia Threat*. New York: HarperCollins Publishers.

Definitions of Terrorism. n.d. "Definitions of Terrorism," UN Office for Drug Control and Crime Prevention. Available from: http://www.undcp.org/terrorism_definitions.html.

Delgado, Juan Manuel. n.d. "The Puerto Rican Prisoners of War." Available from: http://www.prisonactivist.org/pps+pows/pr-pows.html.

De Lutiis, Giuseppe. 1984. *Storia dei Servizi Segreti in Italia*. Rome: Editori Riuniti.

Dempsey, James X., and David Cole. 2002. *Terrorism and the Constitution: Sacrificing Civil Liberties in the Name of National Security*. New York: New Press.

Dershowitz, Alan M. 2002. *Why Terrorism Works*. New Haven, CT: Yale University Press.

Dillon, Martin. 1989. *The Shankill Butchers*. London: Hutchinson.

Dillon, Martin. 1990. *The Dirty War*. London: Hutchinson.

Dillon, Martin, and Dennis Lehane. 1973. *Political Murder in Northern Ireland*. London: Penguin.

Dobkin, Bethami A. 1992. *Tales of Terror*. New York: Praeger.

Dobson, Christopher. 1974. *Black September.* New York: Macmillan.
Dobson, Christopher. 1977. *The Carlos Complex*. New York: Putnam.
Dobson, Christopher, and Ronald Payne. 1986. *War Without End.* London: Harrap.
Dodd, Vikram. 2002. Al-Qaida Suspect Hidden by UK Agents. *Guardian,* July 8.
Domestic Terrorists at Work. 1993. *Atlanta Constitution.* Editorial, Oct. 4.
Downey, Sarah, and Michael Hirsh. 2002. A Safe Haven? *Newsweek,* September 30
Drake, Richard, 1995. *The Aldo Moro Murder Case.* Cambridge, MA: Harvard University Press.
Dwyer, Jim. 1995. *Two Seconds Under the World*. New York: Ballantine Books.
Dyer, Joel. 1998. *Harvest of Rage: Why Oklahoma City is Only the Beginning.* Boulder, CO: Westview Press.
Early Warnings. 2002. Early Warnings. *New York Times,* May 19.
Egan, Timothy. 1995a. Seeking a National Conspiracy. Abortion Task Force is Set Back. *New York Times,* June 18.
Egan, Timothy. 1995b. Shooter Falls Silent about Anti-Abortion Terrorism. *Tacoma News-Tribune,* June 18.
Eggen, Dan. 2002. U.S. Report Faulted Anthrax Prober: FBI Official in Charge of Case Avoided Discipline Over Ruby Ridge Study. *Washington Post* August 24.
Eggen, Dan, and Susan Schmidt. 2002. Mueller: Clues Might Have Led To Sept. 11 Plot—New Memo Details FBI Pilot's Warning. *Washington Post,* May 30.
Elliott, Michael. 2001. What If Saddam Did It? *Time*. Oct. 29.
Emerson, Steven. 1988. *Secret Warriors.* New York: Putnams.
Emerson, Steven, and Brian Duffy. 1990. *The Fall of Pan Am 103.* New York: Putnams.
Emerson, Steven. 2000. *International Terrorism and Immigration Policy. Testimony to Hearing on International Terrorism and Immigration Policy, January 25, 2000. Judiciary Subcommittee on Immigration and Claims.* House Subcommittee on Immigration and Claims. United States House of Representatives. Washington, DC: G.P.O.
Emerson, Steven. 2002. *American Jihad: the Terrorists Living Among Us.* New York: The Free Press.
Emerson, Steven A., and Cristina del Sesto. 1991. *Terrorist*. New York: Villard.
Erlanger, Stephen, and Chris Hedges. 2001. Terror Cells Slip Through Europe's Grasp. *New York Times*, December 28.
Esposito, John L. 2002. *Unholy War*. New York: Oxford University Press.
Evans-Pritchard, Ambrose. 1997. *The Secret Life of Bill Clinton*. Washington: Regnery Pub.
Ezekiel, Raphael S. 1996. *The Racist Mind: Portraits of American Neo-Nazis and Klansmen*. New York: Penguin.
Faligot, Roger, and Pascal Krop. 1989. *La Piscine*. Oxford: Blackwell.
Richard A. Falkenrath, Robert D. Newman, and Bradley A. Thayer. *America's Achilles' Heel*. Cambridge, Mass: MIT Press.
Farrell, William Regis. 1990. *Blood and Rage*. Lexington, Mass.; Lexington Books.
FBI profile says anthrax mailer. 2001. FBI Profile Says Anthrax Mailer Is a Male Loner With a Grudge. *St. Louis Post-Dispatch*, Nov 10.
Fenster, Mark. 1999. *Conspiracy Theories.* Minneapolis: University of Minneapolis Press.

Feuerlicht, Roberta Strauss. 1971. *America's Reign of Terror*. New York: Random House.
Five Draw Long Sentences. 1987. Five Draw Long Sentences for Terrorism Scheme. *New York Times*, December 31.
Follain, John. 1998. *Jackal*. New York: Arcade.
Foner, Philip S., ed. 1995. *The Black Panthers Speak*. New York: Da Capo Press.
Frankfort, Ellen. 1984. *Kathy Boudin and the Dance of Death*. New York: Stein and Day.
Freed, Donald. 1973. *Agony in New Haven*. New York: Simon and Schuster.
Freed, Donald, and Fred S. Landis. 1980. *Death in Washington*. Westport, CT: Lawrence Hill.
Freedman, Lawrence, and Efraim Karsh. 1995. *The Gulf Conflict, 1990–1991*. Princeton, NJ: Princeton University Press.
Gee, Marcus. 2001. Rumours, Conspiracies and Hatred. *Globe and Mail*, October 7.
Geifman, Anna, 1993. *Thou Shalt Kill*. Princeton, NJ: Princeton University Press.
Geifman, Anna. 2000. *Entangled in Terror*. Wilmington, DE: SR Books.
Gelbspan, Ross. 1991. *Break-Ins, Death Threats, and the FBI*. Boston: South End Press.
George, John, and Laird Wilcox. 1996. *American Extremists: Militias, Supremacists, Klansmen, Communists, and Others*. Amherst, NY: Prometheus Books.
Geraghty, Tony. 2000. *The Irish War*. Baltimore, MD: Johns Hopkins University Press.
Gerard, Philip. 2002. *Secret Soldiers*. New York: Dutton.
Gerson, Allan, and Jerry Adler. 2001. *The Price of Terror*. New York: HarperCollins
Gertz, Bill (2002) *Breakdown: How America's Intelligence Failures Led to September 11*. Washington DC: Regnery Publishing.
Gibson, James William. 1994. *Warrior Dreams*. New York: Hill and Wang.
Ginzburg, Carlo. 1999. *The Judge and the Historian*. New York: Verso.
Goldberg, Robert Alan. 2001. *Enemies Within*. New Haven, CT: Yale University Press.
Goleman, Daniel. 1986. The Roots of Terrorism are Found in Brutality of Shattered Childhood. *New York Times*, September 2.
Golway, Terry. 2001. *For the Cause of Liberty*. London: Simon and Schuster.
Goulden, Joseph C. 1984. *The Death Merchant*. New York: Simon and Schuster.
Grathwohl, Larry. 1976. *Bringing Down America*. New Rochelle, NY: Arlington House.
Greer, Steven C. 1995. *Supergrasses*. New York: Oxford University Press.
Griffin, Robert S. 2001. *The Fame of a Dead Man's Deeds*. 1stBooks Library.
Gunaratna, Rohan. 2002. *Inside Al Qaeda*. New York: Columbia University Press.
Gunning for Saddam. 2002. "Gunning for Saddam" PBS *Frontline* Documentary. Available online from: http://www.pbs.org/wgbh/pages/frontline/shows/gunning/.
Halberstam, David. 2001. *War in a Time of Peace*. New York: Scribner.
Halpern, Thomas. 1995. *Beyond the Bombing: the Militia Menace Grows*. New York: Anti-Defamation League.
Hamm, Mark S. 1993. *American Skinheads*. West Point, CT: Praeger.
Hamm, Mark S, et. al. 1997. *Apocalypse in Oklahoma*. Boston, MA: Northeastern University Press.

Hamm, Mark S. 2002. *In Bad Company.* Boston: Northeastern University Press.
Hamzah, Khidr Abd Al-Abbas, and Jeff Stein. 2000. *Saddam's Bombmaker.* New York: Scribner.
Harel, Amos. 2001. Israel Prepares for Expected United States Attack on Iraq. *Ha'Aretz,* October 11.
Hayden, Tom. 1970. *Trial.* New York: Holt, Rinehart and Winston.
Haynes, John Earl, and Harvey Klehr. 1999. *VENONA: Decoding Soviet Espionage in America.* New Haven, CT: Yale University Press.
HBO Slanders Islam in *Path to Paradise.* 1997. "HBO Slanders Islam in *Path to Paradise.*" Available from: http://www.themodernreligion.com/assault/hbo-ptp.html.
Hedges, Chris. 2001. A Glimpse Behind the Plot Against the American Embassy in Paris. *New York Times,* October 28.
Heehs, Peter. 1993. *The Bomb in Bengal.* Delhi/Oxford: Oxford University Press.
Henneberger, Melinda. 2002. Rome Embassy May Have Been Bomb Target. *New York Times,* February 25.
Henze, Paul. 1985. *The Plot to Kill the Pope.* New York.: Charles Scribners' Sons.
Herman, Edward. 1982. *The Real Terror Network.* Boston: South End Press.
Herman, Edward S., and Gerry O'Sullivan. 1989. *The "Terrorism" Industry.* New York: Pantheon.
Herzstein, Robert E. 1994. *Roosevelt and Hitler.* New York: John Wiley.
Hewitt, Christopher. 2002. *Understanding Terrorism in America: from the Klan to al Qaeda.* New York: Routledge.
Heymann, Philip B. 1998. *Terrorism and America: A Commonsense Strategy for a Democratic Society.* Cambridge, MA: MIT Press.
Hill, Ray, and Andrew Bell. 1988. *The Other Face of Terror.* London: Grafton.
Hilliard, Robert L. and Keith, Michael C. 1999. *Waves of Rancor.* Armonk, NY: M.E. Sharpe.
Hinckle, Warren, and William W. Turner. 1992. *Deadly Secrets.* New York: Thunder's Mouth Press.
Hiro, Dilip. 1991. *The Longest War: the Iran-Iraq Military Conflict.* New York: Routledge.
Hiro, Dilip. 2001. *Neighbors, Not Friends: Iraq and Iran After the Gulf Wars.* London: Routledge.
Hirschberg, Peter. 2002. Background/CNN Blinks First in Battle with Israeli Officials. *Ha'aretz,* June 23.
Hitchens, Christopher. 1998. "They Bomb Pharmacies, Don't They?" *Salon,* September 23. http://www.salon.com/news/1998/09/23news.html.
Hitler's Commando Order. 1942. "Hitler's Commando Order." Available from: http://www.wwiitech.net/main/germany/archives/hitlerscommandoorder/.
Hoffman, Bruce. 1990. *The Ultimate Fifth Column.* Santa Monica, CA: RAND.
Hoffman, Bruce. 1998. *Inside Terrorism.* New York: Columbia University Press.
Holland, Jack. 1988. *The American Connection.* New York: Penguin.
Horne, Alistair. 1977. *A Savage War of Peace: Algeria, 1954–1962.* New York: Viking Press.
Horowitz, David. 1999. "Letter to the Past." *Jewish World Review,* December 13. Available from: http://www.jewishworldreview.com/cols/horowitz121499.asp.

Howard, Clark. 1980. *Zebra.* New York: Berkley.

Hudson, Rex A. 1988. *Castro's America Department.* Washington, DC: Cuban American National Foundation.

Hudson, Rex A. 2002. *Who Becomes a Terrorist and Why*. Guilford, CT: The Lyons Press.

Hunt, Albert R. 2002. Anthrax: A Botched Investigation? *Wall Street Journal,* May 9.

Hutchinson, Martha Crenshaw. 1978. *Revolutionary Terrorism.* Stanford, CA: Hoover Institution Press.

Ibrahim, Yossef. 1990. Trial of Accused Mastermind of Bombings Opens in Paris. *New York Times*, January 30.

Ijaz, Mansoor. 2001. Clinton Let Bin Laden Slip Away and Metastasize. *Los Angeles Times*, December 6.

Ingram Carl. 2001. State Security Chief Ready to Face Home-Grown Terrorism. *Los Angeles Times,* December 25.

Interview with Sabah Khodada (2001) Interview with Sabah Khodada, broadcast on PBS *Frontline*, available at http://www.pbs.org/wgbh/pages/frontline/shows/gunning/interviews/khodada.html

Interview with Salah Sh'hadeh. 2002. "Interview with Salah Sh'hadeh." Available from: http://www.memri.org/bin/latestnews.cgi?ID=SD40302.

Iraqi Wanted in US for Eighteen Years is Seized. 1991. Iraqi Wanted in US for Eighteen Years is Seized. *New York Times,* January 19.

Iraq's Terrorist Allies. 1990. Iraq's Terrorist Allies. *Terror Update,* #16, September.

Isikoff, Michael. 2002a. A Spy Story Tying Saddam to 9-11 is Looking Very Flimsy. *Newsweek,* May 6.

Isikoff, Michael. 2002b. Unheeded Warnings: FBI Agent's Notes Pointed to Possible World Trade Center Attack. *Newsweek.* May 20.

Isikoff, Michael. 2002c. The Informant Who Lived With the Hijackers. *Newsweek,* Sept. 16.

Jaber, Hala. 1997. *Hezbollah: Born with a Vengeance.* New York: Columbia University Press.

Jackman, Tom. 2002. Ex-Army Scientist Denies Role in Anthrax Attacks. *Washington Post,* August 11.

Jacobs, Harold, ed. 1971. *Weatherman.* Berkeley: Ramparts Press.

Jacobs, James B., and Kimberly Potter. 1998. *Hate Crime.* New York: Oxford University Press.

Jacobs, Ron. 1997. *The Way the Wind Blew*. London: Verso.

Jacquard, Roland 2002. *In the Name of Osama bin Laden*. Durham, NC: Duke University Press.

James, Caryn. 1996. Choices and No Choices in the Abortion Wars. *New York Times,* December 18.

James Jesus Angleton and the Kennedy Assassination. n.d. "James Jesus Angleton and the Kennedy Assassination." Available from: http://www.webcom.com/ctka/pr700-ang.html.

Jamieson, Alison. 1989. *The Heart Attacked.* London: M. Boyars.

Jenkins, Brian. 1985. *International Terrorism: The Other World War.* Santa Monica, CA: RAND Corporation.

Jenkins, Loren. 1998. "Is bin Laden a terrorist mastermind—or a fall guy?" *Salon*. August 27. http://www.salon.com/news/1998/08/27news.html.

Jenkins, Philip. 1986. The Assassins Revisited. *Intelligence and National Security* 1:459-471.

Jenkins, Philip. 1988a. Under Two Flags: Provocation and Deception in European Terrorism. *Terrorism: an International Journal* 11:275-287.

Jenkins, Philip. 1988b. Whose Terrorists? Libya and State Criminality. *Contemporary Crises* 12:5-24.

Jenkins, Philip. 1989. Evidence and Ideology: the Assassination of Olof Palme. *Contemporary Crises* 13:15-33.

Jenkins, Philip. 1991a. Strategy of Tension: The Belgian Terrorist Crisis of 1982–6. *Terrorism: an International Journal* 13:299-309.

Jenkins, Philip. 1991b. Spy Fiction and Real Terrorism. In *Spy Fiction, Spy Films and Real Intelligence,* ed. Wesley K. Wark, 185-203. London: Frank Cass.

Jenkins, Philip. 1992. *Intimate Enemies*. Hawthorne, NY: Aldine de Gruyter Publishers.

Jenkins, Philip. 1994. *Using Murder*. Hawthorne, NY: Aldine de Gruyter Publishers.

Jenkins, Philip. 1996. *Pedophiles and Priests*. New York: Oxford University Press.

Jenkins, Philip. 1997. *Hoods and Shirts*. Chapel Hill, NC: University of North Carolina Press.

Jenkins, Philip. 1998. *Moral Panic*. New Haven, CT: Yale University Press.

Jenkins, Philip 1999a. *Synthetic Panics*. New York: New York University Press.

Jenkins, Philip. 1999b. Fighting Terrorism as if Women Mattered. In *Making Trouble: Cultural Constructions of Crime, Deviance and Control,* eds. Jeff Ferrell and Neil Websdale, 319-346. Hawthorne, NY: Aldine De Gruyter Publishers.

Jenkins, Philip. 2000. *Mystics and Messiahs*. New York: Oxford University Press.

Jenness, Valerie, and Kendal Broad. 1997. *Hate Crimes*. Hawthorne, NY: Aldine De Gruyter Publishers.

Johnson, Loch. 2000. *Bombs, Bugs, Drugs and Thugs*. New York: New York University Press.

Johnston, David. 1991. Scrutiny of Iraqis and Other Arabs in the US is Stepped Up. *New York Times*, January 8.

Johnston, David. 2002a. F.B.I. Says Pre-Sept. 11 Note Got Little Notice. *New York Times*, May 9.

Johnston, David. 2002b. Pre-Attack Memo Cited Bin Laden. *New York Times,* May 15.

Johnston, David. 2002c. Apartment Searched Anew in F.B.I.'s Anthrax Inquiry. *New York Times,* August 2.

Johnston, David, and Elizabeth Becker. 2002. C.I.A. Was Tracking Hijacker Months Earlier Than It Had Said. *New York Times*, June 3.

Johnston, David, and James Risen. 2001. Officials Say Plot May Have Involved 2 More Jets. *New York Times,* September 19.

Johnson, Larry C. 2001. The Declining Terrorist Threat. *New York Times*, July 10.

Jones, J. Harry. 1968. *The Minutemen*. Garden City, NY: Doubleday, 1968.

Jones, Stephen, and Peter Israel. 1998. *Others Unknown*. New York: Public Affairs.

Juergensmeyer, Mark. 2000. *Terror in the Mind of God.* Berkeley: University of California Press.

Kahane, Meir. 2000. *The Story of the Jewish Defense League*. New York: Institute for Publication of the Writings of Rabbi Meir Kahane.

Kamiya, Gary. 2001. "The Patriot." *Salon,* April 9. http://www.salon.com/books/2001/04/07/mcveigh/

Kaplan, Jeffrey. 1996. *Cult at the End of the World.* New York: Crown Publishers.

Kaplan, Jeffrey, and Leonard Weinberg. 1999. *The Emergence of a Euro-American Radical Right.* New Brunswick, NJ: Rutgers University Press.

Karsh, Efraim, and Inari Rautsi. 1991. *Saddam Hussein: a Political Biography.* New York: Free Press.

Kasrils, Ronald. 1993. *Armed and Dangerous.* Oxford, England: Heinemann.

Katz, Samuel M. 2000. *The Hunt for the Engineer.* New York: Fromm International.

Katz, Samuel M. 1993. *Israel Versus Jibril.* New York: Paragon House.

Katz, Samuel M. 2002. *Relentless Pursuit.* New York: Forge.

Katzenell, Jack. 2002. Palestinian Accused of Planning Mass Cyanide Poisoning of Israelis. (Associated Press) *Boston Globe,* August 1.

Keller, Bill. 1992, A Bomber Lives with his Guilt in a Land of Scant Innocence. *New York Times,* October 18.

Kempton, Daniel R. 1989. *Soviet Strategy Toward Southern Africa: The National Liberation Movement Connection.* New York: Praeger.

Kempton, Murray. 1974. *The Briar Patch.* New York: Dell.

King, Wayne. 1988. FBI Papers Portray Inquiry Fed by Informer. *New York Times,* February 13.

Kishkovsky, Sophia. 2002. Russian Novelist Scoffs at Post-Soviet Leaders. *New York Times* August 25

Kitson, Frank. 1971. *Low Intensity Operations.* Hamden, CT: Archon Books.

Knight, Peter. 2001. *Conspiracy Culture.* New York: Routledge.

Knight, Peter, ed. 2002. *Conspiracy Nation.* New York: New York University Press.

Koring, Paul, and Stephanie Levitz. 2001. 5th Hijack Team May Have Been Thwarted. *Globe and Mail,* September 15.

Kramer, Jane. 2002. *Lone Patriot.* New York: Pantheon 2002.

Kramer, Martin S. 2001. *Ivory Towers on Sand.* Washington, DC: Washington Institute for Near East Policy.

Kristof, Nicholas D. 2002a. Connecting Deadly Dots. *New York Times,* May 24.

Kristof, Nicholas D. 2002b. Anthrax? The F.B.I. Yawns. *New York Times,* July 2.

Kristof, Nicholas D. 2002c. The Anthrax Files. *New York Times,* July 12.

Kristof, Nicholas D. 2002d. The Anthrax Files. *New York Times,* August 13

Kupperman, Robert, and Tamara Kupperman. 1991. The Politics of Pan Am 103. *New York Times,* November 16.

Kushner, Harvey W. ed. 1998. *The Future of Terrorism,* London: Sage Publications.

Kux, Dennis. 2001. *The United States and Pakistan, 1947–2000.* Baltimore: Johns Hopkins University Press

LaBrecque, Ron. 1987. *Lost Undercover.* New York: Dell.

Lahoud, Lamia. 2002. 80.6% of Palestinians support continuing terror campaign. *Jerusalem Post,* September 28.

Lamy, Philip. 1996. *Millennium Rage: Survivalists, White Supremacists, and the Doomsday Prophecy.* New York: Plenum Press.

Landau, Elaine. 2002. *Osama bin Laden: A War Against the West.* Brookfield, CT: Twenty-First Century Books.

Langewiesche, William. 2001. The Crash of EgyptAir 990. *Atlantic Monthly.* Available from: http://www.theatlantic.com/issues/2001/11/langewiesche.htm.

Laqueur, Walter. 1987. *The Age of Terrorism.* Boston: Little Brown.
Laqueur, Walter. 2001. *History of Terrorism*. New Brunswick, NJ: Transaction Publishers.
Laqueur, Walter. 1999. *The New Terrorism*. New York: Oxford University Press.
Laqueur, Walter. 1979. *Terrorism.* Boston, MA: Little, Brown.
Ledeen, Michael 2002a. *The War Against the Terror Masters*. New York: St. Martin's Press.
Ledeen, Michael 2002b. Dead Terrorist in Baghdad. Available at http://www.nationalreview.com/ledeen/ledeen082002.asp
Lee, Martha. 1995. *Earth First! Environmental Apocalypse*. Syracuse, NY: Syracuse University Press.
Lehr, Dick, and Gerard O'Neill. 2001. *Black Mass*. New York: Harper Perennial.
Lernoux, Penny, 1980. *Cry of the People.* Garden City, NY: Doubleday.
Ian O. Lesser et al. 1999. *Countering the New Terrorism*. Santa Monica, CA: RAND Corporation.
Levin, Jack, and Jack McDevitt. 1993. *Hate Crimes: The Rising Tide of Bigotry and Bloodshed*. New York: Plenum Press.
Levine, Daniel. 1991. *The Birth of the Irgun Zvai Leumi.* Jerusalem, Israel: Gefen Publishing House.
Lewis, Paul H. 2002. *Guerillas and Generals: the Dirty War in Argentina.* Westport, CT: Praeger.
Lichtblau, Eric. 1999. Clinton Asserts Executive Privilege in Clemency Case. *Los Angeles Times,* September 17.
Lichtblau, Eric. 2002. I.N.S. Ignored Possible Link of Airport Killer to Terrorists. *New York Times,* September 25.
Lifton, Robert. 1999. *Destroying the World to Save It*. New York: Henry Holt and Company.
Linenthal, Edward T. 2001. *Unfinished Bombing*. New York: Oxford University Press.
Livingstone, Neil C. 1982. *The War Against Terrorism.* Lexington, MA: Lexington Books.
Livingstone, Neil C. 1990. *The Cult of Counter-Terrorism.* Lexington, MA: Lexington Books.
Livingstone, Neil C., and T. E. Arnold, eds. 1986. *Fighting Back.* Lexington, MA: DC Heath.
Livingstone, Neil C. 1988. *Beyond the Iran-Contra Crisis*. Lexington, MA: Lexington Books.
Loftus, John, and Emily McIntyre. 1989. *Valhalla's Wake*. New York: Atlantic Monthly Press.
Longman, Jere. 2002. *Among the Heroes*. New York: HarperCollins.
Longworth R. C. 2002. Possible Meeting of Atta, Iraqi Fuels Debate on Attack. *Chicago Tribune,* May 10.
Lukas, J. Anthony. 1997. *Big Trouble*. New York: Simon and Schuster.
Maas, Peter. 1986. *Manhunt*. New York: Random House.
McAlister, Melani. 2001. *Epic Encounters*. Berkeley: University of California Press.
McCann, Eamonn. 1974. *War and an Irish Town*. London: Penguin.
McCuen, Gary E., ed. 1997. *Abortion Violence and Extremism*. New York: Gem.

McDaniel, Denzil. 1997. *Enniskillen*. Dublin, Ireland: Wolfhound Press.
MacDonald, Andrew. 1980. *The Turner Diaries*. 2d ed. Arlington, VA: National Vanguard Books.
MacDonald, Andrew. 1998. *Hunter.* Hillsboro, WV: National Vanguard Books.
MacFarquhar, Neil. 2002. A Cairo Storyteller With Time to Dream. *New York Times* September 16.
McGee, Jim. 1983. New Breed of Anti-Castro Militant Moves to Miami. *Miami Herald,* December 30.
MacKey, Sandra. 2002. *The Reckoning: Iraq and the Legacy of Saddam Hussein*. New York: W.W. Norton and Company.
Malley, Robert. 1996. *The Call from Algeria*. Berkeley: University of California Press.
Mandel, Daniel. 2001. "Muslims on the Silver Screen." *Middle East Quarterly* Available from: http://www.meforum.org/article/26/.
Marchak, M. Patricia. 1999. *God's Assassins.* Montreal: McGill-Queen's University Press.
Marighela, Carlos. 1971. *For the Liberation of Brazil*. Harmondsworth: Penguin Books.
Martin, David C., and John Walcott. 1988. *Best Laid Plans*. New York: Harper and Row.
Martinez, Luis. 2000. *The Algerian Civil War*. New York: Columbia University Press.
Marx, Gary T. 1988. *Undercover: Police Surveillance in America.* Berkeley: University of California Press.
Matthiessen Peter. 1983. *In the Spirit of Crazy Horse*. New York: Viking Press.
Meade, Robert C., 1990. *Red Brigades: The Story of Italian Terrorism*. New York: St. Martin's Press.
Medved, Michael. 2002. "Admit Terrorism's Islamic Link" *Jewish World Review,* July 2. Available from: http://www.jewishworldreview.com/cols/medved1.asp.
Melley, Timothy. 1999. *Empire of Conspiracy*. Ithaca, NY: Cornell University Press.
Melman, Yossi. 1987. *The Master Terrorist*. New York: Avon.
Merkl, Peter H., ed. 1986. *Political Violence and Terror: Motifs and Motivations*. Berkeley: University of California Press.
Michel, Lou, and Dan Herbeck. 2001. *American Terrorist*. New York: Harper Collins.
Miller. Abraham H., ed. 1982. *Terrorism: the Media and the Law.* Dobbs Ferry, NY: Transnational Publishers.
Miller, John, and Michael Stone. 2002. *The Cell*. New York: Hyperion.
Miller, Judith, Stephen Engelberg, and William Broad. 2001. *Germs.* New York: Simon and Schuster.
Miller, Judith. 1996. *God Has Ninety-Nine Names*. New York: Simon and Schuster.
Miller, Judith. 1986. French Say Suspect Gives Clues on Terror Network. *New York Times,* May 18.
Miller, Judith. 1987. The Istanbul Synagogue Massacre. *New York Times Magazine,* January 4.
Miller, Judith. 2001. An Iraqi Defector Tells of Work on at Least 20 Hidden Weapons Sites. *New York Times,* December 20.
Miller, Judith, and Laurie Mylroie. 1990. *Saddam Hussein and the Crisis in the Gulf.* New York: Times Books.

Miller, Judith, Jeff Gerth, and Don Van Natta. 2001. Many Say U.S. Planned for Terror but Failed to Take Action. *New York Times*, December 30.

Miller, Judith, and Don Van Natta. 2002. In Years of Plots and Clues, Scope of Qaeda Eluded U.S. *New York Times*, June 9.

Miller, Mark, and Daniel Klaidman. 2002. The Hunt for the Anthrax Killer. *Newsweek*, August 12.

Miniter, Richard. 2002. Did the CIA Leak the News About 9/11? *New Republic*, June 3.

Mishal, Shaul, and Avraham Sela. 2000. *The Palestinian Hamas*. New York: Columbia University Press.

Mitchell Jr., Richard G. 2002. *Dancing at Armageddon*. Chicago: University of Chicago Press.

Louis R. Mizell, and James Grady. 1998. *Target U.S.A.* New York: John Wiley and Sons.

Jack B. Moore. 1993. *Skinheads Shaved for Battle.* Bowling Green, KY: Bowling Green State University Press.

Moss, David. 1989. *The Politics of Left-Wing Violence in Italy, 1969–85.* New York: St. Martin's Press.

Moss, Robert. 1972. *The War for the Cities*. New York: Coward, McCann and McGeoghegan.

Moynihan, VENONA and Truman. 1999. "Moynihan, VENONA and Truman." *Secrecy and Government Bulletin*, 77, March. Available from: http://www.fas.org/sgp/bulletin/sec77.html.

Mylrole, Laurie. 2000. *Study of Revenge*. Washington, DC: AEI Press.

Mylroie, Laurie. 2001. "Iraqi Complicity in the World Trade Center Bombing and Beyond." *Middle East Intelligence Bulletin* 3(6) June. Available from: http://www.meib.org/articles/0106_ir1.htm.

Nacos, Brigitte. 1996. *Terrorism and the Media*. New York: Columbia University Press.

Nacos, Brigitte. 2002. *Terrorism, Counterterrorism, and the Mass Media*. Lanham, MD: Rowman and Littlefield.

National Commission on Terrorism. 2000. "Countering the Changing Threat of International Terrorism." Available from: http://w3.access.gpo.gov/nct/.

Neiwert, David. 1999. *In God's Country.* Pullman, WA: Washington State University Press.

Neiwert, David. 2001. "A Saddam Connection?" *Salon*, Sept 21. http://dir.salon.com/politics/feature/2001/09/21/iraq/index.html.

Netanyahu, Benjamin, ed. 1986. *Terrorism: How the West Can Win*. New York: Farrar, Straus Giroux.

Netanyahu, Benjamin. 1997. *Fighting Terrorism.* New York: Noon Day Press.

Neuffer, Elizabeth. 2002. Training Tapes Depict Attacks Planned for US. *Boston Globe*, January 13.

Newton, Huey P. 1995. *Revolutionary Suicide.* (originally published 1973) New York: Writers and Readers Publishing.

Norval, Morgan. 1990. *Inside the ANC: The Evolution of a Terrorist Organization*. Washington, DC: Selous Foundation Press.

Nutter, John Jacob. 2000. *The CIA's Black Ops.* Amherst, NY: Prometheus Books.

O'Ballance, Edgar. 1997. *Islamic Fundamentalist Terrorism, 1979–1995: The Iranian Connection.* New York: New York University Press.

O'Callaghan, Sean. 1998. *Informer*. New York: Bantam Books.

Oliker, Olga. 2001. *Russia's Chechen Wars 1994–2000*. Santa Monica, CA: RAND Corporation.

Oliphant, Thomas. 2002. FBI'S Shifting Versions on Missed 9/11 Warnings. *Boston Globe*, June 2.

Olmsted, Kathryn. 1996. *Challenging the Secret Government*. Chapel Hill: University of North Carolina Press.

O'Neill, Patrick. 2002. "Those Who Speak and Those Who Don't." *Independent Online,* May 1. Available from: http://indyweek.com/durham/2002-05-01/trotline.html.

O'Sullivan, Noel, ed. 1986. *Terrorism, Ideology and Revolution*. Boulder, CO: Westview.

Otis, Ginger Adams. 2001. The Homegrown Anthrax Blitz. *Village Voice*, October 19.

Oziewicz, Estanislao, and Tu Thanh Ha. 2001. Canada Freed Top al-Qaeda Operative. *Globe and Mail* (Canada), November 22.

Page, Michael Von Tangen. 1998. *Prisons, Peace, and Terrorism.* New York: St. Martin's Press.

Paletz, David L., and Alex P. Schmid, eds. 1992. *Terrorism and the Media*. Newbury Park, CA: Sage.

Payne, Cril. 1979. *Deep Cover*. New York: Newsweek Books.

Payne, Leslie, and Tim Findley. 1976. *The Life and Death of the SLA.* New York: Ballantine Books.

Pelletiere, Stephen C. 1992. *The Iran-Iraq War*. New York: Praeger.

Peterson, Scott. 2002. Ex-Smuggler Describes Iraqi Plot to Blow Up US Warship. *Christian Science Monitor*, April 3.

Phillips, Don, and Dan Eggen. 2001. Sweeps Find Box-Cutters on Two More Airliners. *Washington Post*, September 22.

Picard, Robert G. 1993. *Media Portrayals of Terrorism.* Ames, IA: Iowa State University Press.

Pierce, William. 1995. "Terror Breeds Terror." Available from: http://www.natvan.com/free-speech/fs955a.html.

Pilger, John. 2002. The Great Charade. *Observer* (London), July 14.

Pillar, Paul R., and Michael H. Armacost. 2001. *Terrorism and U.S. Foreign Policy.* Washington, DC: Brookings Institution.

Pluchinsky, Dennis. 1982. "Political Terrorism in Western Europe", in Alexander and Myers, supra.

Poland, James M. 1997. *Understanding Terrorism.* Englewood Cliffs, NJ: Prentice Hall.

Porth, Jacquelyn S. 1998. "U.S. Has Chemical Weapons-Related Soil Sample from Sudan Plant." Available from: http://www.fas.org/man/dod-101/ops/docs/98082503_ppo.html.

Posner, Steve. 1987. *Israel Undercover.* Syracuse, NY: Syracuse University Press.

Priest, Dana, and Dan Eggen. 2002. 9/11 Probers Say Agencies Failed to Heed Attack Signs. *Washington Post,* September 19.

Purdy, Matthew. 2002. New Jersey Laureate Refuses to Resign Over Poem. *New York Times,* September 28.
Pyke, Nicholas. 2002. "Aide Says Nidal Confessed to Lockerbie bombing," Guardian, August 23.
Quandt, William B. 1998. *Between Ballots and Bullets.* Washington: Brookings Institution Press.
Ra'anan, Uri et al. 1986. *Hydra of Carnage.* Lexington, MA: Lexington Books.
Randal, Jonathan C. 1983. *Going All the Way*. New York: Viking Press.
Rapoport, David. 2001. *Inside Terrorist Organizations.* 2d. ed. Portland, OR: Frank Cass.
Rapoport, David, and Yonah Alexander, eds. 1989. *Morality of Terrorism.* 2d ed. New York: Columbia University Press.
Reader, Ian. 2000. *Religious Violence in Contemporary Japan*. Honolulu: University of Hawaii Press.
Reeve, Simon. 2001. *The New Jackals*. New ed. London: André Deutsch.
Reeve, Simon. 2000. *One Day in September.* New York: Arcade Publishing.
Reich, Walter, and Walter Laqueur, eds. *Origins of Terrorism*. Washington, DC: Woodrow Wilson Center Press.
Reiter, Jerry. 2002. *Live from the Gates of Hell*. Amherst, NY: Prometheus Books.
Reuter, Peter. 1982. *Licensing Criminals: Police and Informants*. Santa Monica, CA: RAND Corporation.
Revell, Oliver "Buck." 1998. *G-Man's Journal.* New York: Pocket Books.
Rich, Frank. 2002. Road to Perdition. *New York Times*, July 20.
Ridgeway, James. 1995. *Blood in the Face.* 2d ed. New York: Thunder's Mouth Press.
Ridgeway, James. 2002. Mondo Washington. *Village Voice*, March 27–April 2. Available from: http://www.villagevoice.com/issues/0213/ridgeway.php.
Riebling, Mark. 1994. *Wedge*. New York: A.A. Knopf/ Random House.
Rimanelli, Marco. 1989. Italian Terrorism and Society 1940s–1980s. *Terrorism: an International Journal* 12: 249-296.
Ripley, Amanda. 2001. The Hunt for the Anthrax Killers. *Time*, Nov 5.
Risen, James. 2001. In Hindsight, C.I.A. Sees Flaws That Hindered Efforts on Terror. *New York Times*, October 7.
Risen, James. 2002a. U.S. Traces Iran's Ties to Terror Through a Lebanese. *New York Times*, January 17.
Risen, James. 2002b. Sept. 11 Suspect May Be Relative of '93 Plot Leader. *New York Times*, June 5
Risen, James. 2002c. Report Faults C.I.A.'s Recruitment Rules. *New York Times*, July 18.
Risen, James. 2002d. Terror Acts by Baghdad Have Waned, U.S. Aides Say. *New York Times*, February 6.
Risen, James. 2002e. C.I.A. and F.B.I. Agree to Truce in War of Leaks vs. Counterleaks. *New York Times,* June 14.
Risen, James, 2002f. U.S. Failed to Act on Warnings in '98 of a Plane Attack. *New York Times,* September 19.
Risen, James. 2002g. F.B.I. Agent Was Tracking Radical Linked to Hijacker. *New York Times* Sept. 24.
Risen, James, and David Johnston. 2002. F.B.I. Account Outlines Activities of Hijackers Before 9/11 Attacks. *New York Times,* September 27.

Risen, James, and Jane Perlez. 2001. New Analysis: Terror, Iran and the U.S. *New York Times,* June 23.

Risen, James, and Judy Thomas. 1998. *Wrath of Angels.* New York: Basic Books.

Rohter, Larry. 2002. Iran Blew Up Jewish Center in Argentina, Defector Says. *New York Times,* July 22.

Rose, David. 2001. Attackers Did Not Know They Were to Die. *Observer,* October 14.

Rose, David, and Ed Vulliamy. 2001. Iraq "Behind US Anthrax Outbreaks." *Observer,* October 14.

Rubinstein, Danny, and Yossi Melman. 2002. Arch terrorist Abu Nidal reported dead in Baghdad. *Ha'Aretz,* August 19.

Rubin, Barry, ed. 1989. *The Politics of Terrorism.* Washington, DC: University Press of America.

Rubin, Elizabeth. 2002. The Most Wanted Palestinian. *New York Times Magazine,* June 30,

Safire, William. 2001a. Prague Connection. *New York Times,* November 12.

Safire, William. 2001b. Enemy of My Enemy. *New York Times,* November 29.

Safire, William. 2001c. Advance the Story. *New York Times,* October 22.

Safire, William. 2002. Mr. Atta Goes to Prague. *New York Times,* May 9.

Said, Edward W. 1978. *Orientalism.* New York: Pantheon Books.

Said, Edward W. 1997. *Covering Islam.* rev. ed. New York: Vintage Books.

Said, Edward W. 2002. "What Israel Has Done." *The Nation.* May 6: 20-23.

Salinger totally sure. 1997. "Salinger 'Totally Sure' TWA 800 Missile Theory Is True." CNN March 13. Available from: http://www.cnn.com/US/9703/13/twa/.

Sanger, David E. 2001. 2 [Two] Leaders Tell of Plot to Kill Bush in Genoa. *New York Times,* September 26.

Sater, William. 1981. *Puerto Rican Terrorists: A Possible Threat to U.S. Energy Installations?* Santa Monica, Calif.: RAND Corporation.

Sayigh, Yazid. 1999. *Armed Struggle and the Search for State.* New York: Oxford University Press.

Scanlan, Margaret. 2001. *Plotting Terror: Novelists and Terrorists in Contemporary Fiction.* Charlottesville, VA: University of Press of Virginia.

Scheer, Robert. 2002. "Will Bush Wag the Dog?" *Salon,* May 8. http://www.salon.com/news/col/scheer/2002/05/08/dog/index_np.html

Schiff, Ze'ev. 2002. Syria has allowed hundreds of Qaida men to settle in Lebanon. *Ha'Aretz* September 2

Schleifman, Nurit. 1988. *Undercover Agents in the Russian Revolutionary Movement.* New York: St. Martin's Press.

Schmalz, Jeffrey. 1989. Furor Over Castro Foe's Fate Puts Bush on Spot in Miami. *New York Times,* August 16.

Schmidt, Susan. 2001. Anthrax Letter Suspect Profiled; FBI Says Author Likely Is Male Loner; Ties to Bin Laden Are Doubted. *Washington Post,* Nov 11.

Schmidt, Susan. 2002. Evidence Lacking as Probe of Scientist in Anthrax Scare Intensifies. *Washington Post,* August 15

Schoofs, Mark. 2001. Killer's Trail: Why Anthrax Probe Is Increasingly Hunting Domestic 'Lone Wolf.' *Wall Street Journal,* November 12.

Schweitzer, Glenn E., and Carole Dorsch Schweitzer. 2002. *A Faceless Enemy.* Reading, MA: Perseus Publishing.

Sciolino, Elaine. 1991. *The Outlaw State*. New York: John Wiley.

Seale, Patrick. 1988. *Asad of Syria*. Berkeley: University of California Press.

Seale, Patrick. 1992. *Abu Nidal: A Gun for Hire*. New York: Random House.

Seely, Robert. 2001. *Russo-Chechen Conflict, 1800-2000*. London; Portland, OR: Frank Cass.

Seger, Karl A. 1991. Is America Next? *Security Management*, April, 30-38.

Serrano, Richard A. 1998. *One of Ours: Timothy McVeigh and the Oklahoma City Bombing*. New York: Norton.

Shackelford, Michael. n.d. "The Black Hand." Available from: http://www.ku.edu/~kansite/ww_one/comment/blk-hand.html.

Shaheed (1996) *Shaheed: The Making of a Suicide Bomber*. Video documentary, directed by Dan Setton.

Shaheen, Jack G. 2001. *Reel Bad Arabs*. New York: Olive Branch Press.

Shakur, Assata. 1987. *Assata: An Autobiography*. Westport, CT: Lawrence Hill.

Shapiro, Bruce. 2000. "The Hyping of Domestic Terrorism." *Salon*, June 12 http://archive.salon.com/news/feature/2000/06/12/terrorism/print.html

Shenon, Philip. 2002. Senate Report on Pre-9/11 Failures Tells of Bungling at F.B.I. *New York Times*, August 28.

Silberstein, Sandra. 2002. *War of Words*. New York: Routledge.

Silj, Alessandro. 1979. *Never Again Without a Rifle*. New York: Karz.

Simon, Jeffrey. 2001. *Terrorist Trap: America's Experience with Terrorism*. 2d ed. Bloomington, Ind.: Indiana University Press.

Sivan, Emmanuel, and Menachem Friedman, eds. 1990. *Religious Radicalism and Politics in the Middle East*. Albany, NY: State University of New York Press.

Slovo, Joe. 1997. *Slovo: The Unfinished Autobiography*. New York: Ocean Press.

Smith, Brent L. 1994. *Terrorism in America*. Albany, N.Y.: State University of New York.

Snow, Robert. 1999. *The Militia Threat: Terrorists Among Us*. New York: Plenum Trade.

Solinger, Rickie, Faye Ginsburg, and Patricia Anderson, eds. 1998. *Abortion Wars*. Berkeley: University of California Press.

Solomon, John. 2001. CIA Cited Risk Before Attack. *Associated Press*, October 4 .

Southern Poverty Law Center. 1996. *False Patriots*. Montgomery, AL: Southern Poverty Law Center.

Stalker, John. 1989. *The Stalker Affair*. New York: Penguin.

Sterling, Claire. 1981. *Terror Network*. New York: Berkley Books.

Sterling, Claire. 1984. *The Time of the Assassins*. New York: Holt, Rinehart, and Winston.

Stern, Jessica. 1999. *The Ultimate Terrorists*. Cambridge, MA: Harvard University Press.

Stern, Kenneth S. 1996. *Force Upon the Plain: The American Militia Movement and the Politics of Hate*. New York: Simon and Schuster.

Stern, Susan. 1975. *With the Weathermen*. New York: Doubleday

Sterngold, James. 2001. An Arrest in Series of Fires in Phoenix Adds a Plot Twist. *New York Times*, June 23.

Stohl, Michael, ed. 1988. *The Politics of Terrorism*. 3d. ed. New York: Dekker.

Stone, Martin. 1997. *The Agony of Algeria*. New York, Colombia University Press.

Szulc, Tad. 1986. *Fidel: A Critical Portrait*. New York: Morrow.

Taheri, Amir. 1987. *Holy Terror.* New York: Adler and Adler.
Tannenbaum, Robert, and Philip Rosenberg. 1979. *Badge of the Assassin.* New York: E. P. Dutton.
Tarock, Adam. 1998. *The Superpowers' Involvement in the Iran-Iraq War*. Commack, NY: Nova Science Publishers.
Taylor, Peter. 1980. *Beating the Terrorists*. London: Penguin.
Trinquier, Roger. 1964. *Modern Warfare*. New York: Praeger.
Trotsky, Leon. 1909. "Why Marxists Oppose Individual Terrorism."Available from: http://www.marxists.org/archive/trotsky/works/1909/tia09.htm.
Tucker, Jonathan B., ed. 2000. *Toxic Terror*. Cambridge, MA: The MIT Press.
Tyler, Patrick E., and John Tagliabue. 2001. Czechs Confirm Iraqi Agent Met With Terror Ringleader. *New York Times*, October 27.
Tyler, Patrick E. 2002. Officers Say U.S. Aided Iraq in War Despite Use of Gas. *New York Times,* August 18
Tyrangiel, Josh. 2002. What Saddam's Got. *Time*, May 13.
U.N.: Child Sex Trade 'A Form of Terrorism.' 2001. "U.N.: Child Sex Trade A Form of Terrorism." CNN, online, December 17. Available at http://www.cnn.com/2001/WORLD/asiapcf/east/12/17/childsex.conference/index.html?relate.
U.S. Commission (1975) *Report to the President by the Commission on CIA Activities within the United States.* Washington, DC: G.P.O.
U.S. Department of Justice, *Terrorism in the United States.* Annual Editions. Washington, DC: Federal Bureau of Investigation.
U.S. Department of State, *Patterns of Global Terrorism.* Annual Editions. Washington, DC: Office of the Coordinator for Counterterrorism. Available from the gateway site for Internet access: http://www.state.gov/s/ct/rls/pgtrpt/.
U.S. House of Representatives. 1974. *Terrorism: hearings before the Committee on Internal Security, Hearings held Feb. 27–Mar. 26, 1974.* House of Representatives, Ninety-third Congress, second session, Washington, DC: U.S. G.P.O.
U.S. House of Representatives. 1979. *The final assassinations report: report of the Select Committee on Assassinations. U. S. House of Representatives.* New York: Bantam Books.
U.S. House of Representatives. 1986. *Abortion clinic violence: Oversight hearings before the Subcommittee on Civil and Constitutional Rights of the Committee on the Judiciary.* House of Representatives, 99th Congress, first and second sessions, March 6, 12, and April 3, 1985; and December 17, 1986. Washington, DC: G.P.O.
U.S. House of Representatives. 1989a. *CISPES and FBI counterterrorism investigations: hearings before the Subcommittee on Civil and Constitutional Rights of the Committee on the Judiciary.* House of Representatives, One Hundredth Congress, second session, June 13 and September 16, 1988. Washington, DC: U.S. G.P.O.
U.S. House of Representatives. 1989b. *The FBI investigation of CISPES: hearing before the Permanent Select Committee on Intelligence.* House of Representatives, One Hundredth Congress, second session, September 29, 1988. Washington, DC: U.S. G.P.O.
U.S. House of Representatives. 1991. *FBI investigation of First Amendment activities: hearings before the Subcommittee on Civil and Constitutional Rights of the Committee on the Judiciary.* House of Representatives, One Hundred First Congress, first session, June 21 and 22, 1989. Washington, DC: U.S. G.P.O.

U.S. House of Representatives. 1993. *Abortion clinic violence: Hearings before the Subcommittee on Crime and Criminal Justice of the Committee on the Judiciary.* House of Representatives, 103rd Congress, first session, April 1 and June 10, 1993. Washington, DC: G.P.O.

U.S. House of Representatives. 1994. *World Trade Center bombing: terror hits home: hearing before the Subcommittee on Crime and Criminal Justice of the Committee on the Judiciary.* House of Representatives, One Hundred Third Congress, first session, March 9, 1993. Washington, DC: U.S. G.P.O.

U.S. House of Representatives. 1996a. *Combating domestic terrorism: hearing before the Subcommittee on Crime of the Committee on the Judiciary.* House of Representatives, One Hundred Fourth Congress, first session, May 3, 1995. Washington, DC: U.S. G.P.O.

U.S. House of Representatives. 1996b. *Nature and threat of violent anti-government groups in America: hearing before the Subcommittee on Crime of the Committee on the Judiciary.* House of Representatives, One Hundred Fourth Congress, first session, November 2, 1995. Washington, DC: U.S. G.P.O.

U.S. House of Representatives. 1998. *H. Con. Res. 254, calling for the extradition of JoAnne Chesimard from Cuba . . . . before the Subcommittee on the Western Hemisphere of the Committee on International Relations.* House of Representatives, One Hundred Fifth Congress, second session, May 13, 1998. Washington, DC: U.S. G.P.O.

U.S. House of Representatives. 1999. *Committee on Government Reform. The FALN and Macheteros Clemency: Misleading Explanations, a Reckless Decision, a Dangerous Message: Third Report.* House report. 106th Congress, 1st session. Washington, DC: G.P.O.

U.S. House of Representatives. 2000a. *Acts of ecoterrorism by radical environmental organizations: hearing before the Subcommittee on Crime of the Committee on the Judiciary.* House of Representatives, One Hundred Fifth Congress, second session, June 9, 1998. Washington, DC: U.S. G.P.O.

U.S. House of Representatives. 2000b. *Clemency for the FALN: a flawed decision?: hearing before the Committee on Government Reform.* House of Representatives, One Hundred Sixth Congress, first session, September 21, 1999. Washington, DC: U.S. G.P.O.

U.S. House of Representatives. 2002. *Counterterrorism intelligence capabilities and performance prior to 9-11: a report to the speaker of the House of Representatives and the Minority Leader / Subcommittee on Terrorism and Homeland Security, Permanent Select Committee on Intelligence.* Washington, DC: Permanent Select Committee on Intelligence, Subcommittee on Terrorism and Homeland Security, 2002. Available from: http://intelligence.house.gov/Word/THSReport071702.doc.

U.S. Senate. 1975a. *Alleged Assassination Plots Involving Foreign Leaders—An Interim Report of the Select Committee to Study Governmental Operations with Respect to Intelligence Activities.* Washington, DC: G.P.O.

U.S. Senate. 1975b. *The Weather Underground: report of the Subcommittee to Investigate the Administration of the Internal Security Act and Other Internal Security Laws of the Committee on the Judiciary.* United States Senate, Ninety-fourth Congress, first session. Washington, DC: U.S. G.P.O.

U.S. Senate. 1975c. *State Department bombing by Weatherman Underground: hearing before the Subcommittee to Investigate the Administration of the Internal Security*

Act and Other Internal Security Laws of the Committee on the Judiciary. United States Senate, Ninety-fourth Congress, first session, January 31, 1975. Washington, DC , U.S.A.: U.S. G.P.O.

U.S. Senate. 1981. *Historical antecedents of Soviet terrorism: hearings before the Subcommittee on Security and Terrorism of the Committee on the Judiciary*. United States Senate, Ninety-seventh Congress, first session, on the historical antecedents of Soviet terrorism, June 11 and 12, 1981. Washington, DC: U.S. G.P.O.

U.S. Senate. 1982. *The role of the Soviet Union, Cuba, and East Germany in fomenting terrorism in Southern Africa: hearings before the Subcommittee on Security and Terrorism of the Committee on the Judiciary*. United States Senate, Ninety-seventh Congress, second session, on the role of the Soviet Union, Cuba, and East Germany in fomenting terrorism in Southern Africa. Washington, DC : U.S. G.P.O.

U.S. Senate. 1989a. *The FBI and CISPES: report of the Select Committee on Intelligence*. United States Senate, together with additional views. Washington, DC: U.S. G.P.O.

U.S. Senate. 1989b. *Inquiry into the FBI investigation of the Committee in Solidarity with the People of El Salvador (CISPES): hearings before the Select Committee on Intelligence of the United States Senate*, One Hundredth Congress, second session . . . February 23, April 13, September 14, 1988. Washington, DC: U.S. G.P.O.

U.S. Senate. 1995. *Violence at women's health clinics: Hearing before a Subcommittee of the Committee on Appropriations*. U.S. Senate, 104th Congress, first session, special hearing. Washington, DC: G.P.O.

U.S. Senate. 1997a. *Terrorism in the United States: the nature and extent of the threat and possible legislative responses: hearings before the Committee on the Judiciary*. United States Senate, One Hundred Fourth Congress, first session, on . . . penalties . . . crime of conspiracy . . . deport suspected terrorists . . . counterterrorism intelligence . . . increased wiretap and infiltration for federal law enforcement, April 27 and May 24, 1995. Washington, DC: U.S. G.P.O.

U.S. Senate. 1997b. *The militia movement in the United States: hearing before the Subcommittee on Terrorism, Technology, and Government Information of the Committee on the Judiciary*. United States Senate, One Hundred Fourth Congress, first session . . . June 15, 1995. Washington, DC: U.S. G.P.O.

U.S. Senate. 1997c. *The Atlanta Olympics bombing and the FBI interrogation of Richard Jewell: hearing before the Subcommittee on Technology, Terrorism and Government Information, of the Committee on the Judiciary*. United States Senate, One Hundred Fifth Congress, first session . . . July 28, 1997. Washington, DC: U.S. G.P.O.

U.S. Senate. 1998. *Foreign terrorists in America: five years after the World Trade Center: hearing before the Subcommittee on Technology, Terrorism, and Government Information of the Committee on the Judiciary*. United States Senate, One Hundred Fifth Congress, second session . . . February 24, 1998. Washington, DC: G.P.O.

U.S. Senate. 2000. *Clemency for FALN members: hearings before the Committee on the Judiciary*. United States Senate, One Hundred Sixth Congress, first session, on examining certain implications of the president's grant of clemency for members of the Armed Forces on National Liberation (FALN), September 15, and October 20, 1999. Washington, DC: U.S. G.P.O. Available from: http://purl.access.gpo.gov/GPO/LPS9560.

U.S. warned in 1995. 2001. "U.S. Warned in 1995 of Plot to Hijack Planes, Attack Buildings." September 18. Available from: http://www.cnn.com/2001/US/09/18/inv.hijacking.philippines.

Van Natta, Don. 1996. Prime Evidence Found That Device Exploded in Cabin of Flight 800. *New York Times*, August 23.

Vetter, Harold, and Gary R. Perlstein. 1991. *Perspectives on Terrorism*, Monterey, CA: Brooks-Cole/Wadsworth.

Wald, Matthew L. 2001. Earlier Hijackings Offered Signals That Were Missed. *New York Times*, October 3.

Wallace, Charles P. 1995. Terrorists Foiled in Plot to Blow Up 11 U.S. Jets. *Atlanta Constitution*, May 28.

Waller, Douglas. 1998. Inside the Hunt for Osama. *Time*, December 21.

Walls, Rodney. 2001. *Lockerbie*. Westport, CT: Praeger.

Walzer, Michael. 2001. Excusing Terror. *American Prospect*, October 22.

Walzer, Michael. 2002. "Five Questions About Terrorism." *Dissent*, Winter. Available from: http://www.dissentmagazine.org/archive/wi02/walzer.shtml.

Wardlaw, Grant. 1989. *Political Terrorism*. (rev. and extended ed.) Cambridge, England: Cambridge University Press.

War on Terrorism. 2001. "War on Terrorism." Available from: http://www.cia.gov/terrorism/ctc.html.

Watson, Peter, and Bryan Monahan. 1973. The Mind of the Terrorist. *Sunday Times* (London), August 19.

Weimann, Gabriel, and Conrad Winn. 1994. *Theater of Terror*. New York: Longman.

Weinberg, Leonard, and William Lee Eubank. 1987. *The Rise and Fall of Italian Terrorism*. Boulder: Westview Press.

Weiner, Tim. 1995. Senators Seek Legal Inquiry on CIA in Guatemala. *New York Times*, September 30.

Weiner, Tim. 1992. Death Squad Alleged in Puerto Rico. *Philadelphia Inquirer*, January 26.

West, Nigel. 2000. *The Third Secret*. London: HarperCollins.

Wheaton, Elizabeth. 1987. *Codename GREENKIL*. Athens, GA: University of Georgia Press.

Whitaker, Brian. 2002. Mystery of Abu Nidal's Death Deepens. *Guardian*, August 22

White, Jonathan Randall. 2002. *Terrorism: An Introduction*. 3d ed. Belmont, CA: Wadsworth Thomson Learning.

Whitmore, Brian. 2001a. Prague Was Rendezvous for Iraqis, Terror Suspect. *Boston Globe*, October 28.

Whitmore, Brian. 2001b. Anti-US Plot in Prague Detailed. *Boston Globe*, Nov 10.

Wieviorka, Michel. 1993. *The Making of Terrorism*. Chicago: University of Chicago Press.

Wilcox, Philip C. 2001. The Terror. *New York Review of Books*, September 19. Available from: http://www.fmep.org/analysis/wilcox_the_terror.html.

Wilkinson, Paul. 1975. *Political Terrorism*. New York: Wiley.

Wilkinson, Paul. 2000. *Terrorism Versus Democracy*. London: Frank Cass.

Wilkinson, Paul. 1986. *Terrorism and the Liberal State*. New York: New York University Press.

Wilkinson, Paul, and Brian Michael Jenkins, eds. 1999. *Aviation Terrorism and Security*. London/Portland, Ore.: Frank Cass.

Willan, Philip. 2001. Terrorists 'Helped by CIA' to Stop Rise of Left in Italy. *Guardian*, March 26.

Williams, Carol J. 2002. German Official Confirms Tunisia Blast Was Attack. *Los Angeles Times*, Apr 23.

Williams, Paul L. 2002. *Al Qaeda: Brotherhood of Terror*. Parsippany, NJ: Alpha.

Willis, Michael. 1996. *The Islamist Challenge in Algeria.* New York: New York University Press.

Wilson, Jamie 2001. US Feared for Luther King killer in British jail. *Guardian* (London) March 21

Wines, Michael. 1991. International Teamwork May Have Foiled Terror. *New York Times*, March 4.

Wines, Michael. 2002. A Film Clip, and Charges of a Kremlin Plot. *New York Times*, March 6.

Wise, David. 1992. *Molehunt*. New York: Random House.

Woodward, Bob. 1987. *Veil*. New York: Simon and Schuster.

Woodward, Bob, and Dan Eggen. 2001. FBI and CIA Suspect Domestic Extremists; Officials Doubt Any Links to Bin Laden. *Washington Post*, October 27.

Woodworth, Paddy. 2001. *Dirty War, Clean Hands*. Cork, Ireland: Cork University Press.

Wren, Christopher. 1990. Days of Murder Dim the Hopes of South Africa. *New York Times*, September 16.

Wright, Joanne. 1991. *Terrorist Propaganda: The Red Army Faction and the Provisional IRA, 1968-86*. New York: St. Martin's Press.

Wright, Robin B. 2001. *Sacred Rage: The Wrath of Militant Islam.* Updated with New Chapters. New York: Simon and Schuster.

Wright, Robin B. 2000. *The Last Great Revolution*. New York: Vintage.

Younis, Mona. 2000. *Liberation and Democratization*. Minneapolis, MN: University of Minnesota Press.

Zadka, Saul. 1995. *Blood in Zion*. London: Brassey's.

Zakin, Susan. 2002. *Coyotes and Town Dogs*. Tucson, AZ: University of Arizona Press.

Zimroth, Peter L. 1974. *Perversions of Justice*. New York: Viking Press.

Zinn, Howard. 2002. *Terrorism and War*. New York: Seven Stories Press .

Zuckerbrot-Finkelstein, Bluma. 1996. "Kindergartens and Killing: A Guide to Hamas." Available form: http://www.adl.org/presrele/IslEx_61/2694_61.asp.

INDEX